P9-DGV-081

RUDENESS
& CIVILITY

Also by John F. Kasson

AMUSING THE MILLION:
Coney Island at the Turn of the Century
(1978)

CIVILIZING THE MACHINE:
Technology and Republican Values in America, 1776–1900
(1976)

RUDENESS

& CIVILITY

Manners in Nineteenth-Century

Urban America

JOHN F. KASSON

ⓦ *Hill and Wang*

A DIVISION OF FARRAR, STRAUS AND GIROUX

NEW YORK

Copyright © 1990 by John F. Kasson
All rights reserved
Published in Canada by HarperCollinsCanadaLtd
Designed by Tere LoPrete
First published in 1990 by Hill and Wang,
a division of Farrar, Straus and Giroux
Printed in the United States of America
First paperback edition, 1991
Fourth printing, 1997

Library of Congress catalog card number: 90-81229

FOR
Peter and Laura
and, as always, for Joy

Acknowledgments

I have accumulated considerable intellectual and moral debts in writing this book and properly owe a multivolume study in return. I have space here only to thank my major creditors for their generous support. I began the project holding concurrently fellowships from the Rockefeller Foundation and the National Humanities Center, and I was sped toward completion by a Pogue Research leave and Research Council grant from the University of North Carolina at Chapel Hill and a fellowship from the Humanities Institute of the University of California at Davis. My brother, Jim Kasson, considerably eased the burden of writing with the gift of two computers. Preliminary versions of portions of the book appeared in Jack Salzman, ed., *Prospects: An Annual of American Cultural Studies* 9 (Cambridge: Cambridge University Press, 1984); *The Henry Ford Museum and Greenfield Village Herald* 14 (1985); and Kathryn Grover, ed., *Dining in America, 1850–1900* (Amherst: University of Massachusetts Press and Margaret Woodbury Strong Museum, 1987). In the course of my research, lecturing, and writing on this subject, numerous individuals have provided valuable aid and advice. Two in particular offered unstinting and crucial support at every stage: my friend Peter Filene and my wife, Joy Kasson. To them especially I wish to express my profound gratitude.

Contents

List of Illustrations

RUDENESS
& CIVILITY

Introduction

> Nothing, at first sight, seems less important than the
> external formalities of human behavior, yet there is
> nothing to which men attach more importance. . . .
> The influence of the social and political system on
> manners is therefore worth serious examination.[1]
>
> —ALEXIS DE TOCQUEVILLE

> The gestures which we sometimes call empty are per-
> haps in fact the fullest things of all.[2]
>
> —ERVING GOFFMAN

This book challenges conventional wisdom in a number of respects.
It opposes, first, the belief that manners have been in a state of
decline for a very long time and are now worse than ever.[3] I argue
that many of the standards of manners we often assume to be age-
old originated surprisingly recently in the nineteenth century. This
book disputes as well the assumption that manners are merely
empty formalities. On the contrary, I contend that they are inextricably tied to larger political, social, and cultural contexts and
that their ramifications extend deep into human relations and the
individual personality. At the same time, the subject cannot be
understood if considered exclusively within national boundaries,
and I have tried throughout this study to remind readers of con-
tinuities and divergences between the American and European experiences. This book also questions the belief that "improvements"
in manners represent an unambiguous good, emphasizing instead
the equivocal character of this achievement. I value highly the
virtues of civility and regard them as an important, indeed indispensable, prerequisite to a democratic society and to everyday social
intercourse. In the pages that follow, nonetheless, I wish to stress
how established codes of behavior have often served in unacknowl-
edged ways as checks against a fully democratic order and in support
of special interests, institutions of privilege, and structures of
domination.

American historians in particular have been slow to take the subject of manners seriously. Within treatments of the nineteenth century, manners have figured mainly as amusing oddities to leaven weightier matters. But along with a variety of sociologists and anthropologists, I would contend that the rituals of everyday behavior establish in important measure the structures by which individuals define one another and interact. In powerful ways they determine what people take their social identities, social relationships, social "reality" to be. More specifically, manners take the historian squarely into the dialectics of social classification—of how the categories of refinement and rudeness, appropriate and inappropriate behavior, operate within a culture and illuminate its boundaries. In the process, one may see how these categories are historically constituted, their hierarchies maintained and challenged.

The manners appropriate to a dynamic republican society were an issue of keen interest in America from the time of independence onward as traditional social divisions and modes of deference came under attack. The issue was a particularly integral aspect of the extraordinary transformations brought by the rise of an urban-industrial capitalist society in the nineteenth century. These transformations affected every region of the country in myriad ways, creating new material conditions and stimulating new practices that profoundly altered the character of everyday life, but they were most intensely expressed in the proximate spaces of the new American metropolises—the centers of the new economic and social order. Not only did the cityscape itself change radically; so, too, did notions of social relationships, appropriate behavior, and individual identity. Alterations in the physical character of streets, commercial districts, parks, theaters, concert halls, and residential neighborhoods—to take only a few examples—were directly linked to changes in the kinds of activities that transpired in these public settings, as well as to a larger redefinition of the character of public and private life. The material development of urban society has attracted considerable scholarly attention. The vital but elusive changes in cultural practices, conduct, and consciousness that attended this physical transformation have, however, too often been ignored.[4]

The recovery of such changes is clearly a difficult matter. For a historian of nineteenth-century America, the effort is rather like looking for salt in the sea: traces are everywhere but usually so thoroughly diluted as to frustrate one's efforts. I have dealt with this problem by sampling many waters, at the same time searching for sources where commentary on urban social standards and practices crystallized.

These sources include writings, both prescriptive and descriptive, concerned with what might be called the semiotics of everyday urban life. Semiotics, the science of signs, acquired its theoreticians (the Swiss linguist Ferdinand de Saussure and the American philosopher Charles Sanders Peirce) only at the end of this period; yet, considered as the broad enterprise of understanding the life of signs and their meanings within society, it was a popular endeavor throughout the nineteenth century, especially in the metropolis. Practitioners include travelers, novelists, detectives, urban journalists and investigators, caricaturists, actors and performers, diarists and autobiographers, and authors of advice literature. But by far the richest single source is the profusion of etiquette manuals that flowed from printing presses beginning in the 1830s and swelled to a torrent between 1870 and the turn of the century. Aimed at a broad readership, they were written by a variety of editors, publishers, popular writers, and leaders of fashionable society. Although these volumes obviously cannot be taken as a complete and accurate portrayal of American social practices, they offer a rich and largely neglected codification of standards that governed social interaction in the rapidly expanding and powerfully influential urban bourgeois culture.

These different sources have usually been considered in discrete categories—to the extent that they have been studied at all. I wish to suggest, however, that we may profitably see them as parts of a common discourse. Together they form an overlooked yet crucial set of representations of urban democratic life, representations that are often in tension with one another but that shaped nineteenth-century urban Americans' social perceptions and experience.

This is an essay, not an exhaustive account. I do not seek to provide a comprehensive history of these materials or of manners in general. Rather, I wish to offer an interpretation of some of this literature's salient aspects as they bear upon key questions about the nature of social conventions, social relationships, and individual identity in the supposedly "free" market and democratic society of the nineteenth-century metropolis. In a nation in which egalitarian assertions (if not conditions) were rampant, what was the nature of authority? What was the role of deference, if any, and how was it to be expressed? What sustained social bonds when democratic individualism and the pursuit of self-interest could so easily dissolve them? What, indeed, held together individual character, responsibility, and accountability in an anonymous, pluralistic society, particularly when the impersonal forces of the market could so dramatically alter a person's lot, lifting some to fortune while others fell suddenly to ruin? What, in short, was the relationship of the symbolic system of economic exchange (money) to the symbolic system of social relationships (manners) in a democracy?

Most of this literature is revealing not in the candor and profundity with which these issues were explored but, on the contrary, in the very ways in which tensions were repressed or blandly ignored. In a number of respects that I will explore, attempts to inculcate a common standard of "polite behavior" masked high ideological stakes. Such efforts sought to respond to democratic aspirations while curbing their egalitarian "excesses" and to mediate the severities of an expansive capitalistic economy while accommodating its larger demands. In the name of civility and self-discipline, the bourgeois code of manners deflected the pressures and inequities of the society back on the individual. Concerned with the proper representation of oneself in social situations, etiquette advisers and other writers on urban middle-class life opened up questions of the nature and authenticity of the self thus represented. Without attempting in the least to resort to a deconstructionist interpretation of these texts, one may observe the ways in which they often deconstruct themselves.

Such materials throw a raking light across American urban culture, starkly illuminating hidden aspects, obscuring others. Although significant regional variations undoubtedly persisted through the nineteenth century, prescriptive literature minimized these in favor of a generalized metropolitan standard, in which the eastern cities such as Boston, Philadelphia, and especially New York figured heavily; and I have followed their emphasis in this book. Similarly, these sources often ignore important temporal developments and defy minute periodization; accordingly, I consider the bulk of the nineteenth century as a unit in much of my analysis, even though I am mindful of the enormous changes it encompassed and have sought to indicate some of these when appropriate. What *does* emerge forcefully from these materials is a rising standard of refinement prescribed and to some extent achieved as well as an increasing segmentation of roles, behavior, and feeling in public and private alike. Middle-class advisers helped establish new codes of civility that profoundly affected social relationships of all sorts, from those of anonymous strangers to those of intimate family members, as they attempted to mediate between the competing claims of social authority and democratic mobility. The experience of the city and of social life generally in this formative period cannot be understood without an appreciation of the cultural demands such codes involved. They built the inequities as well as the opportunities of life in a democratic capitalist society into the minute structures of everyday conduct: presenting oneself at home and on the street; mingling with strangers and greeting acquaintances; expressing pleasure and affection, anger and conflict; dining with family or guests; attending a concert or theatrical performance.

Still more inclusively, the values of these codes radiated both outward and inward. They provided standards by which to assess entire social classes, ethnic groups, and cultures (often justifying their subordination), while at the same time they extended deep into the individual personality. The rituals of polite behavior and interaction helped to implant a new, more problematic sense of identity—externally cool and controlled, internally anxious and conflicted—and of social relationships. In the anonymous metropolis and within a market economy, individuals grew accustomed to offering themselves for public appraisal. At the same time they scrutinized others to guard against social counterfeits. Paradoxically, the very rituals intended to fortify individual character undermined a sense of personal coherence and gradually led the way toward the "anticipatory self," which continually depends upon the products of the consumer culture for its completion.[5] With the advent of this consumer culture in the early twentieth century, manners and urban experience assumed a distinctively different character and the nature of middle-class aspirations and authority decisively changed. So it is here that I end my account, although an epilogue touches upon the vexed issues of civility and rudeness in our own time.

CHAPTER ONE

Manners before the Nineteenth Century

Manners are generally a subject for anecdote, rarely for analysis. But a half century ago, in *The Civilizing Process*, Norbert Elias placed the study of manners on an entirely new footing with his treatment of the phenomenal changes in standards of deportment and expression since the Middle Ages. Norms of polite conduct, he insisted, could not be understood in isolation. Rather, they were intimately tied to the structures of feeling, human relations, and the larger society of which they were a part. Taking the extensive European literature on manners from the fifteenth to the nineteenth century as pivotal to his analysis, Elias noted how strange, even shocking, many admonitions in the earlier works appear to a modern reader. Fifteenth- and sixteenth-century guides for refined nobles at court earnestly addressed concerns that now appear both too gross and utterly superfluous to mention at all:

Before you sit down, make sure your seat has not been fouled.

Do not touch yourself under your clothes with your bare hands.

Do not blow your nose with the same hand that you use to hold the meat.

A man who clears his throat when he eats and one who blows his nose in the tablecloth are both ill-bred, I assure you.

Do not spit on the table.

In attempting to suppress a fart, no less an authority than Erasmus advised:

> If it is possible to withdraw, it should be done alone. But if not, in accordance with the ancient proverb, let a cough hide the sound.

Similarly, the Wernigerode court regulations of 1570 cautioned:

> One should not, like rustics who have not been to court or lived among refined and honorable people, relieve oneself without shame or reserve in front of ladies, or before the doors or windows of court chambers or other rooms.

A 1609 edition of Della Casa's *Galateo* warned:

> One should not sit with one's back or posterior turned toward another, nor raise a thigh so high that the members of the human body, which should properly be covered with clothing at all times, might be exposed to view. . . . It is true that a great lord might do so before one of his servants or in the presence of a friend of lower rank; for in this he would not show him arrogance but rather a particular affection and friendship.

With regard to sleeping, even as late as 1729, one reads:

> If you are forced by unavoidable necessity to share a bed with another person of the same sex on a journey, it is not proper to lie so near him that you disturb or even touch him; and it is still less decent to put your legs between those of the other.[1]

Instead of condemning such instances as evidence of "barbaric" or "uncivilized" behavior, Elias put aside value judgments in order to focus on what the process of "civilization" entailed. He assigned key importance to the changing requirements of daily life from the decentralized, rank-structured, hierarchical social relationships of the Middle Ages to the rise of the modern state: "As more and more people must attune their conduct to that of others, the web of action must be organized more and more strictly and accurately, if each individual action is to fulfil its social function. The individual is compelled to regulate his conduct in an increasingly differentiated, more even and more stable manner." All societies, he acknowledged, demand that individuals exercise some controls over the gratification of their feelings. Yet in comparison to more recent times, Elias argued, people in the late Middle Ages expressed their emotions—joy, rage, piety, fear, even the pleasure of torturing and killing enemies—with astonishing directness and intensity. As the state gradually assumed a monopoly over physical power and violence, individuals were expected to cultivate reserve and mutual consideration in their dealings. Once normal, even refined practices came to be regarded as offensive. First in social settings among their superiors, then increasingly among equals and inferiors and at all times, adults were expected and eventually children taught to discipline their desires and bodily gratifications. Particularly intimate bodily activities—eating, coughing, spitting, nose blowing, scratching, farting, urinating, defecating, undressing, sleeping, copulating, inflicting pain on animals or other human beings—became governed by especially exacting standards and were assigned their special precincts, for the most part behind closed doors. Innovations in polite behavior—epitomized in the rise of the such "implements of civilization" as the fork, the special nightdress for sleeping (replacing day clothes or nakedness), the handkerchief, the chamber pot and later the water closet—expressed this growing delicacy of feeling, a rising threshold of embarrassment, and correspondingly greater stress upon individual self-control. As a result, human affect and behavior were divided into aspects that might appropriately be displayed in public and others, especially sexuality, that had to be kept private and "secret." This split, as Elias emphasized, has enormous implications for the formation of modern personality, with its internalization of prohibitions and its exquisite sensitivity to embarrassment, shame, and guilt.[2]

Elias's account is open to a number of criticisms.[3] His insistence upon the crucial role of the rise of the modern state in the "civilizing process" was far too sweeping and undeveloped to be entirely satisfactory. Arguably, too, the role of the court was ultimately of less importance than that of the bourgeoisie in carrying forth the rising standards of refinement. His starting point in the late Middle Ages conveniently overlooked classical antiquity. Nor did he account sufficiently for the lessening of standards of reserve and growing informality in the twentieth century. Granting when he wrote in the 1930s that "a certain relaxation is setting in," Elias contended it was "merely a very slight recession," and "only possible because . . . the individual capacity to restrain one's urges and behavior in correspondence with the more advanced feelings for what is offensive, has been on the whole secured."[4] In the half century since Elias wrote these words, we have traveled sufficiently far to feel a double sense of distance, not only from the relative lack of refinement of earlier times, but also from what many would regard as the *over*refinement of the Victorian era. For each generation takes its own norms of behavior and feeling as objective.

Nonetheless, Elias opened the door to a new kind of cultural history, keenly attuned to changing standards of emotional expression, bodily control, and personal interaction, and seeking to correlate these with larger changes in social structure. Belatedly discovered by scholars with its republication and translation decades later, including a two-volume English translation in 1978 and 1982, *The Civilizing Process* encouraged fresh explorations of historical terrain, including the transformation of American life from the colonial period through the nineteenth century.

The "Civilizing Process" and Colonial America

Even though the "civilizing process" Elias described had substantially advanced by the seventeenth and eighteenth centuries in the American colonies as well as in northern Europe, an unmistakable divide separates this period from the nineteenth. Almost all books on manners in colonial America were reprinted from English and French sources. Not only do they contain an emphasis on "superiors" and "inferiors" that would dramatically lessen in the course of the nineteenth and twentieth centuries, but they also preserve striking remnants of the sort of advice Elias identified, which later generations would regard as shockingly crude. The most widely circulated of these colonial works was Eleazar Moody's *School of Good Manners*, based on a French courtesy book of 1564. It was first printed in New London, Connecticut, in 1715 and ran through at least thirty-three editions before the mid-nineteenth century.[5] Intended for children, this short work contained a mixture of instruction on worldly deportment and Christian doctrine that would soon go out of fashion. The 1786 edition admonishes the reader:

> Grease not thy fingers or napkin more than necessity requires.
>
> Bite not thy bread, but break it; but not with slov[en]ly fingers, nor with the same wherewith thou takest up thy meat.
>
> Smell not of thy meat nor put it to thy nose.
>
> Foul not the table cloth.
>
> Put not thy hand in the presence of others to any part of thy body not ordinarily discovered.
>
> Spit not in the room but in the corner, or rather go out and do it abroad.[6]

Similarly, the fifteen-year-old George Washington, working from a French Jesuit *Rules of Civility and Decent Behaviour* of 1595 that was widely circulated in various languages and first translated into English in 1640, dutifully copied such maxims as:

> Put not off your Cloths in the presence of Others, nor go out of your Chamber half Drest
>
> Spit not in the Fire, nor Stoop low before it. . . .
>
> . . . bedew no mans face with Spittle by appr(oaching too nea)r him (when) you Speak
>
> Kill no Vermin as Fleas, lice ticks &c in the Sight of Others, if you See any filth or thick Spittle put your foot Dexteriously upon it[;] if it be upon the Cloths of your Companions, Put it off privately, and if it be upon your own Cloths return Thanks to him who puts it off
>
> Being set at meat Scratch not neither Spit Cough or blow your Nose except there's a Necessity for it
>
> Cleanse not your teeth with the Table Cloth Napkin Fork or Knife but if Others do it let it be done w/t a Pick Tooth[7]

Other sources confirm this sense of very different standards and practices of conduct in the colonial period—in some respects, particularly in more rural areas, continuing well into the nineteenth century. "Virginians do not use napkins," the French traveler Brissot de Warville marveled in 1788, "but they wear silk cravats, and instead of carrying white handkerchiefs they blow their noses either with their fingers (I have seen the best-bred Americans do this) or with a silk handkerchief which also serves as a cravat, a napkin, etc." Three years later, in 1791, another Frenchman visiting the resort of Bath, Virginia, observed "an elderly American" at a five o'clock tea, "after taking a cup in one hand and slices of bread and butter in the other, opened his mouth and told the servant to fill it for him with smoked venison."[8]

As for the sharing of beds by adults as well as children, strangers as well as relatives, usually but not always of the same sex, that practice continued throughout the colonial period and at least up to the time of the Civil War, though it clearly offended members of the gentry by the eighteenth century, particularly when they found themselves in forced intimacy while traveling. Often a household lacked even a bed, and in William Byrd's phrase, the entire family "pigg'd lovingly together" on the floor. The English clergyman Andrew Burnaby expressed his distaste in relating a story he learned during his American travels in the 1750s:

A gentleman some time ago travelling upon the frontiers of Virginia, where there are few settlements, was obliged to take up his quarters one evening at a miserable plantation; where, exclusive of a Negroe or two, the family consisted of a man and his wife, and one daughter about sixteen years of age. Being fatigued, he presently desired them to shew him where he was to sleep; accordingly they pointed to a bed in a corner of the room where they were sitting. The gentleman was a little embarrassed, but being excessively weary, he retired, half undressed himself, and got into bed. After some time the old gentlewoman came to bed to him, after her the old gentleman, and last of all the young lady."[9]

A century later, travelers both domestic and foreign were still complaining of strange bedfellows. In *Moby-Dick* (1851) Herman Melville devoted two brilliantly comic chapters to Ishmael's predicament in sharing a bed with a decidedly exotic harpooner, Queequeg, for whom tattoos serve as pajamas. But others thought nothing of the practice. When, for example, as a young man Abraham Lincoln first arrived in Springfield, Illinois, in 1837, lacking family, friends, or money, he went to the store of Joshua Speed to buy materials to make a bed—on credit. When he learned the cost, however, Lincoln looked so melancholy that Speed suggested he save his money by sharing Speed's own room and "very large double bed."

> "Where is your room?" asked he. "Upstairs" said I, pointing to the stairs, leading from the store to my room. Without saying a word, he took his saddle-bags on his arm, went up stairs, set them down on the floor, came down again, and with a face beaming with pleasure and smiles exclaimed "Well Speed I'm moved in."

Lincoln stayed two or three years.[10]

Just as Elias observed with respect to late-medieval and early-modern Europe, so in eighteenth-century America—and much later in the backcountry and frontier—a more relaxed sense of human boundaries and bodily controls was accompanied by fewer inhibitions toward direct personal violence and cruelty. The fierce "rough-and-tumble" fighting in the Southern backcountry that began at least as early as the mid-eighteenth century and flourished through the antebellum period offers a particularly disturbing example. By the time of the American Revolution, the legislatures of Virginia, North Carolina, and South Carolina testified graphically to the carnage of such contests by making it a felony to "cut out the Tongue or pull out the eyes," slit, bite, or cut off the nose, kick or stomp upon "the King's Liege People." The provocations for such brawls give further insight into very different norms of conduct and of honor. On the day of two "fist Battles" in 1774, Philip Fithian, the tutor at Robert Carter III's grand household in Tidewater Virginia, wrote in his journal:

> The Cause of the battles I have not yet known; I suppose either that they are lovers, & one has in Jest or reality some way supplanted the other; or has in a merry hour call'd him a *Lubber*, or a *thick-Skull*, or a *Buckskin*, or a *Scotsman*, or perhaps one has mislaid the others hat, or knocked a peach out of his Hand, or offered him a dram without wiping the mouth of

the Bottle; all these, & ten thousand more quite as trifling &
ridiculous, are thought & accepted as just Causes of immediate
Quarrels, in which every diabolical Strategem for Mastery is
allowed & practiced, of Bruising, Kicking, Scratching, Pinching, Biting, Butting, Tripping, Throtling, Gouging, Cursing,
Dismembring, Howling, &c.[11]

The historian Elliott Gorn has argued that such fights were cru-
cially connected to the "premodern" character of intensely local,
kin-based communities that preceded or, as the nineteenth century
advanced, remained on the margins of the booming capitalist society. Brawling was part of a larger male culture of violent sports
and vengeful action, heavy drinking and immediate pleasure-seek-
ing, a culture much closer in key respects to the easy laughter and
impulsive anger of the late Middle Ages as described by Elias than
to the life of "the modern middle-class individual, with his subdued,
rational, calculating ways."[12]

Looking Backward

By the late nineteenth century the "civilizing process" had so advanced among the urban middle classes that those who seriously
contemplated daily life in colonial America increasingly felt themselves looking backward over a great divide to what was in significant respects a coarser age.

Charles Francis Adams, Jr. (1835–1915), offers a striking case in
point. As the grandson and great-grandson of Presidents and member of one of the most distinguished families in America, he had
every reason to kneel before the world of his forebears in filial piety.
Yet when in the 1890s he wrote the history of his ancestral town
of Quincy, Massachusetts, he scorned those who idealized New
England's colonial past "as a simpler, a purer, and a better time
. . . sterner and stronger, less selfish and more heroic." Making no
effort to avoid value judgments as Elias would later, Adams declared
bluntly:

The earlier times in New England were not pleasant times in
which to live; the earlier generations were not pleasant generations to live with. One accustomed to the variety, luxury

and refinement of modern life, if carried suddenly back into the admired existence of the past, would, the moment his surprise and amusement had passed away, experience an acute and lasting attack of home-sickness and disgust.[13]

Sources of disgust, as Adams chronicled them, were ubiquitous: the drunkenness afflicting all ranks of society that came from a steady diet of beer and, later, hard cider,[14] supplemented, particularly among laborers, with vast quantities of rum; the brutality of corporal punishment, including routine beatings of children, both at home and school; the chaining of maniacs like dogs; the "primitive simplicity" of the early New England houses, even of the landed gentry, which "had none of the modern appliances of luxury, and scarcely those now accounted essential to proper cleanliness or even decency." Regarding this last point, Adams noted that the most thorough ablutions commended by Cotton Mather in 1726 to candidates for the ministry were "daily to wash your Head and Mouth with Cold Water." In Adams's own town of Quincy, no bathroom existed before 1820, "and it is very questionable whether there was any utensil then made for bathing the person larger than a crockery hand-bowl." In the course of the nineteenth century, Adams believed, Americans had climbed an immense stairway of material, intellectual, and moral progress, so that to live as did his colonial ancestors would be intolerable torture.[15]

Other writers shared Adams's sense of distance and revulsion from the crudities of life in colonial times. In 1893 Alice Morse Earle, who could also claim prominent New England forebears, chronicled with mixed fascination and horror the region's "rude" colonial folk customs, from "bundling" courting couples, hazing the bride and groom and even putting them to bed, to public executions, wolf and bear baitings, and drinking copious quantities of rum at funerals. In 1925 a third New England Brahmin, George Francis Dow, summarized the response of such historians in declaring, "Our New England ancestors . . . had standards of living far below those of today. The common speech was gross in the extreme. Crowded living led to familiarity [and, he suggested shortly, even immorality]. There was more drunkenness, profanity, loose living and petty crime in proportion to the population than at the present time, and by no means did every one go to meeting on Sunday."[16]

Southern writers of this period were more inclined to enshrine the image of the Old South as a nobler time than the present; yet even some of them agreed that the most common standards of daily conduct were of comparatively recent origin. As the influential novelist and essayist Thomas Nelson Page declared, "While courtesy is a growth of ancient days, delicacy is a refinement of modern times and is scarcely to be traced further back than the eighteenth century."[17]

Indeed, recent historians have emphasized that in Europe and America alike the eighteenth century saw "a watershed in the history of emotion." By its end a new standard of refinement and feeling emerged prominently. Romantic love assumed new importance in entering marriage, and children were treated with new solicitude. There arose a heightened empathy toward pain and suffering extending to the deaf and blind, the enslaved and deranged, and even to animals, who had earlier been regarded as fit objects on which to inflict pain at will. Emotional control came to be considered an essential aspect of gentility, as the transatlantic popularity of Lord Chesterfield's celebrated *Letters* testifies. The precise reasons for such a transformation are notoriously difficult to specify. Historians have pointed to a variety of factors to account for it: changes in the character of family life that promoted a new stress on affectionate ties, including, especially in America, a rising birth rate; the rise of Protestantism and particularly eighteenth-century evangelicalism in America, with its encouragement of familial affection and self-discipline; the Enlightenment emphasis upon tolerance and rational, just, and humane treatment of all sentient beings; the erosion of local autonomy with the increase of population and the growth of the modern state; the egalitarian spirit associated with the emergence of liberal Western democracies; the rise of a modern capitalist economy with its gradual displacement of the family economy and redefinition of human relationships in terms of the market.[18] Related especially to these last factors, recent historians of colonial America have called attention to a variety of manifestations of a new sense of self, individual privacy, and personal space, as well as changing patterns of social deference and individual ambition—all of which are inextricably related to the movement from a rank-structured, deferential society to a more market-oriented class society.

Life in a Rank-Ordered Society

The rank-ordered conception of society of colonial America derived especially from England. In this hierarchical (and patriarchial) framework each man took his assigned place according to his "quality" or essence in an accepted order of precedence. Commanding the summit were lord, knight, squire, and gentleman—all of whom had sufficient income so that they were above the requirements of daily labor and could devote themselves to their interests and pleasures. Beneath them in the middling ranks were yeoman, husbandman, small merchant, and craftsman, who controlled their means of production but were obliged to work for a living. Then came the propertyless "lower orders": laborer, servant, sailor, vagrant, beggar, and outlaw. In preindustrial England virtually all the actors in this social drama knew their places and the parts assigned to them. They enacted them in their clothes and deportment, their word and gesture, houses and furnishings, food and drink. Each actor always remained mindful of his relation to his immediate "superiors" and "inferiors," and of the ties of patronage and obligation that linked members up and down the social scale. Except among the gentry, he was far less concerned with those who might be counted his equals. Samuel Johnson summarized this conception of society when he warned of the anarchy that would result if England were not governed by "fixed, invariable external rules of distinction of rank, which create no jealousy, since they are allowed to be accidental." But if the rules were fixed, the aristocracy remained open. It created new places to accommodate the rise of new family fortunes. "Gentility is nothing but ancient riches," declared Sir John Holles as early as the reign of Elizabeth I, and later he purchased his own earldom. By the eighteenth century few English peers could trace their titles back through the male line to a feudal grant; their status rested upon royal recognition of their family property.[19]

Colonial British-American society was defined by this set of terms, although the social pyramid was in many respects dramatically different. By the mid-eighteenth century, wealthy merchants and planters stood at the apex in America, unrivaled by any older nobility, even one elevated through "ancient riches" as in England.

Toward the base lay a growing number of urban poor, and at the very bottom in the Southern colonies, an immense population of slaves. The shape of the pyramid was further altered by the fact that in America, freeholding families worked 70 percent of the land, reversing the proportions in England, where freeholders controlled only 30 percent and the nobility and gentry leased the remainder to tenants.[20]

Viewing American society in the rank-ordered terms of England, the colonial landed and commercial gentry sought to emulate the style of their English counterparts and to assume their places at the top of the social hierarchy. They expressed their ambitions by seeking to exert cultural as well as political leadership and eagerly demonstrated their cosmopolitan taste. Beginning with the Governor's Palace in Williamsburg, Virginia (1706–14), they built a succession of great houses designed especially for lavish formal entertainments, modeled on the town and country houses of England. They followed all English styles closely and demanded the latest London fashions in their household furnishings and clothes. Englishmen visiting the American colonies from the late seventeenth century on repeatedly expressed amazement at the speed and extent of their success. As the English historian John Oldmixon wrote in 1741, "a Gentleman from *London* would almost think himself at home at *Boston*, when he observes the Number of People, their Houses, their Furniture, their Tables, their Dress and Conversation, which perhaps is as splendid and showy, as that of the most considerable Tradesman in *London*."[21]

Less often remarked is the important history of the houses and furnishings of common people in the colonial period. Folk housing varied by region much more than did the high-style houses of the gentry; but a typical house in the tobacco-growing region of Tidewater Virginia and Maryland in the seventeenth century was a one-story frame dwelling of two rooms, with additional space in the attic. In such tight and relatively undifferentiated quarters, dwellers did not have the luxury of setting aside special spaces for particular tasks or individual use. Nor did they have many specialized pieces of furniture. Household inventories indicate that more than half the families of the time owned personal property valued at sixty pounds or less. Of these families, only one in four owned a table to sit at; only one in three had chairs and benches—and only one in seven both. Most of necessity were "squatters or leaners," slumping on the floor or crouching on boxes and chests in their waking hours. They ate out of bowls held up with one hand, using spoons as their only cutlery. They lacked not only bedrooms; less than one in seven owned a single bedstead. Most took mattresses and blankets and slept on the floor in groups. Such households did not encourage a highly individuated sense of self with its characteristic need for privacy.[22]

In the course of the eighteenth century the physical structure of the house of the common folk in the Tidewater changed only slowly in the direction of greater domestic space and its segmentation into distinct spheres of activity—in the case of the very poorest, including slaves, perhaps not at all. Household furnishings such as bedsteads, tables, and chairs increased, subtly altering the relationships of the inhabitants to one another. Yet inventories show that one in five households for which records exist from the 1750s did not own both a table and chairs. A similar proportion still lacked knives and forks.[23]

New England had its poor as well, who lived in similar circumstances. Though we still lack the kind of detailed studies we have of the Chesapeake area, the journal kept by Sarah Kemble Knight during a trip she made from Boston to New Haven in late 1704 provides a vivid description of the house of one farmer, his wife, and two children in the Narragansett country:

> This little Hutt was one of the wretchedest I ever saw a habitation for human creatures. It was suported with shores enclosed with Clapboards, laid on lengthways, and so much asunder, that the Light come throu' everywhere; the doore tyed on with a cord in ye place of hinges; the floor the bear earth; no windows but such as the thin covering afforded, nor any furniture but a Bedd with a glass Bottle hanging at ye head on't; an earthen cupp, a small pewter Bason, A Bord with sticks to stand on, instead of a table, and a block or two in ye corner instead of chairs. . . . Nothwithstanding both the Hutt and its Inhabitance were very clean and tydee.[24]

Among the more prosperous majority of southern New Englanders who owned and worked their own lands and occupied the "middling" orders of society, the process of segmentation and accumulation was considerably more advanced by the beginning of the eighteenth century. As Robert St. George has recently shown, New England yeoman families based their initial houses on those they had known in the eastern counties of England and gradually developed an "up-and-back" plan. Most seventeenth-century yeomen's houses had between four and eight rooms, dividing domestic space so as to present a "clean social front" in the hall and parlor near the front door, while pushing the kitchen to a rear lean-to and other working and storage areas into lean-tos at the sides and rear, as well as garret and cellar. The yeoman family ate in the hall, with the head of the household seated in a great armchair (if they could afford it) at the end of the table and others arranged near him on benches, stools, or smaller chairs in order of social status. In the parlor especially, the family affirmed its social standing through its display of possessions, a hint of the beginnings of a new consumer culture that would gradually transform the old rank-ordered society. These items included the great bed—not yet regarded as a private and intimate possession to be kept from public view, but arrayed with coverings as elaborate as the family could muster— as well as perhaps a large cupboard displaying the family's silver, pewter, and glassware. In such ways the houses of New England yeomanry grew more segmented, with rooms increasingly assigned specific functions. By the early eighteenth century even separate "dining rooms" and "children's rooms" appear with greater frequency in inventories.[25]

As the possibilities for material possessions and concern with gentility increased in the eighteenth century, the American colonies offered abundant scope for social ambition—and frequently for comic confusion as well. The script remained that of English rank-ordered society, but actors frequently failed to dress their parts, learn their lines, or keep to their assigned roles. This sort of drama emerges most clearly in first-person narratives of the period, and the remainder of this chapter will consider three of them, which reflect in turn the confounded expectations of a Scottish-born gentleman, the uncertain first steps toward gentility by a rustic Virginian, and the apprenticeship of a canny merchant of appearances in Philadelphia.

Adventures of an Eighteenth-Century Gentleman

The best single portrait of the confusion of gentility and vulgarity in the mid-eighteenth century is by the cultivated Edinburgh-bred physician Alexander Hamilton, who settled in Annapolis in 1739 and left a vivid account of a trip he made from Maryland to Maine and back in 1744. Hamilton traveled as befitted his gentlemanly status. He dressed in elegant clothes, laced hat, and sword and rode on horseback, attended by his personal servant, a slave named Dromo. By no means an arrogant man, he nonetheless expected the quiet deference and honor that were his proper due. Instead, to his irritation, he found himself an object of vulgar curiosity. When he entered the town of Trenton, New Jersey, for example, he "was treated . . . with a dish of staring and gaping from the shop doors and windows, and I observed two or three people laying hold of Dromo's stirrups, enquiring, I suppose, who I was and whence I came."[26]

Other times a hail of questions fell on Hamilton directly. As a sample of many such conversations, he recorded the comic dialogue he enacted with a fellow traveler on the road to Portsmouth, New Hampshire:

He was very inquisitive about where I was going, whence I came, and who I was. His questions were all stated in the rustick civil stile. "Pray sir, if I may be so bold, where are you going?" "Prithee, friend," says I, "where are you going?" "Why, I go along the road here a little way." "So do I, friend," replied I. "But may I presume, sir, whence do you come?" "And from whence do you come, friend?" says I. [*sic*] "Pardon me, from John Singleton's farm," replied he, "with a bag of oats." "And I come from Maryland," said I, "with a portmanteau and baggage." "Maryland!" said my companion, "where the devil is that there place? I have never heard of it. But pray, sir, may I be so free as to ask your name?" "And may I be so bold as to ask yours, friend?" said I. "Mine is Jerry Jacobs, att your service," replied he. I told him that mine was Bombast Huynhym van Helmont, att his service. "A strange name indeed; belike your a Dutchman, sir—a captain of a ship, belike." "No, friend," says I. "I am a High German alchymist." "Bless us! You don't say so; that's a trade I never heard of; what may you deal in sir?" "I sell air," said I. "Air," said he, "damn it, a strange commodity. I'd thank you for some wholesom air to cure my fevers which have held me these two months."[27]

Such rusticity amused Hamilton still more when it pretended to gentility. In Saybrook, Connecticut, his landlady styled herself *Madam* Lay, a title of noble rank. Its adoption struck Hamilton as especially ludicrous since the woman looked as common as clay: "the homliest piece both as to mein, make, and dress that ever I saw," "round shouldered . . . pale faced and wrinkly," and dressed "in the coarsest home spun cloth." "But," he added dryly, "it is needless to dispute her right to the title since we know many upon whom it is bestowed who have as little right as she."[28]

At a Newcastle, Delaware, inn Hamilton came upon another bit of social farce performed by a man named William Morison, "a very rough spun, forward, clownish blade, much addicted to swearing, att the same time desirous to pass for a gentleman." Conscious of his lapses in manners, Morison both apologized for and defended them, saying, " 'Damn me, gentlemen, excuse me; I am a plain, honest fellow; all is right down plain dealing, by God.' " The landlady, observing Morison's "greasy jacket and breeches and a dirty worsted cap" as well as his crudity, mistook him for a plowman or cart driver and served him a menial's breakfast of cold veal scraps. The would-be gentleman was enraged. " 'Damn [me],' " Morison thundered; only respect for " 'the gentleman in company' "—Hamilton himself—kept him from hurling the breakfast out the window and breaking the landlady's "table all to pieces should it cost him 100 pounds for damages." Then he pulled his worsted nightcap off his head, clapped on a linen one in its stead, and declared, " 'Now, . . . I'm upon the border of Pennsylvania and must look like a gentleman; 'tother was good enough for Maryland.' " Eager to regain his status in the eyes of his fellow travelers, Morison blustered that "tho he seemed to be but a plain, homely fellow, yet he would have us know that he was able to afford better than many that went finer: he had good linnen in his bags, a pair of silver buckles, silver clasps, and gold sleeve buttons, two Holland shirts, and some neat nightcaps; and that his little woman att home drank tea twice a day." Morison himself "lived very well," he concluded, "and expected to live better"—as soon as the "old rogue" who owned a coveted piece of land died and he could gain title to it![29]

In effect, Morison appealed to a new measure of social status, one that determined rank not according to fixed "qualities" compounding ancestry, power, learning, and prestige, but instead on the basis of the *quantity* of a family's wealth. As the new capitalist society began to take shape, gentility itself became something to be purchased, and such items as linen, silver, and tea were for rising men such as himself powerful symbols of its achievement. Though Hamilton clearly viewed Morison as a vulgar braggart and a bumpkin, who could never be a gentleman no matter what his wealth, Morison probably told the story as one in which he triumphantly put the landlady in her place and shone before the rest of the company. Standards of refinement would soon change so dramatically that some of Hamilton's own responses to Morison would be regarded as gross. He described himself, for example, as so amused by a ludicrous dispute between Morison and another traveler that "I retired into a corner of the room to laugh a little, handkerchef fashion, pretending to be busied in blowing my nose; so I slurd a laugh with nose blowing as people sometimes do a fart with coughing."[30] As we have seen, to conceal a fart in this way was considered by Renaissance writers on courtesy, including Erasmus, to be a mark of refinement. But the entire subject would become unmentionable a century later.

Just as Hamilton charted the difference between a gentleman and an ambitious yeoman in his account of breakfast with Morison, he measured the even greater gulf between his status and that of a humble ferryman along the Susquehanna by describing the ferryman's family dinner. Yet Hamilton could not even dignify the meal by calling it dinner, speaking of the family instead as "at vittles" and eating "their mess." They sat around a bare table before "a homely . . . fish without any kind of sauce," served in "a dirty, deep, wooden dish." Lacking "knife, fork, spoon, plate, or napkin," they ate "with their hands, cramming down skins, scales, and all." Though the family invited Hamilton to eat, "I told them I had no stomach." Both fascinated and disgusted, he could comprehend such an existence only by creating an aesthetic distance, viewing it "as a picture of that primitive simplicity" of ancient times before "luxury and elegance" were known. In fact, the furnishings of the ferryman's table represented a historic improvement over what their lot might have been only two generations before—at least they had a table to eat off. In any case, as an eighteenth-century gentleman rather than a nineteenth-century middle-class reformer, Hamilton did not propose changing the family's way of life. Accustomed to a world of sharp social distinctions, he assumed that civility and refinement varied according to rank. Of another ferryman, he remarked, "he seemed to be a man of tollerable parts for one in his station," and he lodged the night in the ferry house, sharing the cramped quarters common to all but the gentry: "I went to bed att 9 att night; my landlord, his wife, daughters, and I lay all in one room." The disparity between a ferryman's condition and his own did not trouble him; he was much more impatient with those who refused to conduct themselves appropriately to their station in life.[31]

From Rusticity to Gentility

Hamilton's graphic sketches of gentility and rusticity in mid-eighteenth-century America are borne out by the recollections of one who started life far lower in the social scale, Devereux Jarratt.[32] Born the son of a Virginia carpenter and small farmer in 1733, Jarratt rose by dint of his ambition and quickness of learning to become a prominent Anglican minister, tract writer, and correspondent of John Wesley. But even as he was ailing and dying in the mid-1790s, he dramatically portrayed the world of his youth more than half a century before. Like Hamilton, Jarratt viewed food and dress as key signs of rank, and though his ancestors always lived "free from real want, and above the frowns of the world," he emphasized the simplicity of his family's lot. His mother made all their clothes, "except our hats and *shoes*, the latter of which we never put on, but in the winter season."[33] Similarly, they grew all their provisions themselves, "except a little sugar, which was rarely used." Tea or coffee, the drink of gentlemen, were altogether unknown to the young Jarratt's family and to all the "simple" folk of their acquaintance. As for "what were called *gentle folks*," he early learned to keep "at a humble distance" and to regard them shyly "as beings of a superior order." "A *periwig*, in those days," Jarratt recalled, "was a distinguishing badge of *gentle folk*—and when I saw a man riding the road, near our house, with a wig on, it would so alarm my fears, and give me such a disagreeable feeling, that, I dare say, I would run off, as for my life."[34]

The critical step in Jarratt's rise from the ranks of "simple" to "gentle folk" was when he was "called from the *ax* to the *quill*" in his nineteenth year. A former neighbor living a hundred miles distant who had heard of Jarratt's skill with books sent word that he would hire him as schoolmaster. Jarratt drew this self-portrait as a young rustic snatching his first token of gentility as he prepared to leave his home community and seek his fortune:

> My whole dress and apparel consisted in a pair of coarse breeches, one or two oznaburgs [coarse linen] shirts, a pair of shoes and stockings, an old felt hat, a bear skin *coat*, which, by the by, was the first coat I ever had made for me, since my childhood. And that I might appear something more than common, in a strange place, and be counted somebody, I got me an old wig, which, perhaps being cast off by the master, had became the property of his slave, and from the slave it was conveyed to me. But people were not obliged, you know, to ask how I came by it, and, I suppose, I was wise enough not to tell them.[35]

Yet so poor was Jarratt's imposture and so great the distance between the worlds of the plowman and the planter that even after two years as a schoolmaster, when he finally went to board with a gentleman's family, "I knew not how to introduce myself . . . and what style was proper for accosting persons of their dignity. . . . The gentleman took me . . . for the son of a very poor man, in the neighbourhood, but the lady, having some hint, I suppose, from the children, rectified the mistake, and cried out, *it is the school-master.*"[36]

Before he arrived at their house, Jarratt had learned that this lady, Mrs. Cannon, was a severe *"New-light"* or evangelical, so that "all levities of every kind must be banished from her presence, and every species of ungodliness must expect a sharp reproof from her." Jarratt's response to this news gives us insight not only to his great ambition but to the politics of social relations at this time. Previously as a lodger he had distinguished himself in *"merriment, banter, buffoonery* and such like." Now he resolved *"to act the hypocrite.* I had no intention of being religious, but wished to appear so, in order to gain her good opinion." He found himself locked in nightly sessions with Mrs. Cannon, in which she read aloud lengthy sermons (he was still too poor a reader to take a turn himself). Jarratt feigned "very close attention," sometimes eagerly asking her to read another, while stifling his drowsy incomprehension. Suddenly, after six or eight weeks, a phrase in one of the readings touched home, and he felt profoundly the degree to which he was "a stranger to God and true religion." The resulting change in his conduct, as might be expected, overjoyed Mrs. Cannon. She had made her first convert, and "she was not willing I should go away, till the year was ended, to board any where else."[37]

The sincerity of Jarratt's conversion is not the issue here; its social context is. It arose out of the need to ingratiate himself with a "benefactress" whose patronage Jarratt correctly intuited could prove vitally important. Indeed, her support enabled him to climb the rungs to a position of gentility himself. He shed his "clownish rusticity" and improved his skills as a reader and speaker so much as to lead, not only the Cannon family prayers, but those of Presbyterians in the community. Eventually, he moved to other, more prestigious positions as tutor, acquired Latin and Greek, traveled to England, where he outshone Oxford and Cambridge graduates in the examinations for ordination, and returned, an Anglican minister, to be selected for the parish of Bath, Virginia. None of this would have been possible without the support of patrons or, on Jarratt's part, a keen social as well as intellectual aptitude. Looking back from the 1790s, Jarratt prized the sharp social barriers he managed to scale. Even while he shook his head at the post-Revolutionary "high *republican times*," in which "there is more *levelling* than ought to be, consistent with good government," Jarratt also thanked God, who "raised me from the depths of obscurity and the lowest walks of life, to some degree of eminence and usefulness among men."[38]

In the Marketplace of Appearances

In this last phrase Jarratt clearly alluded to a newly published book that may well have inspired him to write his memoirs in the first place, Benjamin Franklin's already celebrated *Autobiography*.[39] But Franklin played upon the theme of gentility and rusticity with a subtlety Jarratt could not hope to match. He could paint such scenes as his bumptious arrival in Philadelphia in 1723, a boy of seventeen dressed in working clothes, "dirty from my Journey[,] my Pockets . . . stuff'd out with Shirts and Stockings," walking along Market Street holding two enormous rolls under his arms and eating a third, precisely because his ultimate rise to greatness was unquestioned. Even between the occasions when Franklin composed his *Autobiography*, beginning in 1771 and ending only with his death in 1790, he continued to move far beyond conventional Anglo-American gentility, learning instead how to forge a distinctive American republican identity that embraced simplicity as a sign of virtue. Brilliantly alert to the impressions he created as diplomat to France during the American Revolution, he discarded wigs for a fur cap and his natural hair, his sword for a wooden staff, the court finery expected of statesmen for the plain dress of a philosopher. Emerging out of a rank-ordered hierarchical society, he embodied the transformation to a republican and capitalist one. A critical element in this shift was Franklin's sensitivity to relationships not only with superiors, but with equals, and to a growing, anonymous, urban market.[40]

Most readers of the *Autobiography* will immediately recall the passage in which Franklin, having as a youth mightily offended the governmental and religious authorities of Puritan Boston and run away to Philadelphia, described how he established himself as a printer in his new community:

> In order to secure my Credit and Character as a Tradesman, I took care not only to be in *Reality* Industrious and frugal, but to avoid all *Appearances* of the Contrary. I dressed plainly; I was seen at no Places of idle Diversion; I never went out a-fishing or shooting; a Book, indeed, sometimes debauch'd me from my Work; but that was seldom, snug, and gave no Scandal: and to show that I was not above my Business, I sometimes brought home the Paper I purchas'd at the Stores, thro' the Streets on a Wheelbarrow. Thus being esteem'd an industrious thriving young Man, and paying duly for what I bought, the Merchants who imported Stationery solicited my Custom, others propos'd supplying me with Books, and I went on swimmingly. In the meantime [Franklin's rival] Keimer's Credit and Business declining daily, he was at last forc'd to

sell his Printing-House to satisfy his Creditors. He went to Barbados, and there lived some Years, in very poor Circumstances.[41]

This passage condenses one of the essential concerns of Franklin's *Autobiography*: how individuals are judged and reputations made and unmade in the geographically and economically mobile world of the eighteenth century. At the outset of this passage, he revealed his awareness and serene acceptance of the gulf between personal character and observable behavior, his keen appreciation that reputation is founded *only* upon what can be deduced from appearances, whatever one's inner merits might be. As a youth growing up in Puritan Boston, Franklin early learned hard lessons in the importance of public appearances, which no doubt pricked his desire to distinguish between "*Reality*" and "*Appearances*." In running away to Philadelphia, he aimed particularly to shed, besides his onerous apprenticeship to his brother James, his unsavory reputation as a political rebel, a social satirist, and an enemy of religion. Personal needs and the evolving opportunities of the culture conjoined as Franklin learned to become an expert manager of impressions: first an apprentice, then a master of self-effacement as a means of advancement. Unlike later thinkers, he displayed not the least anxiety about the nature of this putative "reality" of character apart from appearances or of the difficulties in reading the character of others if appearances could so easily be separated.

While certainly nowhere in the *Autobiography* did Franklin directly advocate deceit, he was notoriously willing, if he could not "boast of much Success in acquiring the *Reality*" of a particular virtue, to be more than satisfied by his success "with regard to the *Appearance* of it."[42] In contrast to seventeenth-century Puritans and Quakers who sought to bring outward social rituals in conformity with inner virtues, Franklin's unruffled readiness to content himself with appearances, at least in some instances, adumbrated the emergent etiquette of developing capitalism. Trundling his papers in his wheelbarrow, he adapted his behavior, especially in public, in accordance with his interests in the marketplace. Though he might still "debauch" himself—but only with a book!—in solitude, the cultural dictates of the marketplace had already captured the public domain and were pressing in upon the private. The youthful Franklin strove for a time to keep his private moral accounts in order, but instead of feeling himself under the omniscient eye of a wrathful God like his Puritan forebears, he basked in the glow of the "Powerful Goodness" to whom he prayed. And when he discovered that to achieve moral perfection was harder than he thought and that considering all the effort, he preferred, as he put it in his famous image, a speckled ax to a brightly polished one, that, too, was his own affair. Indeed, he concluded with characteristic irony, it was better to have a few blots on one's moral accounts in order to appease public opinion: "a perfect Character might be attended with the Inconvenience of being envied and hated; and . . . a benevolent Man should allow a few Faults in himself, to keep his Friends in Countenance."[43]

As Franklin learned to negotiate between the requirements of his ambition and the sensitivities of his audiences, he helped pioneer the strategies of etiquette that would be so widely disseminated in nineteenth-century America. With social equals as well as superiors, he curbed his considerable appetite for disputation and acquired

> the Habit of expressing myself in Terms of modest Diffidence, never using when I advance any thing that may possibly be disputed, the Words, *Certainly, undoubtedly*, or any others that give the Air of Positiveness to an Opinion; but rather say, *I conceive*, or *I apprehend* a Thing to be so or so, *It appears to me*, or *I should think it is so or so for such and such Reasons*, or *I imagine* it to be so, or *it is so* if *I am not mistaken*. This Habit I believe has been a great Advantage to me, when I have had occasion to inculcate my Opinions and persuade Men into Measures that I have been from time to time engag'd in promoting."[44]

The "Habit . . . of modest Diffidence" had other applications as well. In this watchful, intensely competitive society, not only the assertion of strong opinions but even the promotion of the public good, if performed too directly in one's own name, invited a swarm of envious detractors. Franklin soon learned "the Impropriety of presenting oneself as the Proposer of any useful Project that might be suppos'd to raise one's Reputation in the smallest degree above that of one's Neighbors, when one has need of their Assistance to accomplish that Project." He developed more self-effacing maneuvers, such as presenting his proposal for a public subscription library as "a Scheme of *a Number of Friends*." Keeping accounts on the returns of this investment in reputation, he gleefully reported:

> The present little Sacrifice of your Vanity will afterwards be amply repaid. If it remains a while uncertain to whom the Merit belongs, someone more vain than yourself will be encourag'd to claim it, and then even Envy will be dispos'd to do you Justice, by plucking those assum'd Feathers, and restoring them to their right Owner.[45]

In such ways Franklin practiced his diplomatic skills, learning to soothe the always truculent envy of others, to flatter it if necessary, rather than to goad it. By such maneuvers, too, he put into practice the market relations described by Adam Smith (who corresponded with Franklin about *The Wealth of Nations* several years before its publication in 1776):

> man has almost constant occasion for the help of his brethren, and it is in vain for him to expect it from their benevolence only. He will be more likely to prevail if he can interest their self-love in his favour, and shew them that it is for their own advantage to do for him what he requires of them. . . . It is not from the benevolence of the butcher, the brewer, or the baker, that we expect our dinner, but from their regard to their own interest. We address ourselves, not to their humanity, but to their own self-love, and never talk to them of our own necessities, but of their advantages.[46]

Not content, however, to leave the workings of Smith's "invisible hand" to the marketplace of society alone, Franklin busied himself behind the scenes to engineer its outcomes.

Franklin's *Autobiography* was a landmark not only in American literature, but in the history of market and social relations. In both realms it encouraged the rational pursuit of self-interest at the dawning of an age when such a view could seem not hackneyed but novel and exciting. Franklin challenged the older view that, in historian Joyce Appleby's words, "human beings were impulsive, fickle, passionate, unruly, and likely to come to no good end regardless of what they did. Self-interest in market transactions presumed a rationality that was actually complimentary to human nature. Men and women made choices that served them well."[47] Though he still spoke with a candor about matters such as his "Intrigues with low women"[48] that would trouble refined nineteenth-century readers, his book became a staple of American self-help literature because it captured so shrewdly the terms of the emerging urban capitalist society. In place of a more patriarchical order in which "superiors" and "inferiors" were still clearly linked by ties of obligation and authority enforced by face-to-face contact, there gradually developed a new kind of society in which individuals felt themselves less and less distinctly related to one another except through the workings of the market. Social hierarchy would persist, of course. Indeed, economic divisions did not ease but *increased* with the beginnings of industrial capitalism in the early nineteenth century.[49] But the transition from a rank-structured society to an impersonal "class" society meant that individuals would experience these divisions and the very notion of social hierarchy in ambiguous new ways. The emerging social order shook loose old titles to offer tantalizing possibilities for individual achievement and anxieties of self-definition.

CHAPTER TWO

Etiquette Books and the Spread of Gentility

The favorite word in America for expressing perfection of personal appearance is *genteel*. It is never out of their mouths.

—MARGARET HUNTER HALL, 1827[1]

"Genteel" and "gentility" are words with notable shifts in meaning. Originally denoting the gentry and more broadly the well-born, they came increasingly in the nineteenth century to refer to elegance, grace, and politeness, but by the early twentieth also to mean excessive conventionality, false delicacy, and exaggerated refinement. The history of these words epitomizes enormous changes in the economy and society. The fundamental distinction between the well-born and the common horde that supported the concept of gentility in traditional rank-ordered society had already grown shaky in colonial America, and the egalitarian thrust of the American Revolution battered it further. Under the pressures of an emergent industrial capitalist society, this concept would fall apart, to be supplanted by a bourgeois order that redefined gentility in its own image. The role etiquette books played in the redefinition and dissemination of gentility in the nineteenth century forms the subject of this chapter. How this understanding of gentility was undermined in its turn, beginning in the 1890s, will be suggested in the Epilogue.

Among the many ironies of the American Revolution was the way in which it ultimately weakened the hold of the very gentry who supported it. Fought in the name of republican virtue against aristocratic privilege, and of rural simplicity against overrefinement, the Revolution stimulated a radical questioning of traditional authorities that deeply troubled many leaders as early as the 1780s and '90s. In one of the first American novels, *Modern Chivalry*, Hugh Henry Brackenridge depicted this stunning democratic upsurge after experiencing its force firsthand when he was voted out of the Pennsylvania assembly in 1787 in favor of an ex-weaver. At the story's outset the protagonist John Farrago, a farmer and militia captain "of good natural sense, and considerable reading," makes a speech to an election crowd against the fitness of a weaver (like Brackenridge's erstwhile opponent) to hold political office. "There is no analogy between knoting threads and framing laws," the captain observes. "It would be a reversion of the order of things." But no sooner does he convince the weaver to withdraw than the people fix their choice upon his servant instead. In defying the captain, a spokesman articulates what to them is the true legacy of the Revolution:

> It is a very strange thing . . . that after having conquered Burgoyne and Cornwallis, and got a government of our own, we cannot put in it whom we please. This young man may be your servant, or another man's servant; but if we chuse to make him a delegate, what is that to you. He may not be yet skilled in the matter, but there is a good day a-coming. We will impower him; and it is better to trust a plain man like him, than one of your high flyers, that will make laws to suit their own purposes.[2]

Brackenridge's dismay at the degeneration of classical republicanism into democratic vulgarity would be reiterated again and again in the late eighteenth and early nineteenth centuries, reaching a climax with the election of Andrew Jackson in 1828. The self-assertive society to emerge from the Revolution was not at all what the Founding Fathers had anticipated, and it led to directions unknown.[3]

A second major blow to the old genteel order came from a revolution of another sort: the interrelated developments in industrialization, transportation, communication, and urbanization that together transformed virtually every aspect of American life. Contrary to popular historical stereotypes, the effect was not to distribute wealth more equally than in the colonial period. Quite the opposite: the most recent and authoritative studies point to a "marked rise" in economic stratification during the first half of the nineteenth century, followed by "six decades of persistent and extensive inequality" from the post–Civil War period to the Great Depression of the 1930s.[4] One result was to restructure drastically the nature of social relations. Though the sense of social cleavage in America remained a good deal less than in Europe, an increasing number of historians have pointed to the emergence by the mid-nineteenth century of working, middle, and upper classes with diverging and at times antagonistic conditions, outlooks, and aspirations. To date, most scholarly attention has focused on the working class, with a much smaller group studying the emergence of a new urban upper class composed of both established families and those of new wealth, eager to acquire cultural capital and to set themselves off as a quasi aristocracy from those below. The sprawling social terrain between the upper and working classes still remains to be mapped in detail; but new studies have traced some of the processes by which industrialization and urbanization helped to shape a new middle class as well.[5]

For example, the historian Stuart Blumin has cogently sketched some of the key converging trends that appear to have defined a distinctive middle-class experience and outlook in the nineteenth century, including the changing nature of work and consumption, the development of middle-class neighborhoods and voluntary associations, as well as child-rearing practices that helped boost their progeny up the social ladder. In the critical realm of work, the distinction rapidly developed between manual and nonmanual labor (preserved in the twentieth century as "blue-collar" and "white-collar" jobs). A hierarchy of specialized nonmanual pursuits proliferated, from store and office clerks and assistants, to intermediate managers of various sorts, to manufacturing and financial executives—all of which were physically and socially segregated from the dirtier, less "refined" work of manual production. In contrast to "handworkers," young clerks and other lower-level nonmanual workers were often encouraged to regard themselves as "businessmen in training," who through character, initiative, and perseverance might climb the ladder to both commercial success and social prominence.[6]

Furthering the development of shared class values and eroding the authority of older conceptions of fixed rank and gentility was the extraordinary transformation in the culture of print and reading in the second quarter of the nineteenth century. Economic and technological developments converged to produce what was arguably "the greatest single advance in . . . [printing] since the fifteenth century."[7] Technological improvements in presses, typecasting, typesetting, papermaking, and bookbinding played an indispensable role in the change. In addition, economic growth and the transportation revolution permitted the rise of larger, centralized publishers able to print more specialized works and to reach distant markets. Hitherto, book publishing in America had been in the hands of small, chronically undercapitalized printers. So severe were their constraints that through the late eighteenth century they typically paid authors with copies of their work (generally 10 percent of an edition) rather than cash, and when they republished British novels or histories, they could normally compete with imported editions only if they stuck to works that were short.[8] Despite the relatively high literacy rate in much of colonial America compared to Britain, English book exporters similarly found "exceeding trifling Profit" in the scattered American market.[9] With the 1830s, however, there came a dizzying leap in the world of print from an age of scarcity to an age of abundance: books, magazines, and newspapers became far more widely available in the United States at far lower prices than ever before. The change would affect all classes, but it had a crucial impact on middle-class life.[10]

The Lost World of Samuel Goodrich

The specific meaning of this change was vividly described by one of the most prolific writers, editors, and publishers of the second quarter of the nineteenth century, Samuel G. Goodrich (1793–1860). Beginning as a bookseller and publisher, Goodrich founded and edited *The Token* (1827–42), an annual gift book including such New England writers as Hawthorne, Holmes, Longfellow, Lowell, Sarah J. Hale, Edward Everett, Lydia Maria Child, Lydia Sigourney, Harriet Beecher Stowe—and Goodrich himself. Also in 1827, Goodrich launched the immensely successful and much imitated Peter Parley stories for children, followed by *Parley's Magazine* in 1833 (later *Robert Merry's Museum*). By the end of his career he could boast, "I am the author and editor of about one hundred and seventy volumes, and of these seven millions have been sold!"[11]

From this perspective, Goodrich looked back on the conditions of his boyhood in Ridgefield, Connecticut, as a vastly different world. Ridgefield around 1800, he estimated, was "rather above the average of Connecticut villages in its range of civilization." But while "all could read and write . . . in point of fact, beyond the Almanac and Watts' Psalms and Hymns, their literary acquirements had little scope." Of roughly twelve hundred inhabitants, not more than four subscribed to a weekly newspaper. Though the town could claim a public library with two hundred books, a source of knowledge much more frequently consulted was passing travelers on the thoroughfare from New York to Boston who carried word of events.[12] For children, books were fewer still. Except for *The New England Primer*, "the main contents of which were the Westminster Catechism . . . and some rhymes, embellished with hideous [wood] cuts of Adam's Fall, in which 'we sinned all,' " Goodrich could "remember none that were in general use among my companions." When at about age ten he received a few children's books that his father had bought during a trip to Hartford, they seemed to him a "revelation."[13]

This setting, in which printed works were relatively scarce and those available chiefly religious, encouraged habits of *intensive* rather than *extensive* reading. Children learned to read in a devotional context at home, church, and school, by reciting and hearing the Bible and other religious texts again and again, and committing large portions to memory.[14] (Eighteenth-century etiquette manuals and other secular advice literature may well have been read in a similarly intensive style.)[15] As was the custom in most Ridgefield families, Goodrich's father, a Congregational minister, read aloud to his family a chapter of the Bible every morning and "thus read that holy book through, in course, thirteen times, in the space of about five and twenty years." As a result, the young Goodrich was steeped in the Bible. Its narrative "formed the greater part of my early knowledge," and its "direct, simple style . . . entered into my heart, and became for a long time my standard of taste in literary composition."[16]

In such a context, readers approached the printed materials, whether sacred or secular, as precious objects:

Books and newspapers . . . were read respectfully, and as if they were grave matters, demanding thought and attention. They were not toys and pastimes, taken up every day, and by everybody, in the short intervals of labor, and then hastily dismissed, like waste paper. The aged sat down when they read, and drew forth their spectacles, and put them deliberately and reverently upon the nose. . . . Even the young approached a book with reverence, and a newspaper with awe. How the world has changed![17]

As Goodrich's memoirs suggest, the changes involved far more than an increase in the sheer volume of print; it also brought a new relation between books and their readers. The books of his Ridgefield childhood largely reinforced the authority and values of the local community, with sacred texts at their center. The volumes most available to them were "steady sellers"—staples of the book trade like Watts's psalms and hymns, *The New England Primer*, and especially the Bible—that stayed in circulation for generations.[18] Printers could afford to publish only a few specialized works for a limited readership. For most people, even the purchase of the cheapest schoolbook still represented a considerable expense, and prior to the Revolution, it amounted to two days' wages for a common laborer.[19] Extensive book ownership and book learning remained through the eighteenth century a badge of the gentry just as did refined manners and mode of dress; a large personal library testified to the gentry's ability to afford what was to most an outlandish expense as well as to possess the education and leisure necessary to read widely.

By contrast, the new age of print in the nineteenth century made available to a wide public the possibility of extensive reading that had hitherto been limited to a relatively narrow economic and social group. As works proliferated and passed into the hands of a new body of readers, the social authority of learning and the major texts of the dominant Protestant culture grew more diffuse. Devotional literature was displaced by a profusion of secular materials, so that not even the Bible could retain its former centrality. By the 1830s the rise of popular fiction, magazines, and the new daily "penny press" encouraged reading as a diversion in which the particular work at hand was often ephemeral—"waste paper," in Goodrich's telling phrase. In dramatizing the vast progress in transportation in his day, Goodrich himself indicated this new function of literature as a way of simply passing time when he contrasted a slow, jolting ride in a stagecoach with "sitting down in a railroad car at New York to read a novel, and before you have finished, to find yourself at Boston!" Although Goodrich could boast of his considerable writings and vigorously defended his claim as the true and sole author of the Peter Parley series, in other moods he recognized that his very quantity of publications suggested their transitory nature and his own mediocrity. With more than simple modesty, he confessed:

> In looking at the long list of my publications, in reflecting upon the large numbers that have been sold, I feel far more of humiliation than of triumph. . . . I have written too much, and have done nothing really well. . . . I know, better than any one can tell me, that there is nothing in this long catalogue that will give me a permanent place in literature.[20]

Goodrich and many of his generation stood in an ambiguous position as the nature of authority changed in the first half of the nineteenth century. Raised a Federalist in politics and Congregationalist in religion, the bedrock beliefs of the old New England order, he became a Whig and a Unitarian, more accommodating convictions for a new age of industrial capitalism. Though he certainly did not wish simply to restore the world of his childhood, Goodrich feared democratic assaults upon the hierarchy of wealth and privilege. Like many other magazine editors and popular advisers of his generation, he aimed in his writings to steer a middle course: by diffusing literature to a broad public and especially to children, he tried also to spread a popular gentility as part of a new civil religion in mid-nineteenth-century America. In place of the Calvinistic orthodoxies of *The New England Primer*, he offered cheerful tales and verse of progress through perseverance adapted to the new mercantile age, like *Make the Best of It*, and "Try, Try Again":

> 'Tis a wisdom you should heed—
> Try, try again,
> If at first you don't succeed,
> Try, try again. . . .[21]

Strongly preferring the plausible and factual over the fantastic, Goodrich also fed the immense hunger among the middle class for knowledge of both a general and an instrumental nature with histories, biographies, and geographies for children and adults, and numerous other works for children, including a book on manners in the Peter Parley series, *What to Do and How to Do It*.[22]

Reading for general knowledge was one important sign of cultivation, but the immense economic and social changes that began in the early nineteenth century also created a vast new market for more specific instruction. The continuity of experience between parents and children and between youth and adulthood that would have made much printed advice superfluous to earlier generations became attenuated in a variety of ways. The burgeoning industrial economy and the integration of agricultural markets opened new jobs to both young men and young women, at the same time squeezing out the family economy. Increasingly with each generation, ambitious youths of both sexes could expect to leave their villages to make their fortunes: to seek work in the cities or the new factory towns, and to train in an expanding array of schools, seminaries, and colleges. Whereas earlier generations characteristically learned their trades from their parents, relatives, or neighbors close at hand in an apprenticeship, beginning in the early nineteenth century more and more youths would leave these models behind as they launched themselves into the "world of strangers" of the commercial cities. Even those who remained in their home communities often found old ways of life changing. The expanding network of transportation, communications, and goods brought new tastes and practices into all but the most isolated areas. For instance, had Samuel Goodrich stayed in Ridgefield instead of leaving at age fifteen for a wider world, he would have soon witnessed his neighbors breaking with the domestic economy of the past, which was already by the beginning of the nineteenth century driving many into debt, in favor of more specialized occupations, the village's social lines hardening, the authority of once respected elders flouted and once deferential bows omitted, the Congregational Church disestablished, old houses gone and larger and more sumptuous new ones raised in their stead, furnished in new styles of fashion and refinement for a more formal and self-conscious social life.[23]

The outpouring of books in the nineteenth century included instructional literature of many kinds. One could learn to act, build,

1. The Urbane New World of Print: Genteel strollers pass through Gleason's Publishing Hall in Boston, "the largest and best publishing room in the country" (1853).

calculate, carve, cook, dance, draw, dye, and so forth through an alphabet of attainments; so too one could through etiquette acquire the habits and knowledge that would lead to a better life.[24] The existence once reserved for the gentry now appeared accessible to many social aspirants. With proper drive, knowledge, and success, an individual or family might climb the social ladder to new heights. Though the path to the summit rose precipitously and was guarded by jealous watchdogs of the upper class, middle-class members might nonetheless emulate some of its forms and manners.

The result was to make gentility increasingly available as a social desire and a purchasable style and commodity. The revolution in print conjoined with and helped to shape profound changes in domestic life and aspirations. An extensive middle-class market quickly developed in antebellum America for mass-produced imitations of costly luxuries: balloon-frame houses with New Haven clocks and Waltham watches, Lowell carpets, upholstered sofas, machine-pressed glassware and cutlery, gilt looking glasses, framed chromolithographs, mahogany bureaus and bookshelves, and other furnishings—items, by and large, beyond the budgets of working-class households.[25] Etiquette writers joined a host of other advisers in teaching those who wished to be thought respectable and successful how to perform various social practices, many of which represented historic innovations in the nineteenth century. These included such newly defined "necessities" as frequent bathing and meticulous grooming;[26] new standards for the accouterments and deportment of both domestic and formal dining; the elaboration of rooms and their increasingly specialized furnishings and functions in a stylish household; the administration of servants; the proper conduct of shopping, business, and social exchanges; and the intricacies of public deportment in the nineteenth-century city. The most fashionable social groups, well aware that their fortunes might easily be eclipsed, tried with mixed success throughout the century to reserve their ranks for those of prominent lineage and inherited prestige. But if the fine points of manners could operate as another means of exclusion at the upper ranks of society, for much of urban middle-class life the cultivation of bourgeois manners served as an instrument of inclusion and socialization. Fundamental to the popularity of manuals of etiquette was the conviction that proper manners and social respectability could be purchased and learned.

Advice in Abundance

On both sides of the Atlantic in the nineteenth century, etiquette manuals appeared in unprecedented numbers, corresponding with the rise of bourgeois culture and the new age of print; but nowhere was this literature more abundant than in the United States. According to the avowedly incomplete enumeration by Arthur M. Schlesinger, "aside from frequent revisions and new editions, twenty-eight different manuals appeared in the 1830s, thirty-six in the 1840s and thirty-eight more in the 1850s—an average of over three new ones annually in the pre–Civil War decades." In the period from 1870 to World War I, he reported, the flow of volumes rose to a rate of five or six a year, "probably involving far larger editions."[27] Even though Schlesinger's definition of an etiquette manual was a generous one, embracing books with not simply specific injunctions on manners and deportment but advice on conduct, character-building, beauty, and household management, the size of this literature was still considerable. Etiquette books clearly constituted a major popular literary genre at this time as never before.[28]

These titles reached a vast readership by a variety of routes. Many became a staple of publishers' lists and were often compiled (sometimes under a pseudonym) by publishers themselves—eloquent testimony to their popularity and profitability. The bulk of American etiquette books bore imprints from the major publishing centers that quickly arose in the 1830s and '40s: Boston, Philadelphia, and especially New York. Others emerged from smaller eastern cities and towns as well as from midwestern cities such as Chicago, Detroit, Cincinnati, and Saint Louis. Virtually none came from the South, which remained notably lacking in publishers throughout this period.

Undoubtedly, most etiquette manuals were sold to people who would never have thought of entering a bookstore. Direct-mail sales were a vital aspect of the book trade throughout the nineteenth century, and publishers placed advertisements in a variety of middle-class magazines, from popular women's and family periodicals to more specialized publications with a young, upwardly mobile readership. For example, a single 1883 issue of a newspaper for telegraphers called the *Operator* carried advertisements for *Mar-*

tine's Hand-Book of Etiquette, and Guide to True Politeness, The Standard Book of Politeness, and *Genteel Behavior*, as well as notices for related publications such as *Young American's Letter Writer* and *Prof. Baron's Complete Instructor in All the Society Dances of America*.[29]

Etiquette books were also an important part of the subscription book trade, which expanded to considerable proportions after the Civil War. Drawing first on former soldiers, subscription publishing mobilized virtual armies of sales agents to sweep through cities, towns, and the surrounding countryside, capturing every possible order for their books. Agents received detailed instructions on tactics and strategy, including how to gain their initial book orders from leading figures in a community and to use their prestige, together with the agent's own unrelentingly courteous demeanor, to overcome all sales resistance. In addition to their own staffs, publishers could call upon distributing firms commanding up to five thousand salesmen, and legions of independent canvassers, standing an estimated twenty thousand strong by 1894 in the city of Chicago alone! To dispatch such mercenaries of print was not worthwhile with low-priced books. Subscription publishers concentrated on what they anticipated would be assured successes among customers aspiring to gentility. They compiled or commissioned books wherein etiquette advice flowed over into tips on housekeeping, medical care, letter writing, child raising, business and legal forms, lessons in elocution and public speaking, and miscellaneous matters. Publishers produced the most IMPOSING (detractors would say *gaudy*), INCLUSIVE (*padded*) volumes they could devise, such as *Modern Manners and Social Forms* by James Smiley, cleverly disguised as "Mrs. Julia M. Bradley" (first published in 1889 and 608 pages long), and James McCabe's massive *National Encyclopaedia of Business and Social Forms* (first published in 1879 and swelling to 872 pages).[30]

Contrasting with these expensive editions, some publishers of etiquette manuals aimed for the dimes rather than the dollars of the mass market with short, cheap books. The house of Beadle, soon to become famous as publisher of hundreds of dime Westerns and other tales of adventure, brought out a thin 72-page *Beadle's Dime Book of Practical Etiquette* in 1859, and the next year a rival publisher, Dick and Fitzgerald, countered with Henry Willis's *Etiquette, and the Usages of Society*, running a trim 64 pages and also costing ten cents.[31]

talk about mixin' fonts

THE

NATIONAL ENCYCLOPÆDIA

OF

BUSINESS AND SOCIAL FORMS,

EMBRACING

THE LAWS OF ETIQUETTE AND GOOD SOCIETY,

AND CONTAINING

PLAIN AND SIMPLE INSTRUCTIONS IN THE ART OF APPEARING TO THE BEST ADVAN-
TAGE ON ALL OCCASIONS; HOW TO DRESS WELL AND TASTEFULLY;
WITH RULES FOR COURTSHIP, MARRIAGE, ETC., ETC.

SHOWING

How to Write a Good Hand,

AND HOW TO EXPRESS WRITTEN THOUGHT IN A CORRECT AND ELEGANT
MANNER, WITH INSTRUCTIONS IN COMPOSITION, ORATORY, WRITING
POETRY, WRITING FOR THE PRESS, ETC., ETC.

BEING

A Practical Guide to the Preparation of Business and Legal Documents,

Bills, Receipts, Commercial Forms, Resolutions for Public Meetings, Private
and Public Correspondence, Letters of Sympathy, Friend-
ship, Courtesy, Affection, etc., etc.

ENRICHED WITH

Full and Carefully Prepared Tables of Reference,

CONTAINING IMPORTANT HISTORICAL, BIOGRAPHICAL, GEOGRAPHICAL, SCIENTIFIC
AND OTHER USEFUL KNOWLEDGE.

ILLUSTRATING

THE ART OF MAKING HOME HAPPY,

With Rules for Games, Recreations, Home Amusements, Tableaux, etc., etc.

CONTAINING

VALUABLE HOUSEHOLD RECEIPTS, AND SHOWING HOW TO MAKE THE MOST OF EVERYTHING.

FORMING

A COMPLETE AND COMPREHENSIVE BOOK OF REFERENCE,

EXPRESSLY DESIGNED TO MEET THE EVERY-DAY WANTS OF THE AMERICAN PEOPLE.

BY JAMES D. McCABE.

AUTHOR OF "THE PICTORIAL HISTORY OF THE WORLD," "THE CENTENNIAL HISTORY OF THE UNITED STATES," ETC., ETC.

PUBLISHED BY

THE NATIONAL PUBLISHING CO.,

PHILADELPHIA, PA., CHICAGO, ILL., ST. LOUIS, MO.
AND ATLANTA, GA.

2. An All-Inclusive Title Page.

Some etiquette manuals published by businesses were either sold at nominal amounts or given away as complimentary copies. Thus Dempsey and Carroll, makers of stationery, encouraged "correct" correspondence and genteel manners by distributing *Art Stationery and Usages of Polite Society*.[32] The Kohler Manufacturing Company, makers of headache remedies, a bottled "nerve comfort," and a "one night corn cure," gave away an 8-page pamphlet, *100 Rules of Etiquette*, to cure customers' social ills as well.[33] Similarly, a Dr. Walker of Rochester, New York, "Specialist in chronic and nervous diseases," published a 32-page booklet, *Points on Good Behavior*, which in addition to advice on deportment included special warnings about "sexual decay" and "self-abuse" (masturbation)—both conditions he professed to cure.[34]

Etiquette books published in the United States also reflected the larger shift from English to American authorship in the nineteenth century. Samuel Goodrich estimated that as late as 1820 only 30 percent of the books published in this country were by American writers and roughly 70 percent of British authorship. He judged the American authors' share to have risen by 1830 to 40 percent, by 1840 to 57 percent, and by mid-century to 70 percent—reversing the proportions of thirty years earlier.[35] Though British authors lost their dominance, a strong Anglo-American literary and intellectual culture remained, ironically buttressed by the lack of an international copyright agreement, thereby encouraging unauthorized editions of British works. Books on etiquette that either reprinted or were heavily based on English originals continued to be published in America throughout the nineteenth century, but their relative numbers and importance declined steadily, and as a group they amounted probably to no more than 10 percent of the total.[36]

Much more anomalous were French works. I have located only one issued by an American publisher in the nineteenth century, *The Gentleman and Lady's Book of Politeness and Propriety of Deportment* (1833), and it is characterized by an acute snobbery of professions and Parisian condescension to the provinces that made it unsuitable for a wide American readership.[37]

So plagiarism has a long rich American history!

Authors

Who, then, wrote these dominant American works? Of the more than one hundred fifty etiquette manuals listed in the Selected Bibliography that were published between 1830 and 1910, approximately half appeared anonymously or pseudonymously. Occasionally these works would nonetheless make claims to the authors' social authority in their signatures: by "an American lady," "a woman of fashion," "a gentleman," "a member of New York's most exclusive social circles," "one of the four hundred," "Censor," "Mentor." Of those instances where the authors revealed their identities or subsequent bibliographers have discovered them— roughly two thirds in all—one finds a microcosm of the creators of the new mass culture of print. They included many who made their living by writing, as well as other figures of influence and prestige: editors and columnists for women's and juvenile magazines such as *Godey's Lady's Book, Arthur's Home Magazine, Harper's Bazar* (inspired by *Der Bazar* of Berlin), *Andrews' American Queen, Home Magazine, Vogue,* the *Delineato,* and *Young Folks' Monthly*; book and magazine publishers; writers of popular fiction, history, and biography; college professors, schoolteachers, and school superintendents (who helped make these books an established part of the curriculum); clergymen; reformers of various stripes; businessmen; actresses; leaders of fashionable society; and female relatives of men in public office (including several daughters of congressmen as well as Rose E. Cleveland, sister of the President and his hostess during his first year in office, and Mary Logan, widow of John A. Logan, who with Blaine lost to the Cleveland ticket in the 1884 election). Overall, there were slightly more women than men.

The pathways that led to authorship of etiquette manuals were manifold. In the period from 1830 through the 1860s, numerous individuals tested the new possibilities for professional writers and editors in America. Especially for middle-class women, few vocational options existed, and some seized upon the emerging field of commercial literature as their only way to address a public audience, while others took up the pen in lieu of the seamstress's needle or the teacher's slate as a means to support themselves and their families. For some writers, etiquette books were a distinct sideline; for others, a major endeavor. Brief profiles of representative figures, taken in chronological order of birth, indicate both the range of literary pursuits and the circumstances that at times compelled them to write.

The story of Eliza Leslie (1787–1858) of Philadelphia suggests a pattern common to many nineteenth-century women writers. The eldest daughter of a famous mathematician and watchmaker, she was educated principally at home. Her father's business declined, however, and after his death in her sixteenth year, she and her mother ran a boardinghouse to support the family. She achieved her first commercial success with a cookbook in 1828 and quickly became a leading writer for children and women's magazines. She edited annual gift books for young women and a short-lived monthly, *Miss Leslie's Magazine*. Concern with American manners, foibles, and pretensions, a prominent theme in her writings, blossomed fully in *Miss Leslie's Behaviour Book: A Guide and Manual for Ladies* (first published in 1853).[38]

Sarah Josepha Hale (1788–1879) turned to a writing career in the 1820s as a young New England widow (wearing black mourning garb the rest of her life) with five children to support. She wrote and edited over fifty books in a variety of genres, including novels, verse, biographies, recipes, and children's rhymes (most famously, "Mary Had a Little Lamb"), as well as serving as an exemplary magazine editor. For more than forty years she presided over the leading women's monthly, *Godey's Lady's Book*, a compendium of colored fashion plates, poetry, songs, fiction, household hints, health advice, and earnest editorials that rigidly excluded all controversial subjects. Characterized by one acquaintance as a woman whose entire career was "a tribute to the respectabilities, decorums and moralities of life, devoid of its enthusiasms," she distilled many of her magazine columns and views into her etiquette book, *Manners; or, Happy Homes and Good Society All the Year Round* (1867).[39]

Catharine Maria Sedgwick (1789–1867), the most popular American novelist of her generation, was the descendant of Connecticut's leading families and the daughter of the prominent Massachusetts Federalist Theodore Sedgwick. Raised in the stern Calvinist tradition, she converted to Unitarianism in 1821 and soon after discovered her vocation as a writer. Beginning with *A New-England Tale* in 1822, she created a succession of domestic fictions, historical romances, magazine pieces, and writings for children, among them *Morals of Manners; or, Hints for Our Young People* (1846).[40]

Eliza Ware Farrar (1791–1870) was raised by American Quaker parents on an elegant Welsh estate, married Harvard mathematics professor John Farrar, and settled in Cambridge, Massachusetts. However, her father lost his fortune, and her husband soon became an invalid. Probably both as an expressive outlet and a source of income, she wrote a number of books for children and adults. Her most popular effort was *The Young Lady's Friend* (first published in 1837 and reprinted as late as 1880), a work influential in its stress upon specific matters of behavior rather than general exhortations on character development and religious principles.[41]

The circumstances of male authors in this period are more idiosyncratic, but they also suggest the multiple routes that might lead to assuming the role of etiquette adviser. For example, Timothy Arthur (1809–1885) rivaled Samuel Goodrich as one of the most prolific and widely read antebellum writers and was an important magazine editor and publisher, as well as an indefatigable creator of over two hundred novels and moral tales. His vivid temperance novel *Ten Nights in a Bar-Room* (1854) earned him special fame and became a best-seller. He also wrote *Advice to Young Men on Their Duties and Conduct in Life* (first published in 1847) and a corresponding *Advice to Young Ladies*.[42]

Samuel Roberts Wells (1820–1875) first studied medicine and then entered a career in writing and publishing through the door of that great antebellum enthusiasm, phrenology. In 1843 in Boston he met the "science's" leading proponent, the self-styled "Professor" Orson Fowler, and his brother Lorenzo. Wells joined in their cause and soon married their sister Charlotte, herself a phrenologist. He ran the thriving publishing house of Fowler & Wells, lectured widely with Lorenzo, edited *The Phrenological Journal*, and wrote various books, among them *How to Behave* (1856), *The New Physiognomy* (1866), and *How to Read Character* (1869).[43]

Philadelphia-born Charles Godfrey Leland (1824–1903) pursued a much more scholarly and variegated literary calling. After graduation from Princeton, three years of study in Europe (including three days on the barricades in France during the revolution of 1848), and a brief tutelage in the law, he embarked upon an illustrious career as a journalist, humorist, poet, essayist, translator, and student of languages, especially Gypsy tongues. In the course of an extraordinarily productive life addressing a wide range of topics, he tossed off a little book on *The Art of Conversation* (1864).[44]

In the period from 1870 to the turn of the century a still more diverse array of advisers emerged, encompassing men from a variety of professions and an increased number of women of fashionable society. Clara Sophia Jessup Moore (1824–1899) offers a case in point. Raised "in an atmosphere of good breeding, charity, and devotion to learning" (in the phrase of one biographer), she pursued all these interests as a wealthy and socially prominent Philadelphian. She became a member of the city's literary circle through her fiction and poetry, but achieved a still-broader reputation as one of the most influential writers on etiquette of the late nineteenth century through works such as *Sensible Etiquette of the Best Society* (first published in 1878 and continuing through twenty editions). She defended good manners as an agent of Christian civilization, promoting not only earthly happiness but "our fitness for the enjoyment of a spiritual existence."[45]

The emphasis of Mary Elizabeth Wilson Sherwood (1826–1903) was more worldly. Like some other women advisers, she first learned the importance of etiquette as the daughter of a politician, New Hampshire Whig congressman James Wilson. This education was supplemented by boarding school in Boston, where, she later recalled, "we learned to be ladies, I hope, for we certainly learned very little else." She served as her father's Washington hostess and later, to support her family, wrote for *Harper's Bazar* and produced assorted novels and handbooks, notably *Amenities of Home* (1881), the especially popular *Manners and Social Usages* (1884), and *The Art of Entertaining* (1892). These books reflected, in the words of her grandson, the playwright Robert E. Sherwood, "a strong mind weakly used," as they defended the dominance of a reigning social elite based on virtue, talent, and money.[46]

The career of Florence Marion Hall (1845–1922) expressed more forcefully than most the relation between etiquette and social reform. The daughter of New England reformer Samuel Gridley Howe and writer Julia Ward Howe, she became an active lecturer and suffragist, as well as author of *Social Customs* (1881), *The Correct Thing in Good Society* (1888), *Social Usages at Washington* (1900), and similar works.

The male writers who published etiquette books in this later period came from an even wider range of backgrounds and experience. One who pursued several careers in the course of his life was Robert Tomes (1817–1882). At various times a New York physician, Panama explorer, surgeon on the Pacific Mail Steamship line, and American consul to Rheims, Tomes was also a prolific author. He wrote on diverse topics from military and naval history to a series of handbooks growing out of his work for *Harper's Bazar*, among them *The Bazar Book of Decorum* (1870).

Thomas Embley Osmun (1826–1908) lacked such a colorful history. His interest in social usages emerged from his concern with proper speech. After graduating from Oberlin College, he spent six years in Europe and became an expert on pronunciation and elocution. He wrote books on these subjects as well as *The Mentor* (1884) on manners—all under the pseudonym Alfred Ayres.

Oliver Bell Bunce (1828–1890) of New York began his literary career as a playwright, then moved into publishing. He became editor of *Appleton's Journal* and a supple essayist on manifold topics, including manners, on which he wrote a short book of injunctions entitled *Don't* (1883). (A sequel, *What to Do*, appeared under his wife's name in 1892.)[47]

Thomas E. Hill (1832–1915) was a more entrepreneurial spirit. An Illinois journalist, publisher, businessman, and onetime mayor of Aurora, Hill also compiled the enormously successful *Hill's Manual of Social and Business Forms* (1873). It sold nearly 400,000 copies by the turn of the century and during his life was last issued in a "new and improved 20th century edition, revised and enlarged," in 1911.[48]

The effort and originality these writers gave to their books varied considerably. Some clearly sought to strike a fresh point of view and tone, to write out of their own observations and in response to direct inquiries. Others forswore any claims of real authorship, saying they had compiled their books from various sources. And in the case of many of these volumes, the longest as well as the shortest, one quickly comes to recognize not just a similarity of materials but frequently a wholesale repetition of passages (with or without quotation marks) from other etiquette books of the period. Still, the consensus shared by these books was more than derivative. The etiquette writers' very investment in social conventions (however much they observed their violation) led them to minimize particularity and novelty. Even while bemoaning the lack of an established American "society," writers tended to place themselves self-consciously as defenders of tradition, to hark back to the ladies and gentlemen of "the old school." They preserved an extraordinary continuity of advice in the period from 1830 to the beginning of the twentieth century, when at last new social and cultural pressures forced changes. Before that time, only reluctantly did writers admit the need for revisions in conduct as new technologies developed (the elevator, the telephone, the automobile) and new social practices obtruded (the growing divorce rate, middle-class working women). This defense of tradition, of course, was a radically selective one, which served to provide "a historical and cultural ratification of a contemporary order."[49] As believers in progress, apostles of refinement, and popularizers of gentility, they stood in a far more ambiguous relationship to the past than they acknowledged.

Readership

The readership of etiquette manuals is obviously a much more speculative and intractable subject than their authorship. Though publishers, booksellers, book agents, businesses, schools, Sunday schools, libraries, parents, relatives, and friends placed these books in the hands of millions, we still don't know precisely *who* read them, *how many* read them, and *what* they took away from their reading. Some may well have read them in the intensive style of older times, slowly, deliberately, and repetitively; others, more quickly and selectively. No doubt in some cases these books were not read at all but merely possessed as badges of gentility—or rueful testimonies to the power of a salesman's pitch. Perhaps some read them as windows into the lives of the privileged, as distilled novels of manners, or even as ludicrous instances of snobbery, roaring with laughter at the authors' expense (as later Albert Einstein reportedly laughed when he read Emily Post's *Etiquette*).[50] Yet the most secure path leading toward an understanding of the interaction between book and reader must begin with an analysis of whom etiquette writers thought they were addressing.

Some etiquette books were directed to specific kinds of readers. Of those listed in the Selected Bibliography, nine spoke particularly to youth and children of both sexes, another eighteen to girls and women, and twelve to young men (two specifying those between fifteen and twenty), bachelors, or men in general. Two books addressed black readers in particular, expressing aspirations of black gentility and hopes of the power of politeness to increase racial harmony even as the era of Jim Crow laws and racial attacks began toward the close of the nineteenth century. *On Habits and Manners* (1888) was written originally for the black students of Hampton Institute, Booker T. Washington's alma mater, then "adapted to general use" by Mary Frances Armstrong. Eleven years later, the black author Elias M. Woods published *The Negro in Etiquette*, a book preaching the power of "the gospel of civility" to overcome rudeness and intolerance among both races.[51] One group is notable for its absence in this outpouring of advice: none of the books in my sample or in the bibliographies I uncovered addressed recent immigrants. Though etiquette authors assumed a Christian readership when they touched upon religious matters, they carefully avoided sectarian issues, and with a few notable exceptions the specific obligations of Christian courtesy were not addressed.[52] Religion had become a private matter in an increasingly secular society.

Most etiquette manuals—roughly 70 percent of those listed—spoke to a general readership within the middle class, though one predominantly young. Authors anticipated a variety of readers who were characterized as much by their subjective needs as by their objective social conditions: those bent on self-improvement and, in many cases, social mobility and metropolitan fluency, or, to put the matter less positively, those seeking to overcome real or imagined "disadvantages" of birth, class, and training, and to avoid social uncertainty, embarrassment, and ineptitude. In this spirit, the *Guide to Good Behaviour* (1856) claimed to be written "for the instruction of the young," as well as "for those who, in their early years, neglected to avail themselves of refinements within their reach," "for persons who had not the advantages of polite learning in youth, but . . . [who now] find themselves possessed of wealth to command the luxuries and elegances of society, but have not the polish to make themselves agreeable." The *Guide* promised to remedy these deficiencies without the humiliation of having to reveal them to others.[53]

Similarly, the author of *The American Code of Manners* (1880), a columnist for *The American Queen* in direct contact with a portion of her readers, declared that she wrote her books in response to letters from young ladies in the West and East; from young house-keepers who are beginning, far from the great cities, the first arduous attempts at dinner-giving; from young men who are rising in the world, and who are beginning to aspire toward that knowledge of society from which they have been debarred by a youth of industry; from elderly people, to whom fortune has come late, but whose children begin to wish to know how to take their places in the gay world.[54]

Another writer offered counsel to young men who had been educated in the country and sought to learn the ways of the city life by less painful means than through suffering "mortifying experiences." "Keep [this etiquette book] for reference," she urged readers, "the same as you do a dictionary."[55] In his novel *The Rise of Silas Lapham* of 1885, William Dean Howells portrayed the newly wealthy Lapham family in a similar situation: anxiously consulting etiquette manuals to overcome the social deficiencies of their rustic Vermont background before dining with the patrician Bostonian Coreys—although in this case they did not escape mortification.[56] Still, the promise continued in book after book: by heeding its instructions a reader could master the usages of what writers variously called "good," "polite," "refined," and "fashionable" society.

All these words were synonyms for "metropolitan" society. Though writers occasionally acknowledged the different manners and customs that characterized various regions of the country, separated town and country life from city ways, and even distinguished individual cities, they minimized these differences and encouraged readers to shed their provincial ways in favor of the cosmopolitan standards of city life. "A strong, local accent," advisers warned, ". . . marks you as underbred."[57] Some books published lists of common faults of speech in which rustic expressions figured prominently. The approved alternative was frequently Latinate rather than Anglo-Saxon, abstract rather than sensual and vivid:

> *All-fired*, for *great* or *enormous*.
> *Draw the wool over the eyes*, for *deceive*.
> *Fork over*, for *pay*.
> *Give in*, for *yield*.
> *Go through the mill*, for *acquire experience*.
> *Go under*, for *succumb* or *perish*.

Goner, for *one who is lost*.
Hang around, for *loiter*.
Hard case, for *worthless person*.
Hopping mad, for *very angry*.
Hush up, for *be silent*.
Kick up a row, for *create a disturbance*.
Odd stick, for *eccentric person*.
Poke fun, for *joke* or *ridicule*.
Raise a racket, for *make a noise*.
Reckon, for *think*.
Run into the ground, for *carry to excess*.
Scoop in, for *inveigle*.
Soft solder, for *flattery*.
Sound on the goose, for *staunch* or *true*.
Spread eagle, for *bombastic*.
Stropped, for *out of money*.
Swap, for *exchange*.
Take the rag off, for *surpass*.
Take on, for *grieve*.
Throw in, for *contribute*.
Tuckered out, for *fatigued*.
Wake up the wrong passenger, for *make a mistake as
  to an individual*.[58]

It is equally true that advisers repeatedly ~~poked fun at~~ ridiculed falsely refined speech as well, such as using *limb* for *leg*, *lady* for *woman*, and (as if not to give away the game too soon) *genteel* for *tasteful* or *well-bred*.[59]

Notably, too, "metropolitan" itself increasingly became a synonym for "New York" as the city's dominance as a commercial and cultural capital grew in the late nineteenth century. An increasing number of etiquette advisers lived there, and several books invoked New York in their titles as a mark of their authority: *Social Etiquette of New York*,[60] *The New York Fashion Bazar Book of Etiquette*,[61] *The Etiquette of New York To-day*.[62] The author of *The Complete Bachelor* (1896) remarked that in his many years answering questions for *Vogue* magazine on points of etiquette from all parts of the country, "my correspondents always wanted these questions answered from the New York stand-point. All this I have attempted to do in this volume."[63]

Etiquette advisers strove to accommodate a range of purses and social positions, including in some cases the upper stratum of the working class. *The Art of Pleasing* (1855), for example, emphasized that it spoke to "the laborer, the mechanic, the clerk" as well as "the merchant, and the man of wealth, leisure, and refinement."[64] Another book added that one might possess all the qualities of a gentleman even though "an artisan or a tiller of the soil; and that as real a lady may be found plying her needle, or labouring in a manufactory, as in the most splendid drawing-room."[65] Many stressed that one could observe the forms of gentility on an extremely modest budget. Though most assumed the presence of household servants, they also counseled the reader who could afford only one, or even did without. Nonetheless, certain class boundaries were unmistakable. Advisers drew the line, for instance, at writing for servants themselves. One adviser sniffed, "As we fear this book may not be consulted by servants as much as we would like, we will reserve our chapter to them for another occasion."[66] In fact, to manage adequately many of the requisite social exchanges of urban middle-class gentility demanded some independence, leisure, a carefully furnished household, a versatile wardrobe, and other expenditures. And particularly in the later nineteenth century, some etiquette advisers addressed an ideal reader who could command numerous servants, an elaborate household, and a great deal of ready cash. Whether writers imagined readers of large or modest means, they guided them along well-trod pathways and bade them knock gently at the gates of older social elites. Manners, not just money, and demure emulation of the socially established, not aggressive self-assertion, were necessary for social success. Etiquette advisers characteristically mediated between the contending—and potentially contradictory—demands for social mobility and preservation of social order in a dynamic age of capitalist expansion.

Republicanism and Rudeness

Though etiquette advisers focused on private and personal matters, they found themselves drawn willy-nilly into issues that were public and political. In the words of political scientist Judith Shklar, "The boundaries between acceptable and intolerable inequalities were a burning issue for Americans from the first. Somewhere there had to be a line that marked off legitimate differences of wealth and talent from unacceptable, undemocratic, and unrepublican political manners and activities."[67] In seeking to trace this line through American society, etiquette advisers and other advocates of refinement found themselves attacked on two opposing fronts: first, by those detractors, both Europeans and Americans with aristocratic pretensions, who derided American society as irredeemably vulgar and viewed republicanism as incompatible with refinement; and second, by democratic critics who heard within hymns to civility the less noble strains of snobbery and class interests.

The numerous descriptions by nineteenth-century English travelers of American bumptiousness and vulgarity such as Basil Hall's *Travels in North America* (1829), Frances Trollope's *Domestic Manners of the Americans* (1832), and Captain Frederick Marryat's *Diary in America* (1839) rankled domestic readers precisely because, however overdrawn, their sketches of the confused state of American manners could not be easily dismissed. The lack of established social traditions in the United States, combined with aggressive assertions of social equality, many foreign visitors believed, made civility as Europeans understood it impossible. What they found instead was a culture of coarse familiarity, ludicrous pretension, and frequent rudeness, particularly among the white working classes. As early as 1795 a disillusioned emigrant to America returned to his native England carrying the sour conclusion "Civility cannot be purchased from them [Americans] on any terms; they seem to think that it is incompatible with freedom."[68] Mrs. Trollope claimed that slavery itself appeared "far less injurious to the manners and morals of the [American] people than the fallacious ideas of equality, which are so fondly cherished by the working classes of the white population in America." Servility, she came perilously close to asserting, was essential for civility.[69] Offenses against propriety, moreover, often went beyond dirty linen and tobacco spitting to rowdiness and riot, as the populace could no longer be depended upon to know its "place." The chaotic reception after Andrew Jackson's inauguration in 1829 offers a case in point. According to one horrified account, "a rabble, a mob of boys, negroes, women, children, scrambling, fighting, romping," swept into the White House, elbowed dignitaries aside, and almost trampled the President himself. In its wake the "mob" left fainting ladies and men with bloody noses, carpets and chairs smeared with muddy footprints, and several thousand dollars' worth of broken glassware and china.[70] The insolence of an egalitarian order, if unchecked, apparently knew no bounds.

Etiquette advisers gave a divided response to these critics. While they avoided the bluntly antidemocratic swipes of Hall, Marryat, Mrs. Trollope, and other foreign travelers and denied that their countrymen were uniquely vulgar, they frequently acknowledged the special need for a culture of civility and an established code of manners in the fluid, pluralistic, and often aggressively egalitarian American society. Most Americans, one etiquette adviser conceded in 1857, appeared to "regard *Rudeness* and *Republicanism* as synonymous terms."[71] It was not that rudeness and vulgarity were absent abroad, another writer observed; but Europe's stratified class structure kept the "rough and unwashed" at a social and often physical distance from the affluent. Snug in a first-class railway car, a European traveler could regard the third-class occupants, for all "their unkempt hair, botched and greasy suits, rude manners, and coarse vernacular," as picturesque elements of the social scene. In the United States, by contrast, where the two classes mingled promiscuously on trains, in hotels, and in society at large, no such detachment was possible. Therefore, he concluded fastidiously, "universal cleanliness and good manners are essential to democracy."[72] Toward the end of the nineteenth century, another American adviser enviously regarded the social deference European shopkeepers and cabmen paid their customers and declared, "No book of etiquette is more needed than one which should teach shopgirls and shop-men the *beauty* and *advantages* of a respectful manner [italics added]." In the absence of such books, significantly, she relied upon the workings of the market economy: the chief "advantage" to such salespeople themselves, she continued, was that they would earn more money. The "beauty," presumably, lay in the eye of the social superior.[73]

As for socially privileged readers of etiquette books in a democracy, they were more often urged to observe the strictures of civility not out of egalitarian conviction but out of sheer self-interest. Writing in the late 1880s, a time when social inequities in the United States had become an issue of enormous urgency in diverse quarters from Populist farmers to striking industrial workers to middle-class reformers such as Edward Bellamy, an etiquette writer named Lydia White remarked blandly, "We are all forced, in spite of individual objections and protests, to put into practice the national theory of equality. We must mix together, and it therefore behooves us, for our own comfort, to make the mixture as smooth and agreeable as possible."[74]

Thus, from the age of Jackson to the age of Cleveland, Harrison, and McKinley, in response to sweeping changes in American society, etiquette writers expressed a persistent concern with instituting an American code of manners that would regulate social interchange and temper what they saw as the excesses of democracy. In the later nineteenth century, this concern appears to have intensified in reaction to pressures from various directions, including the influx of new immigrant populations and the presence of a self-assertive new plutocracy. Searching for analogies that would express what they saw as etiquette's importance, several writers in the 1880s and '90s defended it as "the machinery of society." The image suggested the values of order, efficiency, regulation, and subordination of the various parts to the whole that they sought. Etiquette, they argued, "keeps every cog and wheel in place, at its own work, which prevents jostling, and carries all things along comfortably to their consummation."[75]

The Laws of Etiquette

But far and away the favorite analogy was with the law. By this comparison, writers aimed to justify the essential function of etiquette in a democracy and to win compliance with its demands. Consider the following examples, beginning with a passage that moves nimbly from society to "good society" and reminds prospective members, particularly the *nouveaux riches*, that if they fail to observe its laws, their punishment will be both swift and just:

> A nation is a number of people associated together for common purposes, and no one questions the right of those people to make laws for themselves; society is also an organized association, and has a perfect right to make laws which shall be binding upon all of its members. Now, what are called the rules of politeness are nothing more than the customs or laws

3. Etiquette as Social Law: Illustration from *Hill's Manual of Social and Business Forms* (1885). Courtesy of the Margaret Woodbury Strong Museum, Rochester, New York.

of good society; and no one, however fine his education, or however great his wealth, power, or fame, should feel himself wronged in the least if this society refuses him admission until he has made himself fully acquainted with its laws.[76]

Next, a defense of etiquette against charges of its arbitrary or aristocratic character:

Etiquette is not a code of laws or forms handed down to us from the courts of Europe. American society has rules of its own which embrace that which is best in all codes, and which are best adapted to the needs of a republican government. The rules of etiquette are by no means a system of torture; they are to society what civil law is to a country; and, as in the exercise of civil law only the offenders are punished, so in the exercise of the social law only those find it unpleasant who violate its requirements.[77]

Like the law, questions of etiquette were not to be treated as matters of individual taste and discretion, but to be strictly observed. Another writer drove the point home:

> Personal preference may guide us in the conduct of our lives, but it is untrustworthy as an instructor in etiquette. The codes of good society are laws to be obeyed without question, in which preference has no part, any more than in the laws concerning life and personal property.[78]

Other counselors on etiquette, elevated by this analogy to legislators, judges, and legal scholars, could play further variations on the theme. One such adviser, perhaps inspired by the famous dictum of Oliver Wendell Holmes, Jr., that the life of the law was not logic but experience, contended that the laws of etiquette, though often illogical, also represented a distillation of historical social experience:

> Despite its many imperfections, the common law surprises us with its accumulation of sound views and its exposition of true principles,—the result of the combined wisdom of many great minds during long centuries. In the same way the laws that govern manners contain many true and unchanging principles mingled with much that is untrue, unimportant, and transitory.[79]

Often writers went still further, insisting that manners were not simply analogous to laws, but essential to them. Seeking to establish conservative bulwarks against social disorder, they frequently and fondly quoted Edmund Burke: "Manners are of more importance than laws. Upon these in a great measure the law depends."[80]

Thus apostles of civility battled for far bigger stakes than how best to eat asparagus. Their enterprise must be viewed within the larger concern of how to establish order and authority in a restless, highly mobile, rapidly urbanizing and industrializing democracy. Seeking to avoid overt conflict, they turned issues of class and social grievance back upon the individual. They redefined issues of social conflict to questions of personal governance, social propriety, and "good taste." The rules of etiquette would extend the laws and teach each individual his social duties. As we shall see, advisers anticipated various means of enforcement; but they placed their greatest stress upon voluntary compliance. Through instruction in etiquette they aimed to carry the theory of "influence"—the belief in the reformative power of moral suasion—into the very ritual structure of interpersonal activities. Exemplary demonstrations in civility and self-restraint, etiquette advisers believed, would ineluctably move others toward similar conduct and bring about voluntary compliance with the "laws" of polite behavior.

Etiquette Writers and Their Critics

In addition to the obstinate presence of rusticity and rudeness with all their feared social consequences, American advisers on etiquette labored against a second set of difficulties: a deep-seated suspicion of their ideal of civility as leading to insincerity, overrefinement, and decadence. This opposition stemmed in part from absorption of a long-standing English distrust of courtly elegance as mere foppery (frequently expressed from the time of Shakespeare to that of Chesterfield); and it was doubly reinforced by radical Protestant antipathy toward social and religious ritual and also by republican distaste for the least trappings of aristocratic luxury.[81] In this spirit a reviewer in the 1870 *Atlantic Monthly* hurled contempt at the whole vulgar notion of compiling an etiquette manual in America:

> All the wisdom needed for the career of the ordinary republican aspirant can be condensed into three rules which he may write down on his reversible paper cuff: 1. Keep out of fine society; 2. Be cleanly, simple, and honest; 3. Never be ashamed of a blunder. Everything beyond these is vanity.[82]

Mark Twain, who delighted in exposing the pretensions of sham gentility, once planned to write a burlesque of a nineteenth-century etiquette manual. It would instruct readers in proper deportment in all occasions, such as the niceties of address and precedence a young gentleman should observe in rescuing a young lady from a fire, beginning with this declaration:

> Although through the fiat of a cruel fate, I have been debarred the gracious privilege of your acquaintance, permit me, Miss

[here insert name, if known], the inestimable honor of offering you the aid of a true and loyal arm against the fiery doom which now o'ershadows you with its crimson wing. [This form to be memorized, and practiced in private.]

This speech could easily be adapted for other disasters.

For instance, in tendering rescue from destruction by hurricane, or earthquake, or runaway team, or railway collision (where no conflagration ensues), the operator should merely substitute "fatal doom" for "fiery doom"; and in cases of ordinary shipwreck or other methods of drowning, he should say "watery doom." No other alterations are necessary, for the "crimson wing" applies to all calamities of a majestic sort, and is a phrase of exceeding finish and felicity.[83]

Against such jibes, numerous American etiquette writers insisted that they espoused no wholesale adoption of European deportment or of artificial conventions but a distinctively American etiquette, appropriate to a republican and Christian civilization, freed of *"imported superfluities."*[84] In fact, American etiquette books were far better suited to certain cultural needs than Mark Twain's burlesque suggested. Writers adapted, transformed, and generalized the older traditions of English and Continental courtesy books to fit the requirements of a professedly egalitarian society in the process of rapid capitalistic expansion, while aiming to soothe its disruptions. The one-sided deference rituals of the court gave way to more symmetrical assurances of mutual respect among the middle classes. While still paying close attention to social "superiors" and "inferiors," bourgeois readers were taught to behave courteously toward all "respectable" people with whom they might come in contact. One may see in this generalization of courtesy the Durkheimian notion that in "modern" (here nineteenth-century) society, the individual self becomes a little god to be treated with proper ritual respect. But one must add that the definition of the sacred in this bourgeois ritualistic order did not devolve upon all individuals equally, and that, moreover, this order was critically connected to the workings of industrial capitalist society in its earlier stages of development. The individual's "sacredness" provided a justification for his isolation, his loneliness, his vulnerability. The ritualistic order provided a means of extending the cultural hegemony of the dominant classes into the very "structure of feeling" of the larger society.[85]

Manners and the Market

Instructors taught how to channel social ambitions into polite emulation, to encase the iron laws of the market within the velvet glove of manners, in myriad ways. Often the crucial element in their teachings lay as much in what was *not* said as in what was. One may see a striking instance in Julia Dewey's *How to Teach Manners in the School-Room* (1888), in which she imagines a model exchange between a teacher and her young pupils. The lesson deserves quotation in full:

LESSON V.

Purpose.—To suggest as a reason for cultivating good manners that we thus make our manners like those of the best people.
Method.—Question and answers.

The Lesson.

Of what did we talk in our last lesson?
"Of kindness."
"And trying to make others happy."
What is it to think of the happiness of others before our own?
"Unselfishness."
And if we practice unselfishness, what can be said of us?
"That we have good manners."
But do all kind and unselfish people have good manners?
(Some are in doubt.) Let us see. I do not think a truly kind heart will allow any one to be rude, but how is it in this case?

It is not thought polite to eat with the knife. Have you ever known kind people to do it?

"Yes, Miss B."

Why do you think they do it?

"Because they know no better."

Can they learn better?

"Yes, Miss B."

How?

"From other people."

How from other people?

"They can watch, and do what they see nice people do."

And how do these nice people know?

"Perhaps they have watched some other nice people."

If one who has used his knife in eating learns better, what ought he to do?

"To stop using it."

And if he continues to use it, what will be thought of him?

"That he is odd or queer."

Should you like to be thought odd or queer?

"No ma'am."

Then what must you do?

"We must watch people who know what good manners are, and try to make our manners like theirs."

What kind of people are polite?

"The best people."

If we learn to do as the best people do, how shall we be considered?

"To be *best* people."

Now tell me one reason why our manners should be good.

"Because the best people have good manners."

And another?

"Because we wish to be considered *best*."[86]

Such children had taken an important step in the acquisition of both the manners and ambitions appropriate to nineteenth-century urban middle-class culture. Like other fields of study, however, the bourgeois codes of civility and politeness entailed greater complexities the further a student advanced. Julia Dewey neatly begged the question of what made "the best people" best, if anything, apart from their good manners. Was it their money? Their inherited social prestige? And what was the connection between them? Students asking such impertinent questions would have been crisply rebuked by the teacher. The relation of manners to class and money was a troubling one, because if the crucial role of money were starkly revealed, then "the best people" would both forfeit their moral authority and the emulation and respect it brought and join in the free-for-all of the market on an equal footing with the rawest newcomers. Manners provided yet another way of avoiding talking openly about the dirty secret of class in America.

Nor was it only in the schoolroom that such discussion was discouraged. Edith Wharton recalled that in her socially privileged New York girlhood in the 1860s and '70s, " 'bad manners' was the supreme offense." Good manners expressed one's " 'good breeding' "; and the material resources that sustained this position were to pass unremarked—among women and girls especially. "One of the first rules of conversation" Wharton's mother taught her was " 'Never talk about money, and think about it as little as possible.' "[87]

Yet as any reader of Wharton's novels will recognize, this was an injunction impossible to follow. Money was not the only basis of social position, certainly; but the fate of characters such as Lily Bart in *The House of Mirth* demonstrates how within the world of fashionable society of the upper middle class it was indispensable, and without it Lily finds life literally intolerable and ultimately commits suicide. Both men and women were ever alert to the rise and fall of the fortunes about them, and if men suffered bankruptcy (significantly, often called "embarrassment" in the nineteenth century), their families' social stock collapsed immediately. Wharton recalled of her father's "set" in New York:

I believe their value lay in upholding two standards of importance in any community, that of education and good manners, and of scrupulous probity in business and private affairs.

New York has always been a commercial community, and in my infancy the merits and defects of its citizens were those of a mercantile middle class. The first duty of such a class was to maintain a strict standard of uprightness in affairs; and the gentlemen of my father's day did maintain it, whether in the law, in banking, shipping or wholesale commercial enterprises. I well remember the horror excited by any irregularity in affairs, and the relentless social ostracism inflicted on the families of those who lapsed from professional or business integrity. In one case, where two or three men of high social standing were involved in a discreditable bank failure, their families were made to suffer to a degree that would seem merciless to our modern judgment.[88]

Outwardly ignoring money, women learned to conduct their social dealings in accordance with the male world of commerce. Such a direct if unspoken linkage between manners and the market clearly served both to enforce codes of financial probity and to comb the newly indigent out of social "sets." Among men of the mercantile class particularly, in the words of one scholar, "simple commercial honesty was . . . the moral axis around which all . . . human relationships were formed."[89] The principle of fidelity-to-contract, fundamental to business transactions, served in important ways as a model for both men and women in social relations as well. And while the bourgeois code of manners might mediate in some respects the fluctuations of the marketplace, ultimately it was tied to them.

Although middle-class girls and women were to think of money as little as possible, the common assumption was that nineteenth-century males could think of little else; and to them etiquette writers and other popular advisers occasionally broke the code of silence. Such manly talk, however, served only to tighten the knot between manners and the market: manners, advisers confided, might lead to wealth! They insisted that the market itself obeyed not simply iron laws but moral ones, and that the cultivation of civility was the first step to both financial and social success. Showing respect to others combined Christian kindness and self-interest, one writer declared: "politeness is power, and . . . for the ambitious man there is no surer road to the highest places . . . than through good manners."[90] Contended another adviser, "No one quality of the mind and heart is more important as an element conducive to worldly success than civility—that feeling of kindness and love for our fellow-beings which is expressed in pleasing manners."[91] The young man on the make, if he followed such advice, would curb his volatile nature and become deferential, cheerful, and tractable. He would remember what one author called "the pecuniary value of obligingness."[92] Writers on success insisted, "A good manner is the best letter of recommendation."[93] Especially for young men, manners were to be regarded as social capital, "a fortune in itself" that if wisely invested would pay enormous dividends. Such assurances further encouraged the commercialization of courtesy and feeling as, in the scornful language of one mid-century social observer, "*smiles & manners*" became "business capital," a man's "suavity . . . [furnished] him with his salary or income," and he was obliged to "appear pleas'd, anxious, indifferent, or sad according to his customer's humor."[94] The efficacy of such advice and the entire relationship between manners and the market would be tested, above all, in the rapidly developing cities of nineteenth-century America. The expanding urban centers held both the greatest opportunities for business and social successes and the most menacing threats to individual character and social stability. They gathered in dense proximity the prosperous and miserable, the refined and rude, the virtuous and depraved. Here the tensions and contradictions of nineteenth-century American society were most vividly revealed—and disturbingly masked. Readers of etiquette and other advice literature also had to learn how to read the city.

CHAPTER THREE

Reading the City: The Semiotics of Everyday Life

Of all the voluminous texts produced in the nineteenth century, among the most massive and challenging were the new metropolises themselves. They were recognized by writers of all sorts as the great signifying structures of the age: vast, intricate repositories, dense with meaning, out of which more specific texts might be created. Observers typically stressed, however, the enormous *difficulty* of reading the city at large and its inhabitants, let alone writing about them. New York, London, Paris, and other cities presented such compressed, tangled, contrasting, chaotic, and often opaque surfaces as to be simply unintelligible in terms of any earlier coherent system of signs. Confronting the city as a text, readers found themselves, in the words of Henry James, striving to decipher in the abundance of facts "the *i*llegible word . . . the great inscrutable answer to questions . . . something fantastic and *abracadabrant*, belonging to no known language." The theme of the city's illegibility was a recurrent one, common to writers as diverse as Balzac, Engels, and Poe. But to learn the language of the modern city and to read it as a text was no mere belletristic act; it was essential to a full and meaningful urban life. Without this ability one would remain perpetually an uncomprehending stranger, baffled by the city's signs and codes, unable to understand others or to represent oneself. The rise of the nineteenth-century city created enormous anxiety over precisely this crisis of meanings, what might be called a semiotic breakdown. In the new urban centers of the Western capitalist democracies, traditional notions of social relations, manners, and appropriate behavior all appeared in disarray. The vision of metropolitan society and culture cherished by etiquette advisers was in fact one of a number of contending definitions of what nineteenth-century urban life would and could be.[1]

This urban upheaval was especially dramatic in the United States, marking an abrupt departure from earlier historical experience. Although port cities were an essential part of colonial life, they were tiny by later standards. The four largest cities—Boston, New York, Philadelphia, and Charleston—grew substantially over the course of the eighteenth century; yet their *combined* populations amounted to only 18,700 in the year 1700, 59,000 in 1750, and 145,500 in 1800—this last only slightly larger than the population of Mexico City in the same year. Relative to the increase in the population at large, America's total urban population (generously defined as those living in towns of above 2,500 inhabitants) actually declined slightly over the course of the eighteenth century, from 7.7 percent in 1700 to 7.2 percent in 1775. The early decades of the nineteenth century saw only a modest upturn in the percentage of the urban population. As late as 1820, only one person in fourteen lived in a community of more than 2,500, and only twelve cities exceeded 10,000.[2]

But if the nation slowly approached the "urban threshold" in the early nineteenth century, it bounded across with dazzling speed, riding the galloping industrial capitalist economy. The following decades recorded, in relative terms, the most rapid urbanization in American history. Between 1830 and 1840, the population living in cities of 2,500 or more grew by 64 percent; between 1840 and 1850, by 92 percent; between 1850 and 1860, by 75 percent. The largest city in 1820, New York, swelled from a population of 125,000 in that year to 800,000 by 1860, over a million including Brooklyn. Philadelphia climbed from 64,000 in 1820 to 566,000 in 1860. Chicago, a tiny frontier settlement in 1832, claimed 20,000 residents by 1848 and 180,000 by 1865. San Francisco, which had scarcely existed prior to the great gold strikes of 1848, exploded to 57,000 in the next dozen years.[3]

Rapid urban expansion continued through the rest of the nineteenth century and into the early twentieth. As of 1880, seventy-seven cities could boast a population of over 25,000, and twenty, of more than 100,000. By 1910, New York, now with its five consolidated boroughs, claimed almost five million residents, Chicago had swelled, astonishingly, to over two million, and Philadelphia had tripled its 1860 population to reach over one and a half million. Not just these great cities but communities of all sizes grew markedly to form a complex system of regional and increasingly national urban networks. Altogether, between 1860 and 1910 America's urban population increased sevenfold and rose in percentage terms from 19.8 to 45.7 percent of the total population of the country.[4]

This enormous urban growth was fueled by migration from the country and smaller towns and increasingly by immigration. By 1860 the fifty largest cities included one and a half million who were foreign-born—roughly 40 percent of their total population— as well as a vast group of native migrants. The great waves of immigrants to the United States in the late nineteenth and early twentieth centuries also landed chiefly in the larger industrial cities. By 1920, in cities of 100,000 or more, 58 percent were foreign-born or the children of foreign-born parents.[5]

This new population inhabited a new cityscape that embodied all the tensions of the emergent economic and social order. In many cities, older mixed neighborhoods gave way to enclaves segregated by class and ethnicity. As pressures for cheap housing increased, the poor and recent immigrants clustered in tenements, cellars, and shanties whose only sanitary provisions were the privy and the gutter. As the geographer David Harvey has observed, "At the very historical moment when the potentiality of the city as 'a place of encounters' . . . was at its apogee, it became a fragmented terrain held down and together under all manner of forces of class, racial, and sexual domination."[6]

Bird's-Eye and Mole's-Eye Views of the City

Such a rapid urban transformation challenged the power of newcomers and longtime residents alike to comprehend the city as an entity. The problem of reading the city dates from this time. Etiquette books offered detailed instructions on how to "read" the character of various people and social situations in an urban context and how to conduct oneself accordingly; but their advice cannot be fully understood unless it is seen in relation to the larger question of the character of American urban life and how best to read the city and its participants. Two primary strategies of such reading emerge in the United States as well as in northern Europe by the mid-nineteenth century: the bird's-eye view and what might be called the mole's-eye view—the splendid urban panorama and the searching urban exploration.

In the broadest sense, bird's-eye views may be taken to encompass a variety of nineteenth-century efforts to rise above the disparate surfaces of the city, either literally or imaginatively, in order to read it as a coherent structure, its various parts subordinated to the whole. Bird's-eye views converted the city into a kind of concrete abstraction, displacing the profusion of sensory experience by the cold, distant grasp of the eye. Such views flattered their beholders' power by subjecting the city for their inspection as privileged readers, conquering tourists. Much of the immense fascination with ever-higher towers, bridges, and, later, skyscrapers lay in the panoramic vision of the city they afforded. During her travels in the United States in the mid-1830s, the English writer Harriet Martineau mounted the highest point available in the cities she visited—Boston's State House, Philadelphia's Pennsylvania Hospital, Washington's Capitol, a new hotel in Baltimore, a church steeple in Charleston, South Carolina, and so on—in order to behold each as a "living map." She earnestly recommended that other travelers follow her example as "their first business in a foreign city": "It is scarcely credible how much time is saved and confusion of ideas obviated by these means." Beginning with the earliest daguerreotypists in the 1830s, photographers took to towers, rooftops, and hills, aiming to capture the city's identity, to restore the legibility lost in the swirl of daily life in the streets. By the 1860s the camera was airborne as photographers in the United States and abroad achieved the first successful city views from balloons.[7]

Yet the most successful and popular urban bird's-eye views were lithographs from imaginary positions in the air. Although the tradition of such views extends back to late-fifteenth-century printed woodcuts, before the mid-nineteenth century a typical American urban view was taken from a ground-level or only slightly elevated perspective across a river or bay. Such a vantage point suited smaller maritime ports but could not capture the nation's extraordinary new cityscapes, and the bird's-eye view rapidly superseded earlier perspectives for both dynamic cities such as Boston, New York, Chicago, Saint Louis, and San Francisco and even fledgling towns such as McGregor, Iowa, and Sunset, Texas. This perspective was especially congenial to the demands of urban capitalist development, and it is little wonder that bird's-eye lithographs were prominently displayed in business offices and banks, hotels and shops, as well as in private homes. In some cases, real estate promoters commissioned city views that projected a flourishing metropolis from a few huts and cabins, leaving hapless investors to discover belatedly that what they beheld was, in the words of one such dupe, merely a "lithographic fiction," an "engraved romance."[8] But even the most accurate depictions were highly selective. With an ease that urban photographers envied, lithographic artists could assume an aerial perspective and exaggerate or diminish aspects of their subject at will while endowing the city as a whole with breathtaking clarity and drama. The cityscape appeared enclosed and defined, with its foreground especially highlighted as a brilliantly legible text, telling a story of dynamic enterprise and unity. The city's great monuments of culture and commerce stood dominant: its parks and boulevards, bridges and harbors, civic buildings and churches. What at street level might appear fragmentary and chaotic here became subsumed into an integrated and bounded order.

However, the holistic vision of the bird's-eye view could be sustained only by ignoring key parts of the city. Scenes of squalor, vice, and want, of congestion and depression, had no place in these images. They were simply effaced in the celebratory portrayal of harmonic order. Nonetheless, the unity of such depictions was contradicted both by many city dwellers' daily experience and, increasingly, by alternative literary and visual representations of the city—mole's-eye views—that myopically traced the dark and hidden tunnels of urban life.

In contrast to the almost utopian vision of the bird's-eye views, these mole's-eye perspectives disclosed a nightmare of fragmentation and corruption. Instead of regarding the city in bright daylight from above to stress its progressive order, they presented the city primarily from the shadowy depths to emphasize its degradation and chaos. Such depictions include numerous treatments of the wicked city in mid-nineteenth-century fiction and melodrama, reformers' investigations into urban poverty, vice, and crime, and journalistic sketches of American cities that flourished in the mid- and late nineteenth century. Inspired by English and French tours of urban lowlife, including Pierce Egan's *Life in London* (1821) and Eugene Sue's *Les Mystères de Paris* (1843), American writers adapted their conventions to local conditions. Their formulaic character is

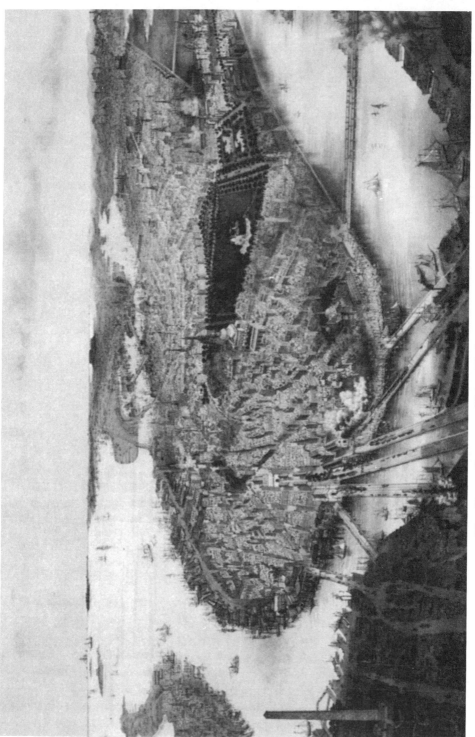

4. The City as Prosperous Unity: Bird's-eye view of Boston, 1877.

5. Mole's-Eye View of New York. Frontispiece from McCabe's *Secrets of the Great City* (1868). The five scenes compress the story of a young man's ruin in the city. At upper left he leaves home for New York; he visits a fashionable saloon at top right, drinks with "fancy" gamblers at center, is robbed and murdered by his companions immediately below, and at the bottom his body is recovered from the river by police.

clear in titles such as: *The Miseries of New York; The Mysteries and Miseries of New York; The Mysteries and Miseries of New Orleans; New York by Gas-Light: With Here and There a Streak of Sunshine; Sunshine and Shadow in New York; New York by Sunlight and Gaslight; Lights and Shadows of New York Life; Lights and Shadows in San Francisco; Chicago by Gaslight*; and *Boston Inside Out! Sins of a Great City!*[9]

Whereas the bird's-eye lithographs presented the city as a clearly legible text of unity and progress, flourishing markets and civic spirit, the "mysteries and miseries" genre showed cities ravaged by the single-minded devotion to gain. Material greed and the pressures of the marketplace, these writers insisted, had created new cities polarized between the greedy, snobbish upper class and the degraded, often vicious poor. Such a city could not be grasped as a totality, since it lacked any moral, social, or physical center. It remained a labyrinth of segmented areas, each with its characteristic social types. In New York, for example, these included the pretentious Fifth Avenue parvenu, the feverish Wall Street speculator, the preening Broadway dandy, the swaggering Bowery fireman, the "fancy" gambler, the grasping Chatham Street Jewish pawnbroker, the alluring prostitute, the defeated drunkard, the wretched and vicious Five Points slum dweller, the street-wise newsboy.

And if the city's sheer intricacy made it difficult for the uninitiated to read, its elaborate deceptions made it impossible. Hypocrisy and immorality reigned among people and establishments of the most impeccable appearance; and hosts of criminals set cunning traps for the unwary. As one book ominously declared: "New York is a great secret, not only to those who have never seen it, but to the majority of its own citizens. Few living in the great city have any idea of the terrible romance and hard reality of the lives of two thirds of the inhabitants." Those who did not know what most city dwellers experienced were, of course, middle-class readers, socially insulated from the very sight of the poor. For those who wished to know, such guidebooks insisted, the pathway they provided in their pages offered the only safe mode of conduct:

[This volume] is designed to warn the thousands who visit the city against the dangers and pitfalls into which their curiosity or vice may lead them, and it is hoped that those who read the book will heed its warnings. The city is full of danger. The path of safety which is pointed out in these pages is the only one—a total avoidance of the vicinity of sin. No matter how clever a man may be in his own town or city, he is a child in the hands of the sharpers and villains of this community, and his only safety lies in avoiding them. His curiosity can be satisfied in these pages, and he can know the Great City from them, without incurring the danger attending an effort to see it.[10]

The hidden city of the poor held a special fascination. The explosive development of slums (in which an estimated three quarters of New York's population lived by the late 1850s) shocked prosperous observers, arousing at once sympathy and disgust.[11] In *New York by Gas-Light* (1850) George G. Foster epitomized the lurid, prurient tones of journalists and other investigators of the poor as he panted with eager and dreadful determination "to penetrate beneath the thick veil of night and lay bare the fearful mysteries of darkness in the metropolis—the festivities of prostitution, the orgies of pauperism, the haunts of theft and murder, the scenes of drunkenness and beastly debauch and all the sad realities that go to make up the lower stratum—the underground story—of life in New York!"[12] Social and sexual repressions converged in these Victorian tours of the city's secret life. Regarding this "underground story" as a dark continent, populated by "primitive" natives, urban explorers typically set out upon their safaris at night, accompanied by police officers and lanterns, to map the region of poverty, vice, and crime as a first step to eradicating it. Its very existence rebuked the bourgeois vision of a regenerated metropolis of neatly enclosed homes and broad avenues swept clean of working-class hawkers, idlers, drinkers, prostitutes, and demonstrators.[13]

Not only were the approach and tone conventionalized; so, too, was the very itinerary of these "gaslight" tours by 1866, when the New York minister Peter Stryker followed the trail of earlier investigators in an excursion to the metropolis's "lower depths" with a party of church officers and policemen. Entering the slums, they pushed into dank cellars to discover a motley cluster of residents, "black and white, men, women and children, all huddled together." Stryker reported: "They evince no surprise at seeing us enter, evidently being well accustomed to the inspection of the police department." At another tenement, Stryker's party beheld what was to their eyes abundant evidence of moral degeneracy and social disorder in the spectacle of racial intermingling—"people of both sexes and every shade of color herding together, exhibiting less taste and refinement than the brute creation"—and additional indications that such sites had already become an established part of the tour. His portentous diction thickened as he continued: "From these miserable abodes we hasten, and as with disgust we turn from the locality, we hear some depraved children, who evidently sur-

6. The City as Polarized Extremities: The mansion of the dry-goods magnate
A. T. Stewart and the notorious slum the Old Brewery at Five Points in New York.
Frontispiece from Matthew Hale Smith's *Sunshine and Shadow in New York* (1868).

mise the nature of our mission, saying in mock solemnity, 'The miseries of New York!' . . ."[14]

In the "lights and shadows" genre and related descriptions of the city, the proliferating "dark" and "secret" enclaves of vice were conventionally contrasted with the "sunshine" or "daylight": the most public and visible realms of changing city life, preeminently the central business and shopping districts, the "downtown" most frequented by middle-class residents and visitors. Both the "light" and the "dark" regions, of course, were manifestations of the expansive industrial capitalist economy—and of its social costs. Yet they challenged middle-class observers' powers of "reading" in very different ways: the "dark" by its deception and wickedness, the "light" by its very blandness and opacity. The difficulties of reading the city posed by both realms extended to reading specific characters within them, not only among the deceitful, but among urban dwellers of all sorts, as the pressures of life erased legible signs of individual attributes.

Faces in the Crowd

Symptomatic of this difficulty was the attention paid to the restless, preoccupied expression of pedestrians in American business districts, which became as prominent a piece of description in urban guides and travelers' accounts as the tenement houses and barrooms. Here are three examples; first, the Austrian diplomat Baron von Hübner in Chicago around 1871:

> I mix with the crowd, which drags me on with it. I strive to read their physiognomies, and I find everywhere the same expression. Everyone is in a hurry, if only to get home as fast as possible to save the few hours of rest, after having made the most of the long hours of work. Everyone seems to suspect a competitor in his neighbor. The crowd is the embodiment of isolation. The moral atmosphere is not charity but rivalry.[15]

And here is Mark Twain exploring New York in 1867:

> A man walks his tedious miles through the same interminable street every day, elbowing his way through a buzzing mul-

titude of men, yet never seeing a familiar face, and never seeing a strange one the second time. . . . Every man seems to feel that he has got the duties of two lifetimes to accomplish in one, and so he rushes, rushes, rushes, and never has time to be companionable—never has any time at his disposal to fool away on matters which do not involve dollars and duty and business.[16]

And, finally, an account of a man arriving in the city in search of a job, as reported in *New York by Sunlight and Gaslight* (1882):

I turned into Broadway at the Bowling Green, and as I did so, found myself in a steady stream of human beings, each hurrying by as if his life depended upon his speed, taking no notice of his fellows, pushing and jostling them, and each with weary, jaded, anxious look upon his face. As I gazed at this mighty torrent I was dismayed. I got as far as Trinity Church-yard, and then I put my valise upon the pavement, and leaning against the railing, watched the people as they passed me by. They came by hundreds, thousands, all with that eager, rest-less gait that I now know so well, all with the weary, anxious, care-worn expression I have mentioned, as if trying to reach some distant goal within a given time. They seemed to say to me, "We would gladly stop if we could and rest by the way; but we must go on, on, and know no rest."[17]

Such descriptions again and again depict a remorselessly commer-cial society that has swept everyone up in its grasp, squeezing out their individual characteristics and turning them into mechanisms, caricatures of themselves. The very impulse to caricature that swelled so prominently in the nineteenth century, both in the United States and in northern Europe, represented an attempt to capture through ludicrous exaggeration this process of social trans-formation. As the French writer Champfleury observed, "The bourgeois never found their portraitist, only their caricaturists." Caricaturists seized upon their lack of individuality, the degree to which they had become mere embodiments of a social type.[18] This loss of individuality was not confined to the city; Thoreau saw it at work in Concord, Tocqueville throughout his travels in America. But the business districts of the city displayed the paradoxes of mid-nineteenth-century American capitalist democracy in their starkest form. The individual's very independence and mobility often brought, not heightened dignity and achievement, but, on the contrary, a sense of anonymity and isolation. The relentlessly commercial character of American culture and its incessant competition for status within an egalitarian ethos produced a self-punishing restlessness and sense of thwarted ambition, a tyranny of collective opinion. As the historian John Diggins has observed, "The more free the individual felt himself to be, the more isolated and lonely he actually became until he craved to forsake his solitude in order to surrender his self to the new invisible authority of society itself. Thus as authority drifted from the once-conscious individual to the collective stupor of mass society, the whole idea of natural rights, the assumption of individual autonomy and freedom characteristic of eighteenth-century thought, was collapsing in the face of nineteenth-century social realities."[19]

Reading the Illegible Man of the Crowd

This conviction that the nineteenth-century capitalist economy and the commercial metropolis in particular were creating new social types, as disturbing and difficult to decipher as the larger urban process of which they were a part, was brilliantly explored in two short stories, Edgar Allan Poe's "The Man of the Crowd" (1840) and Herman Melville's "Bartleby, the Scrivener. A Tale of Wall-Street" (1853). Each story focused upon a key aspect of the new geography of the commercial metropolis: in Melville's case the financial district, the center of the city by "daylight" and of its widening control and rationality; in Poe's story the city by "gaslight," the labyrinth of squalor, vice, and misery that urban capitalism had created. Beginning like so many other fictions, journalistic investigations, travelers' accounts, and advice books by attempting to "read" character in the city, both stories ultimately exposed the problems in the observer's attempt—and by extension, that of all readers of city life and literature—to retain a detached, rational stance or to come to any satisfactory resolution.

Poe's story begins and ends with a quotation concerning an early German book that " 'er lasst sich nicht lesen' "—it does not permit itself to be read"; and the tale concerns the adequacy of the metaphor of the text as a paradigm for the interpretation of human character and behavior in the modern city. The narrator begins in the languid, contemplative posture of the *flâneur*, sitting at the window of a London coffeehouse as he recovers from an illness. From "poring over advertisements" in his newspaper, he turns his attention increasingly to the passersby in the crowd outside. He first regards them not as individuals but—as in so many urban descriptions—as social types, whose inner character may be easily read by their outward traits "of figure, dress, air, gait, visage, and expression of countenance" in the tradition of physiognomics stimulated by Johann Kaspar Lavater, as well as the literature of *moeurs* of such writers as Jean de La Bruyère, from whom Poe takes his story's epigraph.[20]

But while most social observers would hazard only a few gross distinctions among the multitude, Poe's narrator reads these figures effortlessly, confidently, pressing beneath their relatively undifferentiated surfaces to disclose subtler nuances of class and character. It is as if the pedestrians were themselves advertisements, each for his profession: those who were "*undoubtedly* noblemen, merchants, attorneys, tradesmen, stock-jobbers"; the "*obvious*" tribe of clerks; pickpockets who the narrator marveled "*should ever be mistaken* for gentlemen by gentlemen themselves"; gamblers, "*still more easily recognisable*"; and so on, in a vast moving social panorama (italics added). Like Balzac, Dickens, and other investigators of the nineteenth-century cityscape, Poe's narrator aims to pierce through the superficial flatness and grayness of the crowd to uncover, in the words of a recent critic, the "latent systems of signification which the surfaces mask." By disclosing the underlying divisions, gradations, and hierarchies within the crowd, the narrator reveals new meanings in the commercial city. Beneath its apparently unremarkable, even banal, features, such as the advertisements he so avidly studies, he discovers "the pathology of social life" (Balzac's proposed volume codifying the "laws of exterior existence") in an intricate subtext.[21]

This subtext grows in interest for the narrator as its materials become more lurid. The comically mechanical expressions and movements of "the decent" (similar to those noted by von Hübner, Mark Twain, and others) do not "greatly excite . . . [his] attention." As the night advances, however, the crowd grows more disreputable, and his scrutiny of passersby correspondingly more intense.

With his brow now pressed to the glass, he sights an old man who challenges his abilities to read and interpret the urban text, the person he will ultimately call "the man of the crowd."[22]

The stranger's "absolute idiosyncracy of . . . expression" confounds the narrator's social typology. He gives forth such wild and contradictory signs as to be illegible. Whereas at the beginning of the story the metaphor of reading the crowd suggested an ability to bring the urban scene easily into congruence with literary experience, to achieve a sense of intelligible continuity and control, to occupy a familiar and privileged interpretive stance as a trained reader, that confidence is now shattered. "Aroused, startled, fascinated," the narrator leaps up to follow him. The stance of a languid, contemplative reader, sitting within the coffeehouse, gives way to the strenuous and prolonged work of pursuit. Poe's narrator becomes the amateur investigator, the detective, the social scientist, determined to follow his quarry until he decodes his message and possesses his secret meaning.[23]

Throughout this quest, the narrator ostensibly retains his stance as the rational observer conducting an urban ethnography with disinterested intent and rigorous care. He accepts the burden of a night-and-day-long investigation with equanimity. He carefully notes at close range every salient detail of the stranger's behavior, while taking pains "not to attract his attention" and so contaminate the results of his investigation. Practical and resourceful in his dress, the narrator adopts a handkerchief as a shield against fog and rain and congratulates himself in wearing rubber overshoes so that he can proceed "in perfect silence." Only at the end of his investigation, as a kind of final experiment, does he abandon his cover and, "stopping fully in front of the wanderer, gaze at him steadfastly in the face." The stranger passes without notice. "At length" the narrator declares the results of his research: "This old man . . . is the type and the genius of deep crime. He refuses to be alone. *He is the man of the crowd.* It will be in vain to follow; for I shall learn no more of him, nor of his deeds." End of case history.[24]

Poe's narrator offers both a virtuoso performance of physiognomic reading and an exposure of its limits. Even if the stranger does not permit his full inner character to be read, the narrator satisfies himself as to its essential evil and torment. Like numerous other nineteenth-century writers, Poe intuited that in the new commercial urban culture, everyone carried his own secret shame from which he sought refuge in the crowd. The narrator eagerly responds to the new opportunities for surveillance and detection this situation afforded, and presents us with what the critic Walter Benjamin has called a kind of "x-ray picture of a detective story." No specific crime occurs, let alone any clues surrounding it. The narrator/ detective needs none. He purports to see the crime's embodiment (whether potential or realized is unclear) in the appearance of the stranger himself. The detective story is distilled to its essence: the pursuer, the crowd, the suspect. Like so many of Poe's tales, how- ever, this one invites the reader to regard the narrator himself with suspicion and, adopting his own methods, to pierce through the surfaces of his account to its hidden motives and meanings. Beneath the social scientist/detective's detached stance toward the object of his investigations, the story suggests a much more interdependent, dialectical relationship. The narrator scrutinizes the crowd and par- ticularly the old man who so fascinates him, not simply through a transparent window but in a mirror of reflexivity and subjectivity as well. Note his description of himself in the coffeehouse: "Peering through the smoky panes into the street," he intensifies his study of the crowd until he is pressing his "brow to the glass . . . when suddenly there came into view a countenance . . . which at once arrested and absorbed my whole attention." It is, of course, the old man; but—the ambiguity of the term "the glass" is telling—the narrator might also be said to behold unwittingly, as in a looking glass, the reflection of his own imagination and repressed identity. The narrator's markedly greater interest in the netherworld of so- ciety than in the conduct of "the decent" suggests a kind of voy- euristic gratification. His literally feverish pursuit of the stranger and eagerness to suspect him of deep crime express the projection outward of his own concupiscent self-interest, shame, and guilt in an elaborate defense mechanism. Early on in his pursuit, he notes significantly, either "my vision deceived me," or else, through a hole in the stranger's cloak, "I caught a glimpse both of a diamond and of a dagger," emblems of wealth and violence, sexual potency and danger. The figure he so avidly stalks is a kind of double: *both* men pursue and emotionally feed on strangers of the urban throng without ever coming into direct contact with them. The final con- frontation between the two is deeply ironic, for it involves *mutual nonrecognition.* It is as if the urban crowd gives way in the story, as in a dream, to a chase down a hall of mirrors, in which the narrator narcissistically pursues his own image without recognizing its likeness. Sententiously intoning his conclusion, the narrator insists to the end upon a sharp split between subject and object. But to whom, "at length," does he speak these results? Has he become a mutterer and gesticulator like the gentry he described at the outset? Certainly he is much more deeply implicated in the grotesque and troubled identities of the urban crowd than he acknowledges; *that* fact as much as his putatively objective findings makes Poe's tale so vivid and disturbing.[25]

A Tragicomedy of Civility

Melville's longer story "Bartleby, the Scrivener" complements and extends many of the themes in Poe's. Both are first-person narratives in which the storyteller attempts to "read" the appearance and behavior of a problematic urban figure who serves as a key "text" for the emerging society and culture of the nineteenth-century city. In both stories, too, what comes to be at issue is less the objective character, the independent "story," of the figure under scrutiny than the dialectic between subject and object and its implications for the nature of social relationships and attachments in the commercial metropolis.[26]

But the contrasts are as telling as the points in common. The narrator of Melville's story is not the idle, manic *flâneur* of Poe but a genial, timid Wall Street lawyer, who, "from his youth upwards, has been filled with a profound conviction that the easiest way of life is the best," and who wishes above all else to protect his peace. Avoiding the turbulence of the courtroom and the public arena, he contents himself with "a snug business among rich men's bonds and mortgages and title-deeds. All who know me, consider me an eminently *safe* man," he adds, punning on the vaults that he protects for his clients. The lawyer thus presents himself as the soul of bourgeois normality and conventionality. He is clearly not one to hang around coffeehouses, studying passersby, let alone to pursue a strange old man night and day. Yet while the lawyer does not seek out the netherworld that so fascinates Poe's narrator, nor confer his curiosity gratuitously upon a stranger, he, too, comes to the reader offering a novel case history of the odd aspects of character within the swelling commercial metropolis. That he locates this history, not in any lurid figure redolent of crime and evil, but within a law-copyist or scrivener, the kind of clerical subordinate that Poe's narrator passed over in a glance, makes his chronicle in some respects all the more disturbing.[27]

As in Poe's tale, so in Melville's, the narrator gives us but a fragment, based upon his firsthand observations. The very fragmentary nature of the report is, in a sense, a mark of its authenticity, since hearsay is suspect both in social science and in law, and, moreover, a badge of its modernity, since a fragmentary literature is the simulacrum of the fragmentary character of modern life. Bemoaning the fact that "no materials exist for a full and satisfactory biography of this man," as in truth Bartleby lacks sufficient materials for a full and satisfactory life, the lawyer reminds us: "What my own astonished eyes saw of Bartleby, *that* is all I know of him, except, indeed, one vague report which will appear in the sequel."[28]

At the time of his "little history," the lawyer held the office of a Master in Chancery, since abolished by the New York State Constitution.[29] He affectionately recalls the easy duties and remuneration of his position, which he had hoped to hold for life, and catches himself on the verge of strong language in denouncing its abrogation as a "———— premature act." But in order to appreciate his story fully one needs to know what the office of Master in Chancery entailed. It was a court of equity in which the Master exercised broad discretionary powers without a jury to determine just and fair measures in cases that lay outside the strict letter of the law. Typical cases included a request to the Chancellor to set aside a decree of divorce by a reconciled couple; an appeal from one with a future contingent interest in an undivided share of real estate for partition of the property; a request by a former owner to negate a sale of his sheep pasture to a buyer who concealed his knowledge that it contained a valuable mine. Chancery was theoretically concerned with "the whole truth" and the merits of the individual case as it adjudicated legal obligations. Opposing such a discretionary view, those who abolished the office aimed, as the eminent jurist Roscoe Pound later observed, "to regulate every act of the judge from the time he enters the court room. It is hardly too much to say that the ideal judge is conceived as a pure machine." The lawyer in "Bartleby" embodies the divided feelings that this social and legal transition represents. His concern for the whole truth and the individual case grows in the course of his involvement with Bartleby, even while he comes to recognize that the whole truth is unattainable and such an individual as Bartleby unknowable. At the same time the lawyer longs for the kind of security and comfort afforded more by general cases than by specific instances and more suited to what was increasingly viewed as the mechanical character of market relations.[30]

Thus situated, he accommodates himself to the eccentricities of his office employees: his two copyists, the alcoholic Turkey and dyspeptic Nippers, and the office boy Ginger Nut. In various ways all of them are victims of thwarted ambition, figures who despite the promise of American mobility and individual achievement have found themselves consigned to subordinate positions with little hope of advancement. Turkey and Nippers, in particular, appear scarcely able to contain their frustration and aggression within the civility and servility their positions demand. In the effort to repress their feelings they have become caricatures of themselves. After intemperate midday dinners, Turkey falls into "a strange, inflamed, flurried, flighty recklessness of activity," and "though the civilest, nay, the blandest and most reverential of men in the morning," in the afternoon he becomes, in the lawyer's timorous phrase, "disposed, upon provocation, to be slightly rash with his tongue, in fact, insolent." By contrast, Nippers's indigestion, the symptom of his frustrated aspirations, seizes him mainly in the mornings, stirring his "nervous testiness and grinning irritability," as he fusses over such details as the height of his copy stand. Reflecting upon these angry adjustments, the lawyer observes, "the truth of the matter was, Nippers knew not what he wanted. Or, if he wanted any thing, it was to be rid of a scrivener's table altogether." The lawyer reconciles himself to these odd behaviors with a mixture of kindly understanding of his employees' foibles, a shrewd sense of their ultimate usefulness, and a temperamental aversion to pressing his demands upon others. Throughout, he patronizingly regards their temperaments, not their situations, as at fault. As he says of Turkey, "He was a man whom prosperity harmed."[31]

The lawyer's duties as Master in Chancery demand a third copyist, and when a young man appears before him, "pallidly neat, pitiably respectable, incurably forlorn," he quickly hires him, "glad to have among my corps of copyists a man of so singularly sedate an aspect." It is, of course, Bartleby.[32]

Secluded behind a screen in the lawyer's inner office, Bartleby sets to work. At first, his employer is gratified by his relentless industry although disquieted by the silent, pale, mechanical manner in which he performs his duties. But then, in response to an order to compare copy, Bartleby utters the first of his repeated demurrers, "I would prefer not to."[33] Soon and in identical terms he declines to run errands, to call Nippers from the next room, to perform any duties at all, to tell anything about himself, or to be discharged, even to leave the corner of the office in which, the lawyer discovers, he has made his home. So, by degrees, Bartleby politely but adamantly refuses to have commerce with the world. In the process he propels a tragicomedy of civility in the nineteenth-century commercial metropolis.

Yet Bartleby is scarcely more of a developed literary "character" than Poe's wandering "man of the crowd." In a story of some sixteen thousand words, he speaks but thirty-seven short lines, a substantial portion merely repetitions of "I would prefer not to." As one critic has observed, "Few characters in fiction, if indeed any exist, have been able to say all they wish in so striking, so nearly speechless a manner."[34] Motionless in contrast to the incessantly moving figure in Poe's story, palely respectable rather than strangely lurid in his appearance, Bartleby nonetheless also becomes an individual radically alienated in the commercial metropolis. If Poe's stranger is indeed "damned," as the narrator insists, Bartleby is, both in his cadaverous appearance and gradual regression from the world of affairs, dead, finally literally so as he demurs from the business of living itself.[35]

Still, as with Poe's "The Man of the Crowd," the center of Melville's story is not Bartleby himself but the narrator's attempts to come to terms with him. While observing the polite forms the lawyer so prizes—he never flatly refuses a request—Bartleby undermines the system of authority and subordination that the codes of civility were intended to support. His bland, opaque resistance, like a mirror, throws back the lawyer's own assumptions and responses: his timid rationalizations, his reluctance to contemplate the darker sides of human existence, as well as his compassion and generosity.

Upon hearing Bartleby first decline his request, the lawyer decides that either one or the other has been misunderstood and repeats it. Twice rejected, he stares at Bartleby in amazement, but, unwilling to press the point in the face of the scrivener's passionless resistance, in each case he allows the matter to pass, pleading to himself the press of business. On the next occasion, he attempts to reason with Bartleby, he appeals to the opinion of his other employees, but to no avail.

Finding that Bartleby is out of the office one Sunday morning, the lawyer unlocks his desk and examines his personal effects like an amateur detective in the manner of Poe. All the while he protests to himself, "I mean no mischief, seek the gratification of no heartless curiosity . . . besides, the desk is mine, and its contents, too, so I will make bold to look within." Bartleby's meager and isolated existence fills him first with pity, then with fear and revulsion, as he concludes that "the scrivener was the victim of innate and incurable disorder. I might give alms to his body; but his body did not pain him; it was his soul that suffered, and his soul I could not reach." The lawyer's statement is perhaps accurate, but it is also an attempt to free himself from the shame and guilt he feels in his dealings with Bartleby.[36]

Deciding that the scrivener "had now become a millstone to me, not only useless as a necklace, but afflictive to bear," the lawyer in a quiet, gentlemanly fashion gives him notice. Yet Bartleby remains. Courteously, the lawyer protests: "Bartleby . . . I am seriously displeased. I am pained, Bartleby. I had thought better of you. I had imagined you of such a gentlemanly organization, that in any delicate dilemma a slight hint would suffice. . . ." But still Bartleby declines to leave. Inwardly outraged by his employee's invincible obduracy, the lawyer imagines himself driven to murder, a fantasy that flatters his sense of power even as it troubles his sense of morality and self-control. He reconciles himself to his situation by endeavoring to see Bartleby as "billeted upon me for some mysterious purpose of an all-wise Providence, which it was not for a mere mortal like me to fathom."[37]

This posture of Christian equanimity, however, soon topples amid the "whisper of wonder" that circulates among the lawyer's professional acquaintances concerning the strange behavior and anomalous position of his scrivener. Again, he is made to feel the shame of his impotence. Since Bartleby steadfastly remains, the lawyer is finally compelled to move to new offices himself in order to be rid of him. Still, ties to Bartleby persist: the new tenant of his former offices holds him responsible for Bartleby, who, evicted from his meager quarters, now haunts the corridors; a mob is feared;

the lawyer himself is threatened with exposure in the press. Vainly he protests that "Bartleby was nothing to me—no more than to any one else." In desperation, the lawyer offers to find Bartleby a position as a copyist, or another kind of job, and, finally, in an extraordinary, even heroic appeal, invites Bartleby to live with him "till we can conclude upon some convenient arrangement for you at our leisure," perhaps, the lawyer must foresee, forever. Bartleby declines all his entreaties. He is subsequently taken to prison as a vagrant, where he spurns the lawyer's last efforts to feed and comfort him, and dies.[38]

Thus, by subverting all normal expectations of the relationship between employer and employee, Bartleby both exposes the lawyer's conventionality and pushes him beyond it. Bartleby forces him to examine what bonds, obligations, and duties link one person to another in the commercial metropolis, what remains in the world of Wall Street when utility no longer exists.[39] Precisely because relationships have become more pluralistic in this society, social bonds and obligations have grown more indeterminate. The structure of specified obligations has broken down. In the case of Bartleby and the lawyer, we have what would seem the clearest possible set of obligations, that established by their work in a free market as employer and employee. But the story shows how such a structure quickly collapses in the experience of the lawyer when pressed at its foundations. Reluctant to allow the rule of a pure ethic of market exchange and utilitarian values, though he is at times sorely tempted, the lawyer cannot bring himself to declare that if for whatever reason Bartleby declines his duties, then he is entitled to nothing; that if he refuses to leave, then he deserves to be coerced; that if he is imprisoned, that is no affair of the lawyer's. In the case of his other copyists, Turkey and Nippers, the lawyer has managed to negotiate between the necessities of business and the claims of human sympathy without being forced to choose absolutely between them. But Bartleby allows no such negotiation. After his initial period of intense industry, he gradually refuses to participate in any system of exchanges or reciprocities, either of services for pay or gratitude for charity. The lawyer is left alternatively indignant and sympathetic, seeking in some way to reestablish the conventional bonds of service and civility. By the end of the story, however, he is forced to suspend this effort, as he gradually moves beyond a kind of minimal altruism that costs relatively little to the

threshold of heroic self-sacrifice, with no expectation of acknowledgment, no hope of reciprocity of any kind.[40] The paradox of
"Bartleby," apprehended as it is from the lawyer's point of view,
is that ultimately not the scrivener's commitments but those of his
employer are put to the test; not the clerk but his superior experiences shame, guilt, and failure as he strives to meet what emerge
as indefinite and potentially limitless obligations. While Poe's narrator assumed a stance of moral indifference under the cloak of
disinterested spectatorship, the lawyer in "Bartleby" struggles under the sort of awkward moral burden increasingly afforded by "the
world of strangers."

The lawyer's situation in "Bartleby" exposes a dilemma of urban
middle-class Americans generally in the nineteenth century. As the
philosopher James Fishkin has recently contended, "an unspoken
assumption" of everyday life in a liberal democracy "is that morality
is reserved for special occasions." Most everyday actions are not
regarded as carrying moral stakes but exist purely as matters of
personal choice and initiative. If it were otherwise, if the press of
moral obligations and conflicting claims were the rule rather than
the exception, "there would be no significant sphere of action where
we could feel at liberty to do as we please." But if each individual
is putatively free to make his own bargains, what general obligations
remain? Is society simply to be governed by the pursuit of individual rights, and are all ties except those of an impersonal market
dissolved? What are specific bonds—whether of family, friendship,
religion, employment, or community—to mean? What becomes of
the public realm? These were issues for all of American society,
but the conditions of urban life gave them special urgency, raising
the scale of potential moral demands in a host of possible actions
and situations and among a multitude of possible recipients.[41] If
one individual could be as morally demanding as Bartleby (even
while directly asking for nothing), what overwhelming possibilities
might an entire city hold!

Social Detection and Concealment

Poe and Melville thus illuminated the perplexities that attended
both the effort to read the character of others in the expanding
commercial metropolis and to maintain one's own balance. As the

precise boundaries between liberty and obligation, public and private, grew problematic, so, too, did the very notion of individual character and the integrity of the self. In different ways, both stories pointed to a crisis of self-representation and social trust.

It may seem a large leap from the fictive world of "The Man of the Crowd" and "Bartleby, the Scrivener," to the world of etiquette manuals and other popular urban advice literature; yet these same issues throbbed beneath the surface of those writings as well—no less so because they were repressed and ignored. In the rapid transition to an industrial economy and a burgeoning urban society, the traditional modes by which individuals defined themselves and recognized one another, always particularly fluid in America, seemed to contemporaries to fall apart. In an anonymous, aggressively commercial culture, older ceremonies of social deference changed their character. Social inferiors in the cities no longer doffed their caps, bowed low, and averted their eyes before superiors, nor did children "mind their manners" (as the phrase was for making obeisance to adults). Often observers despaired of locating others neatly in social niches by either appearance or manners. How was one to tell a solid gentleman from a social counterfeit? How communicate one's own good intentions while shielding oneself from the piercing scrutiny of public inspection?

Etiquette advisers, together with a host of other figures from novelists to detectives, addressed these questions—though they could never fully answer them. As one adviser asserted, "Society has its grammar as language has, and the rules of that grammar must be learned." Etiquette writers set themselves up as grammarians, usage experts, and instructors in the intricate and, for many, foreign language of social ritual. In what Edith Wharton would later call "a kind of hieroglyphic world, where the real thing was never said or done or even thought, but only represented by a set of arbitrary signs," they promised to identify these signs and discern their meanings. To interject the critical vocabulary of our own time, they were on a popular level semioticians of social ritual—a stance that led them to some unanticipated positions.[42]

A central problem that etiquette writers found themselves forced to confront (along with their readers and participants in the new pluralistic urban-industrial culture generally) involved the moral meaning of conventions of etiquette and the basis upon which the signs of ritual discourse could be read and relied upon. Were the

rituals of politeness and civility grounded in a moral order, whether
that of society, of class, or of individual character (the lady, the
gentleman)? Or were they merely a matter of appearance, subject
to hypocritical manipulation? As etiquette writers explored the nature of the "set of arbitrary signs," they risked demystifying the
ritual order and the social order it supported. By emphasizing the
power of ritual, the efficacy of etiquette to refine and even transform
a social situation, they unintentionally threw into question the degree to which human character was the determining force in social
activities. Although there is a certain perversity in linking etiquette
writers with modern semioticians, there is also a strange aptness.
In etiquette literature as in much contemporary criticism, "as meaning is explained in terms of systems of signs—systems which the
subject does not control—the subject is deprived of his role as source
of meaning. . . . the self is dissolved as its various functions are
ascribed to impersonal systems which operate through it."[43] Seeking
to provide props for individual "character"—defined in the oft-
repeated phrase of Emerson as "moral order through the medium
of individual nature"—etiquette writers unwittingly began to pull
the concept apart.[44] They naïvely began the investigations that
Erving Goffman and other recent scholars have pursued so avidly,
in which the self—far from existing apart from society in any kind
of transcendental power—is largely a series of dramatic effects.[45]

This anxiety about the meaning of social signs, particularly of
human expression and character, in the new capitalist metropolis
affected both nineteenth-century Europe and the United States.
What might be broadly called a semiotic approach proliferated in
the human sciences and in everyday social experience. The novel,
the most popular literary form of the age, took as one of its principal themes the concealment and unmasking of character and its
problematic relationship to appearances. In this respect the concerns of fiction were closely linked to developments in a number
of areas, as the semiotics of everyday life transformed fields from
art connoisseurship to criminology to the nascent discipline of psychoanalysis. By the turn of the century, such brilliant investigators
as the Italian art historian Giovanni Morelli, Arthur Conan Doyle's
fictional detective Sherlock Holmes, and Sigmund Freud had developed analogous strategies of detection, in which they assigned
less importance to the manifest content of the objects before them
than to the latent meaning of apparently insignificant details. Mo-

FRA FILIPPO. FILIPPINO. SIGNORELLI. BRAMANTINO.

MANTEGNA. GIOVANNI BELLINI. BONIFAZIO. BOTTICELLI.

7. Expression in Trifles: Characteristic depiction of ears by various masters from Morelli's *Italian Painters*.

relli, for example, in attempting to distinguish genuine paintings by old masters from misattributions, copies, and outright forgeries, did not concentrate on a work's obvious features, for these would be carefully imitated. Instead, he closely examined the most trivial details, such as the treatment of earlobes, hands, and toes—all those inadvertent gestures in which an artist dropped his guard and revealed through his distinctive habits his true identity. "Even details, in themselves insignificant," he declared, "may lead us to the truth." Doyle's Sherlock Holmes similarly trained his eye upon the apparently insignificant details that escaped others' notice, insisting in case after case that "there is nothing so important as trifles." And Freud, who had read Morelli, made the scrutiny of involuntary gestures, slips of the tongue, and other inadvertencies a key element in psychoanalysis. In a passage from his famous case history of "Dora" that recalls Holmes, Freud put the claim most sweepingly:

> He that has eyes to see and ears to hear may convince himself that no mortal can keep a secret. If his lips are silent, he chatters with his finger-tips; betrayal oozes out of him at every pore. And thus the task of making conscious the most hidden recesses of the mind is one which it is quite possible to accomplish.[46]

Morelli, Freud, and Holmes were exemplary figures who sought to put their respective disciplines upon the solid footing of science, but the approach they pursued so brilliantly built upon age-old folk wisdom and also the distinctive culture of nineteenth-century urban life. As Poe's "The Man of the Crowd" suggests, the modern city afforded new possibilities both for cloaking one's own identity and scrutinizing, even shadowing, strangers met by chance. The dual arts of detection and concealment came to be regarded as necessary skills for urban living.

Etiquette and related advice literature promised to teach these arts, insisting that by their mastery one could decode the baffling appearances of everyday life and effortlessly read another's character. "The habits of the soul become written on the countenance," Samuel G. Goodrich assured his young readers; "what we call the expression of the face is only the story which the face tells about the feelings of the heart." Others frequently extended the argument from facial expression to manners in general: "Manners are the outward expression of the internal character." By attending carefully to the expressions and gesture of others, one could pierce the cloak of anonymity and know their inmost hearts. Villainy would stand revealed and hence lose its power.[47]

The basis of much of these claims lay in a faith in the power of physiognomy, the science of reading temperament and character from the appearance of the body and particularly the face. It was a pursuit that thrived in the social conditions of the metropolis, which brought a vast array of human types into intimate proximity. Reading a face in the crowd could become a quasi-literary activity itself. The distinguished philosopher Charles Sanders Peirce offered one virtuoso demonstration of such an act of physiognomic reading and urban detection when, finding himself on a streetcar without a book in hand, he focused instead on his own woman of the crowd:

> Street cars are famous *ateliers* for speculative modeling. Detained there, with no business to occupy him, one sets to scrutinizing the people opposite, and to working up biographies to fit them. I see a woman of forty. Her countenance is so sinister as scarcely to be matched among a thousand, almost to the border of insanity, yet with a grimace of amiability that few even of her sex are sufficiently trained to command:— along with it, those two ugly lines, right and left of the compressed lips, chronicling years of severe discipline. An expression of servility and hypocrisy there is, too abject for a domestic; while a certain low, yet not quite vulgar, kind of education that is evinced, together with a taste in dress neither gross nor meretricious, but still by no means elevated, bespeak companionship with something superior, beyond any mere contact as of a maid with her mistress. The whole combination, although not striking at first glance, is seen upon close inspection to be a very unusual one. Here our theory declares an explanation is called for; and I should not be long in guessing that the woman was an ex-nun.[48]

more revelatory about writer than his subject

(Reading back from this portrait to its author, one would not be long in guessing him a male Protestant of education and social prestige.)

Similarly, an 1871 work entitled *New Physiognomy* encouraged readers to learn how a man's walk reveals his character by shadowing their own men of the crowd:

> Would you know the character of a man by his walk? Fall upon his trail, observe his motions when yourself unobserved; take on his manner and step, and by following him a short distance, you will feel as he feels, and soon become *en rapport* with him. If he put on airs and attempt to show off in the character of a "swell," you will do the same, and for the moment lose your own individuality or identity, and be swallowed up by him. . . .

Lest this exercise turn into the sort of merging of identities that Poe described, the writer added immediately:

> . . . but your second thoughts will make you heartily disgusted with this false or assumed character, and you will then return to yourself. If he be noble, manly, generous, and dignified, you will take on the same spirit by imitating his walk. If he be a rogue, fleeing from justice, and you closely watch his movements, you will soon get into the same spirit, and feel like the wicked who "flees when no man pursueth."[49]

Etiquette books express this intense new interest in reading character from appearances, particularly in the street, and indicate how high the stakes might be, how piercing the scrutiny: "Persons on the street attract the attention of every passer-by by their dress, their conduct, and their manner of walking. Some critics say that character may be read by any of these as readily as by the features of the face. Nothing so quickly points out the low-bred as loudness of conduct or flashiness of dress on the street." In a passage that recalls the emphasis upon incidental gestures by Morelli and Freud, a second etiquette adviser declared:

> The *manner* in which a person says or does a thing, furnishes a better index of his character than *what* he does or says, for it is by the *incidental expression* given to his thoughts and feelings, by his looks, tones and gestures, rather than by his words and deeds, that we prefer to judge him, for the reason that the former are *involuntary* [italics added].[50]

Etiquette advisers coached their readers to cultivate the art of urban detection in whatever social situation they found themselves: on the street, in omnibuses and other public conveyances, as well as in social gatherings. "When people talk of themselves," an 1833 guide counseled young men, "lend both your ears . . . for, let men be ever so much upon their guard, it is odds if some such escape is not made, as is a sufficient clue to the whole character." Then the writer added significantly, "We need not observe to you, that, for the very same reason, you are never to make yourself the subject of your own conversation: though, we hope, you will have no vices to conceal, all men have infirmities; and it is as unnecessary as impolitic to expose them." But still more important than ear and tongue in social detection was the eye. As another adviser urged, "You should not only have attention to everything, but a quickness of attention, so as to observe at once all the people in the room, their motions, their looks, and their words; and yet without staring at them, and seeming to be an observer."[51]

Such caution seemed particularly necessary in the heterogeneous urban society where superficial appearances could deceive the unwary. For example, the urbane Philadelphia diarist Sidney George Fisher demonstrated his own highly practiced ability to appraise a scene at a glance during a visit at the Union Hotel in Saratoga, New York, in 1867:

> To the Union flock the men & women of the vulgar fashionable world, gamblers & demi-reps, some of the latter unmistakably women of the town. I went there two or three times & walked in the evening through the immense drawing rooms, I was never more disgusted. There was no elegance or beauty, but coarse, low, vice & vulgarity. The men looked like thieves & the women like the whores that many of them were. I here saw John Morrisey, the noted pugilist, gambler, *burglar*, rowdy, & member of Congress, & with him Heenan, the celebrated prize fighter. The latter, a fine specimen of athletic strength, a magnificent animal; the former of powerful make & with a gross brutal countenance & most depraved & guilty look.[52]

Yet in the fragmented and shifting world of the nineteenth-century city, social detection was not always so easy. The economic and social interests of many figures lay precisely in eluding discovery in order to exploit for their own selfish ends the possibilities of unstable and illegible identity as well as the ambiguous relationship between the social exchanges of respectable society and the economic exchanges of the marketplace. Despite attempts by various popular writers to formulate a science of character based upon outward expression and to establish a system of stable meanings between outward signs and inner substance, social counterfeits did a brisk business—and one with an occasionally disturbing kinship to putatively legitimate activities.

Social Counterfeits

Such counterfeits assumed a variety of forms. On the lowest level, they included alms seekers who claimed to be defeated in the urban marketplace. Without the least pretense to gentility, these beggars violated the benevolence of pedestrians by asking charity for sham afflictions, as rogues have for centuries. Shameless self-advertisers, cunning merchandisers of their own misfortune, some indeed had reversible tin signs hanging across their breasts, allowing them to choose which calamity might earn greater reward in a particular locale.[53]

Far more sinister were those who infiltrated the world of the respectable urban middle classes to prey upon them from within. These included prostitutes masquerading as ladies, seducing gullible men, corrupting family life, and tainting virtuous women. Overwhelmingly of working-class origins, such prostitutes were involved in a masquerade of class as well as of virtue. Prostitutes of many kinds invaded the public spaces and seeped into the private spheres of the middle class. The vice "no longer confines itself to secrecy and darkness," lamented Dr. William Sanger in his massive report on New York prostitution of 1859, "but boldly strikes through our most thronged and elegant thoroughfares, and there, in the broad light of the sun, it jostles the pure, the virtuous, and the good. It is in your gay streets, and in your quiet, home-like streets; it is in your squares, and in your suburban retreats and summer resorts; it is in your theatres, your opera, your hotels; nay, it is even intruding itself into the private circles, and slowly but steadily extending its poison, known but to few, and entirely unsuspected by the majority of our citizens." Sanger and others noted with fascination and alarm the lot of the most favored courtesans. "Selected for their beauty, grace, and accomplishments," these women led duplicitous lives, wrote one urban guide.

They dress in great elegance, and quite as decorously as females generally do at balls, parties, or at concerts. Meet them in the streets, or at picture galleries, or at a fashionable soirée, and there is nothing about them to attract attention. No person who knows them or their character can in any way recognize

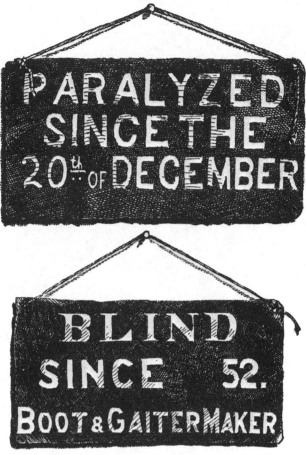

8. Counterfeit Calamities: A beggar's reversible sign.

them in public. These women have their pew in a fashionable church; some attend Sunday school, and have their own religious homes.

In the elegant houses of prostitution in which they boarded, this deceptive gentility prevailed, as "quiet, order, and taste abound." Their patrons included "prominent citizens," government officials, and visiting merchants, many of whom insisted on making the rounds of the city before they would conduct business. Other "fallen women of the higher classes," urban guidebooks warned, mingled even more promiscuously with the respectable middle

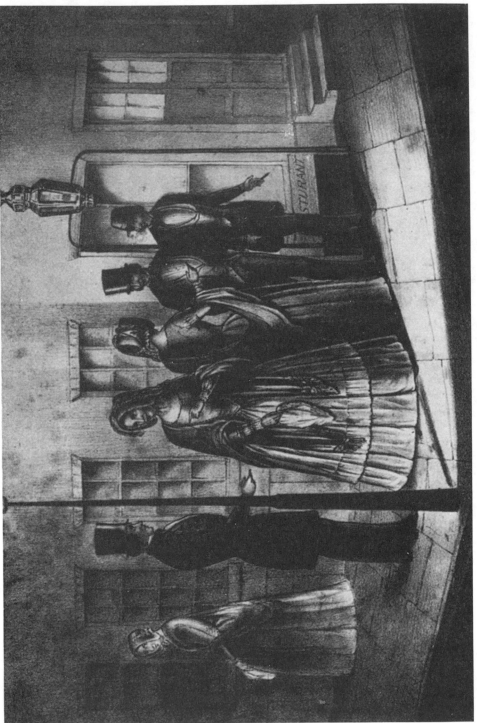

9. Ladylike Prostitutes and Gentlemanly Customers in New York.

class. They lodged in prominent hotels and virtually all boarding-houses, and used fashionable restaurants to arrange their assignations.

> A quiet, but close observer will frequently see a nod, or a smile, or a meaning[ful] glance pass between most respectable-looking persons of opposite sexes, and will sometimes see a note slyly sent by a waiter, or dropped adroitly into the hand of the woman as the man passes out. Some of these nominally respectable places are so largely patronized by this class, that a virtuous woman is in constant danger of being insulted should she chance to enter one of them.[54]

Some of these prostitutes and their procurers further added to their duplicity by being blackmailers. According to highly charged exposés of urban vice, they contrived various ingenious traps to snare respectable men and women in compromising positions. An actual seduction was not always necessary; anything that might lend itself to the *appearance* of scandal, no matter how innocent in fact, served their purposes equally well. An upright businessman or even a minister might be naïvely led to a house of prostitution. Similarly, a "handsome and fashionably dressed street-lounger" might lure a respectable wife on a carriage ride, then sweep her away to a house or restaurant where he would endeavor to ply her with "wine and wiles," and ultimately, whether his seduction was successful or not, threaten to inform her husband.[55]

Still another kind of social counterfeit that achieved particular prominence in mid-nineteenth-century urban America was the confidence man. Scoundrels have gulled credulous victims throughout history, but the term "confidence man" was apparently coined only in 1849, and it instantly achieved widespread currency. It originated in the story of a swindler of "genteel appearance" and remarkable audacity called (among various aliases) Samuel Thompson. He would approach a well-dressed stranger on the streets of a city and greet him as if he were an old acquaintance. After a brief conversation Thompson would ask, "Have you confidence in me to trust me with your watch until to-morrow?" The victim, embarrassed to have forgotten this affable gentleman and reluctant to deny such a forthright request, would lend his watch. Then the "confidence man" walked off laughing, never to return. He was finally caught

10. Enticement and Blackmail as Depicted in the *National Police Gazette*: "Almost Trapped: An Episcopal Minister in New York Just Misses Becoming the Victim of a Horrible and Scandalous Blackmailing Racket."

by the police only after a dupe happened upon him a second time by chance.[56]

Four days after Thompson's arrest in New York City on July 7, 1849, a biting satire appeared in the *New York Herald* underscoring the ironic parallels between this brazen swindle and the manipulations of the most stupendously successful capitalists. All were confidence men, the writer charged, but while one was satisfied with minor larceny from individuals, the others tricked great fortunes in stocks and bonds from companies, stockholders, legislatures, and the public at large. The trouble with Thompson was not that he was too audacious, but that he was too timid:

His genius has been employed on a small scale in Broadway. Theirs has been employed in Wall street. That's all the difference. He has obtained half a dozen watches. They have pocketed millions of dollars. He is a swindler. They are exemplars of honesty. He is a rogue. They are financiers. He is collared by the police. They are cherished by society. He eats the fare of a prison. They enjoy the luxuries of a palace. He is a mean, beggarly, timid, narrow-minded wretch, who has not a sou above a chronometer. They are respectable, princely, bold, high-soaring "operators," who are to be satisfied only with the plunder of a whole community.[57]

Others, however, viewed the victims of confidence men generally not as innocents (though Thompson's appear to have been) but as fools who expected something for nothing and were tricked by their very greediness. As part of a lengthy definition of the confidence man, an 1859 "rogue's lexicon" observed, "He knows his subject is only a knave wrongside out, and accordingly he offers him a pretended gold watch at the price of a brass one; he calls at the front door with presents from no where, as none could be expected; he writes letters in the most generous spirit, announcing large legacies to persons who have no kin on the face of the earth who cares a copper for them." Such confiding victims *deserved* to be deceived. Without their cupidity, confidence men could not exist.[58]

Others who swelled the ranks of urban impostors included pickpockets, shoplifters, "sneak thieves" who depended upon stealth for their crimes, blackmailers, forgers, and the like. Together with confidence men, such figures raised the stakes of urban detection to new heights. Their exposure and apprehension required not simply amateur readers of character and the idle musings of *flâneurs*, but the piercing scrutiny of professional detectives and police.

These detectives in turn strengthened the intricate ties between reading books and reading the appearance of strangers as they publicized their exploits in volumes for a middle-class audience; but unlike etiquette and physiognomic guides, they emphasized the extreme *illegibility* of these criminals, their deceptive opacity to all but the most trained eye. Such writing drew most immediately upon the growing popularity of American pulp fiction on detectives and criminals; but it also had abundant precedents in Europe, particularly in the literature of roguery that flourished in late-sixteenth- and early-seventeenth-century England, when "cony-catching" pamphlets classified rogues by their specialized deceptions, such as fraters (proxy beggars), dommerers (sham deaf-mutes), whipjacks (fake shipwrecked sailors), and Abraham men (dissembling mad-men). Nineteenth-century American chroniclers of roguery, in effect, revised this literature for an age of modern urban capitalism and middle-class professionalism. They stressed how skillfully the most nefarious criminals counterfeited the appearance and manners of respectable ladies and gentlemen. A multitude of cases in point are contained in three books published in the 1870s and 1880s: *Criminals of America* by Philip Farley; *Thirty Years a Detective* by Allan Pinkerton, the founder of the famous private detective agency; and *Professional Criminals of America* by New York City's inspector of police and chief of detectives Thomas Byrnes.[59]

Byrnes, for example, presented a rogues' gallery of over two hundred photographs in which he insistently corrected popular misconceptions of criminals as set apart by their suspicious and forbidding appearance. Although some figures indeed looked unsavory, many assumed the guise of models of respectability. Most pickpockets, he maintained, would not by their aspect or dress excite the least curiosity. One pickpocket, sneak thief, and forger he described as "generally clean-shaven, and affects a staid and religious air during his operations," and another, a pickpocket and shoplifter, appeared "quite a clerical-looking old fellow." Often working as a team or "mob" of as many as four, such pickpockets operated with minute precision to maneuver their "mark" into position, all the while maintaining the appearance of middle-class respectability. Confidence men, Farley and Byrnes agreed, counterfeited the semblance of gentlemen still more thoroughly:

[They] are very careful in their personal appearance, and avoid anything remarkable in their dress, and endeavor to attain an easy respectability in effect, rather than the assumption of a man of fashion. Professional confidence men have more than once declared that a tinge of gray in their side whiskers would be a great advantage to them, and a bald head a fortune. The man who loiters about the offices and corridors of the principal hotels awaiting his prey, appears as the best-natured man in the world. He is invariably to be found with a smile on his

RUFUS MINOR,
ALIAS RUFE PINE,
BANK SNEAK.

DAVID C. BLISS,
ALIAS DOCTOR BLISS,
SNEAK.

GEORGE CARSON,
ALIAS HEYWOOD,
BANK SNEAK.

ALEXANDER C. BRANSCOM,
FORGER AND CONFIDENCE MAN

FRANKLIN J. MOSES,
EX. GOV. MOSES,
SWINDLER

DAVID SWAIN,
CONFIDENCE.

11. Criminals of Gentlemanly Appearance: Mug shots from Byrnes's *Professional Criminals of America*.

face, and in moving out of the way of the guests and porters passing to and fro, politely bows at every turn.[60]

With regard to bank sneaks, forgers, hotel thieves, and other burglars, these detectives drove home the same point. Such criminals included men of the most gentlemanly appearance and refined demeanor, high intelligence, and sometimes excellent education. One bank forger and counterfeiter, Byrnes reported, studied chemistry at Yale College; a hotel and boardinghouse thief attended Oxford, earned a medical degree, and spoke five languages; Franklin J. Moses, a Reconstruction governor of South Carolina, became a

12. Pickpockets Stalk an Unwary Victim: An illustration from Pinkerton's *Thirty Years a Detective.* The bearded man has just been seen withdrawing a large sum of money from the bank. Two thieves, apparently reading a magazine, serve as "front stalls" blocking the "mark's" way for a moment. Another stall, with a mustache, close behind the man pushes him on his left side, both distracting him and also turning him more toward the "tool" or "hook," who will pick the pocket, using his coat to conceal his hand—and his plunder.

swindler passing bogus checks.[61] Although some petty thieves might be easily discernible, all the most accomplished and dangerous criminals carried "no suggestion of their calling about with them." Rather they were men who led "double lives," assuming an aspect of quiet respectability in their homes and with their families, which they supported by cool, professional villainy. Indeed, as Pinkerton particularly emphasized, many of the qualities of leading criminals, including their shrewdness, daring, intelligence, and enterprise, if used in honorable pursuits would have won them considerable reputation and wealth, even greatness.[62]

Although the relatively few female criminals in these accounts generally presented a less refined appearance than the men, they, too, included disturbing instances of counterfeits capable of penetrating deep into polite society. Readers learned, for example, of the case of Helen Graham, a woman of great beauty, education, and taste, "who might have . . . shone in the most brilliant circles of refined society," but was in fact a debauched and promiscuous blackmailer. Female pickpockets as a whole, Philip Farley maintained, "dress well, put on a quiet, unassuming demeanor, and slip modestly into a crowd at a shop window or in a store, and feel around until they have discovered the hiding-place of a well-filled purse." If in these rogues' galleries male criminals appeared dark parodies of business rationality ruthlessly exploiting the opportunities of urban capitalist society, their female counterparts were portrayed as perversions of middle-class consumption, yielding to the myriad temptations of sensual desire and greed that metropolitan life laid before them. The new department stores and other shops that catered especially to women, for example, not only provided easy targets for the confirmed shoplifter with her concealed bag and especially crafted muff, but also were the scenes of silent seduction of the weak. In Byrnes's lurid description, police records bulged with instances in which a wife and mother from an honest, pious home succumbed in a shop to her "sex's fondness for finery" and was so enamored of some trifle, though she had already spent all her money, "as to risk home, honor, everything to secure it."

> It is so exposed. There is no one about. It would be such a simple thing to take it and conceal it. Conscience stifled by cupidity is dormant, and the lust of possession is all that possesses her. A moment more and the article is under her cloak, and all of a tremble she is edging away, half frightened, half regretful, yet wholly swayed by the securing of the moment's idol.

But she has not yet learned the dissembling arts of her more hardened sisters. "Everything about her rises to betray her—her frightened glance, her sneaking attitude, the closer clutch she has upon her cloak." She is apprehended, searched, and exposed as a thief. The line that separated a shopper from a shoplifter, a gentleman from a confidence man, and respectability from criminality, could be disturbingly thin.[63]

On a number of grounds, then, the presence of such criminals as described in these books undermined basic assumptions of middle-class life. They suggested that character was not permanent but malleable, that identity was not coherent but fragmented, and that social appearances were not dependable but subject to the most cynical manipulation. "Perhaps the real crime of the confidence man," the sociologist Erving Goffman has observed, "is not that he takes money from his victims but that he robs all of us of the belief

13. "A Fashionable Thief—Shoplifting."

that middle-class manners and appearance can be sustained only by middle-class people." The more successfully criminals carried out their impostures of middle-class respectability, the more they weakened "the moral connection between legitimate authorization to play a part and the capacity to play it."[64] A Gresham's law of social currency might result whereby bad faith drove good out of circulation. And if the face value of polite respectability could be counterfeited too easily and plentifully, then the currency of social exchange would be worthless.

While fanning the anxieties of readers, Farley, Pinkerton, and Byrnes assured them of their own ability to detect such impostors, however ingenious their disguises, through expert scrutiny of their portraits and thorough knowledge of their practices and peculiarities.[65] Yet reliance upon the detective's expertise was not altogether consoling. It might, indeed, only deepen the crisis of self-representation and social trust the detective was called upon to solve. For in the name of restoring justice and stability to society, the detective hid his own identity under multiple disguises and lived a more radically fragmented, isolated, theatrical life than the most deceitful villain. Pinkerton in particular prided himself in being a master of disguise and boasted that "nine-tenths of the actors on the stage . . . would do well to take lessons in their own profession" from the detective. He encouraged his agency's operatives to assume a role in shadowing a suspect, in which one appeared "the careless, ordinary individual" or even a fellow criminal. Pinkerton's model detective was a confidence man in reverse, who infiltrated a stratum of criminal society and skillfully employed every subterfuge at his command to gain the information necessary to betray it. "He must at all times be upon his guard, ever ready to take advantage of the most trifling circumstances, and yet, with an outward demeanor that dispels suspicion and invites the fullest confidence." His ability to beat criminals at their own game, however, came at the cost of his own alienation. During his life as an active investigator, he would never step off the stage of his manifold roles and be his true self. "The great essential," Pinkerton emphasized, "is to prevent his identity from becoming known, even among his associates of respectable character, and when he fails to do this; when the nature of his calling is discovered and made known, his usefulness to the profession is at an end, and failure, certain and inevitable, is the result." The problem Poe and Melville addressed in their short stories (and that Melville treated at greater length in his novel *The Confidence-Man: His Masquerade*) was endemic to the culture. The dilemmas of trust and doubt, confidence and suspicion, easily led to an impasse.[66]

CHAPTER FOUR

Venturing Forth: Bodily Management in Public

If the attempt to read the character of others could open up a bewildering world of deceptive appearances and multiple identities, so, too, could the experience of falling under the gaze of anonymous strangers, to feel *oneself* read and appraised. This offering of self to public scrutiny was one of the central adjustments of nineteenth-century urban life. It affected both sexes, but especially middle-class women, who only gradually widened the narrow compass of their late-eighteenth-century forebears, who had been substantially restricted from venturing forth in the city streets unattended by men. For men and women both, especially among the uninitiated, the unemployed, the insecure, the anxious, or the neurotic, the glare of exposure could be overwhelming. Theodore Dreiser provides a fictional instance when, newly arrived in late-nineteenth-century Chicago, Carrie Meeber begins to look for a job:

> As she contemplated the wide windows and imposing signs, she became conscious of being gazed upon and understood for what she was—a wage-seeker. She had never done this thing before and lacked courage. To avoid conspicuity and a certain indefinable shame she felt at being caught spying about for some place where she might apply for a position, she quickened her steps and assumed an air of indifference supposedly common to one upon an errand. In this way she passed many manufacturing and wholesale houses without once glancing in.[1]

Here her shame is directly tied to her position as one without a secure economic niche in the capitalistic order of production, her status and need nakedly exposed. To conceal that need she plays a minor identity game of her own: pretending to be on an errand rather than looking for work. Although this tactic allows her to save face momentarily, it defeats her larger purpose.

The anxieties of urban life could assume many forms. Even such a great claimant of "the imperial self" as Ralph Waldo Emerson wrote in his journal in 1838:

> It is strange to me how sensible I am to circumstances. I know not how it is but in the streets I feel mean. If a man should accost me in Washington street [in downtown Boston] & call me base fellow! I should not be sure that I could make him feel by my answer & behaviour that my ends were worthy & noble. If the same thing should occur in the country I should feel no doubt at all that I could justify myself to his conscience.[2]

A New York carpenter, writing in 1833 about his first experiences in the city on his own, described his feelings even more vividly:

> I became excessively nervous, so that I was continually full of apprehensions of danger, afraid of everything, and starting with alarm at almost everything. If anything came upon me suddenly, it affected me very much . . . I often became so much embarrassed and confused, that I would lose the power of speech; and frequently, when in conversation, I used suddenly to lose my thoughts in the midst of a sentence, and totally forgot what I was talking about . . . When out from home I was often attacked with these turns in the street, and became so much confused and bewildered, that it was with great difficulty that I could find my way to my house.[3]

The agoraphobic anxiety of this description reveals the acute vulnerability an individual could feel in the new urban setting. It is hardly surprising that agoraphobia (from the Greek *agora*, or "marketplace") emerged as a neurosis in the nineteenth century. Agoraphobic anxiety attacks were spurred by the sharp discontinuities between public and private life. To leave the support of home for an anonymous city street could topple an already fragile sense of self. Agoraphobia represented in extreme form the emotional repression, segmentation, and insecurity of identity (who one is, what work one does, how one is related to others and to society at large, how one will react in various situations) that urban-industrial capitalist society demanded. Structural changes in society contributed to changes in individual personality and created "a built-in identity crisis."[4]

Although, obviously, not all urban Americans became agoraphobes, embarrassment became a normal, even an essential, part of American urban life.[5] Embarrassment thrives upon the unfulfilled expectations of the kind that frequently occurred in novel social situations and with individuals of shifting or indeterminate status. On the street and in social encounters, individuals projected various claims about their identity, claims that in a pluralistic, mobile society might frequently be denied. In such situations embarrassment could act as a powerful instrument of social regulation, guarding privileged social pathways and taking the place to some degree in a modern industrial society of older codes of social deference. It served as a subtle and routine form of discipline, all the more effective because the individual felt his own inadequacy exposed and participated in meting out his own punishment without consciously discerning the system of exposure involved.[6]

This sensitivity to embarrassment reflected the unstable, altered context of honor, shame, and reputation in the market economy and democratic ethos of the nineteenth-century city. The traditional notion of honor that flourished in more locally based, preindustrial societies—and which historian Bertram Wyatt-Brown has found so fundamental to antebellum rural Southern life—was based upon the individual's prideful regard of social reputation among those who knew him within a hierarchical order. "Honor," Wyatt-Brown writes, "resides in the individual as his understanding of who he is and where he belongs in the ordered ranks of society," adding that "when society has pretensions that there are no ranks, honor must necessarily be set aside or drastically redefined to mean something else." This is precisely what happened. Outside the Old South, honor shed its overwhelming concern with the public recognition of inner and especially manly worth; it was redefined to mean "domestic and civic virtue," in a word, respectability, and applied more equally to both sexes. In the pluralistic world of the nineteenth-century commercial metropolis, especially, individuals still submitted to public evaluation, but not by their neighbors in a rank-ordered society, but by a largely fluid and anonymous multitude. A new kind of embarrassment and sense of shame emerged as a result, one that fed upon uncertainties of status, of belonging, of living up to often ambiguous standards of social performance in a society in which all claims of rank were subject to challenge.[7]

The intense bourgeois concern with "rudeness" in the nineteenth century must be viewed in relation to this altered context of shame and embarrassment. Rudeness in this culture constituted a kind of social obscenity, a violation of the codes of civility in such a way as to make public that which should remain private, to single out for special attention that which should remain inconspicuous, or else to cast public actions, conduct, and individual actors in an unworthy or degrading light.[8] At a time when the segmentation of public and private life was rapidly increasing, the public arena was fraught with special concern as a problematic realm. As one etiquette adviser bemoaned, "Every one with whom we come in contact, however much beneath us, and indifferent to us, possesses the power to pain us by unguarded and unpleasant words." Indeed, rudeness threatened not simply in words but in the slightest expression—a gaze held too long, an insolent gesture, an overly familiar smile, an unwelcome touch. The new social settings of an urban-industrial age created a kind of ecology of embarrassment and increased the sense of vulnerability to possible rudeness. On crowded streets, in shops and hotels, on omnibuses, streetcars, trains, and steamboats, and in elevators, strangers were promiscuously amassed in intimate proximity. Such scenes were rife with potential obtrusions from which defense or escape could be difficult.[9]

The codification of etiquette books provided a measure of relief from the uncertainties of "correct" behavior and the shameful uncertainties of self that lay beneath them. By defining rules and transgressions, etiquette advisers offered to some degree a structure of innocence and guilt that was less indeterminate and hence less continually punishing than the structure of shame. As one writer declared decisively, "Etiquette is the machinery of society. . . . It prevents the agony of uncertainty, and soothes even when it cannot cure the pains of blushing bashfulness. If one is certain about being correct, there is little to be anxious about."[10]

There was, of course, still much to be anxious about. The ritual order of public interaction was premised upon this sensitivity to shame and fear of self-exposure. Individuals developed various ways to protect themselves in public—first and most obviously, by avoiding situations where shame and exposure might likely occur (a strategy that particularly restricted the movement of women); by taking refuge in a depersonalized role or adhering strictly to a norm of behavior; or if an embarrassing incident did in spite of all occur, either ignoring the lapse if possible or ceremonially mending the situation so that social identities were restored. To avoid exposing and shaming others and also to avoid participating in their shame became a major principle of public conduct.[11]

The advice and admonitions of etiquette books were built around these strategies. In the process the social codes of tactful civility subtly varied from the moral codes of truthfulness and justice. Etiquette writers (and presumably their readers) were reluctant to recognize this shift, for it contained particularly disturbing implications for the development of American society.[12] Lord Chesterfield's social Machiavellianism potentially opened up a society of hypocrites and poseurs, and to close this breach American writers frequently asserted that manners and morals were one. As the epitome of the gentleman, etiquette advisers cited no less a model than Jesus, and their most common single affirmation was that the first and greatest principle of politeness lay in the blessed Golden Rule. But while these invocations remained fashionable throughout the nineteenth century and into the twentieth, other conceptions tugged the code of public manners away from its moral base. Numerous protective and defensive practices, summarized as "tact" and "respect for privacy," came into play as etiquette writers prepared their readers for social encounters. Rather than Christian charity and sympathy, etiquette served as social armor against intrusion: "It is like a wall built up around us to protect us from disagreeable, underbred people who refuse to take the trouble to be civil." The right of individual privacy, under new pressures in the brashly inquisitive metropolis and subject to the development of new technologies of intrusion and publicity, was elevated to sacred status, which everyone was bound to respect. Bluntly formulated, the social command became something very different from the Golden Rule—the Iron Rule of Public Civility, an etiquette of laissez-faire for a capitalist culture: "All rights, and the essence of true politeness, are contained in the homely maxim, 'MIND YOUR

OWN BUSINESS'; which means, by a pretty evident implication, that you are to let your neighbor's business alone." In this terse injunction the writer defended an ideal of conduct that bound together propriety, privacy, and property. Implicitly, he accepted the boundless market as the model for all exchange, social as well as economic, in urban capitalist society.[13]

Street Behavior, Bodily Management, and Gender Ideals

Such advice, in effect, responded to the crisis of social representation and the instability of identity in the public realm by abandoning as far as possible any notion of legitimate, specifically public, interchange or fellowship, and addressing only the pursuit of personal affairs. In public the individual uneasily pretended to be in private. To shield against the public gaze and guard against the intruders and deceivers who pervaded the metropolis and made your business their own, etiquette advisers urged a strategy of self-discipline to the end of self-effacement.

On the city street this strategy applied in varying degrees to both sexes, but particularly to women, who still faced substantial limitations upon their participation in everyday public life. Only gradually did the customs loosen that had bound fashionable urban ladies in the late eighteenth century to their houses unless accompanied by a male escort. When the travel writer Mrs. Anne Royall visited New York City in the 1820s, for example, she reported that "ladies of the better sort" consciously set themselves apart from the women of Broadway: "from motives of delicacy, [they] were never seen in the street on foot . . . [and] they always took a carriage be the distance ever so small." And a New Yorker amusedly recalled how as late as 1835, a confection shop on Broadway languished in neglect as "society ruled that it was not proper [for ladies] to enter and partake." Well into the nineteenth century, men did most of the shopping for the household, and some business districts were considered almost exclusively male terrain. Other public acts, such as speaking before large mixed secular audiences, as did the various abolitionists and feminists beginning with the radical egalitarian Frances Wright in 1828, would continue to be branded as shameless and unwomanly. If the ideal for both men and women was to be completely inconspicuous in public, for women the stakes were much higher and the possibilities for transgression much greater.[14]

In matters of dress, both ladies and gentlemen avoided elaborate shows of finery on the street, favoring wardrobes that were cloaks of genteel anonymity. Let us consider, first, appropriate street dress for a man.

The polite gentleman stepped onto the street as if onto a public stage, with gloves and hat on and all minor adjustments completed. A gentleman so far avoided turning "a public thoroughfare into a private dressing-room" that he did not have his boots polished on the street. He was impeccably clean and neat, his collars and cuffs "faultlessly white, and the clothes well brushed." He dressed soberly, shunning the affectations of the social-climbing "swell" and, still more, the fashion-conscious dandy, who strove to be conspicuous above all else. In his mid-nineteenth-century incarnation, the dandy affected tight trousers, an exaggeratedly stylish overcoat "with monstrous buttons and wide sleeves," gigantic tie and shirt collar, glossy hat, bright green gloves, a light walking stick, and an eyeglass to inspect any curiosity along the way. Etiquette advisers scorned such elaborate finery as a badge of effeminacy. "Don't . . . wear anything that is *pretty*," one manual told its male readers. "What have men to do with pretty things?"[15]

This view was a historic innovation. Before the nineteenth century, both in Europe and colonial America, men's clothing was often every bit as elaborate—even as "pretty"—as women's. As late as 1782 John Hancock appeared at midday dressed in "a blue damask gown lined with velvet, a white stock, a white satin embroidered waistcoat, black satin small-clothes, white silk stockings and red morocco slippers." On his head he wore not one but two caps: "a red velvet cap within which was one of fine linen, the last turned up two or three inches over the lower edge of the velvet."[16]

In the course of the nineteenth century the image of the ideal gentleman rapidly shed the remnants of eighteenth-century courtliness and assumed the aspect of the solid, substantial, inexpressive businessman. The colors of his wardrobe grew progressively somber. The New York Knickerbocker Abram Dayton recalled that by the 1830s "black was the prevailing color" among fashionable young men of the city; "it was worn for promenade, parlor, church, ball, business," and "in such uniformity of style, as effectively to destroy all individuality." By mid-century, an etiquette adviser noted, "nineteen-twentieths of all coats are black. . . . Dress pan-

14. A Dandy—and His Detractors.

taloons must also be black, or white; but in the morning, drabs, grays, and plaids are worn." Evening suits were also black. Both coats and trousers were cut fuller, concealing the outlines of the body, while heavy shoes or boots encased the feet and dark hats gave weight and dignity to the head. By the later nineteenth century the modern suit developed in Europe and America and became the requisite costume—virtually the anonymous uniform—of the business culture. In the words of one modern critic, "It was the first ruling class costume to idealise purely *sedentary* power. The power of the administrator and conference table." The costumes of previous elites originated in the requirements of active pursuits such as hunting, riding, dueling, or dancing. "Essentially the suit was made for the gestures of talking and calculating abstractly." Concealing individual bodies and personalities, it subordinated the wearer to the workings of the marketplace. Almost immediately,

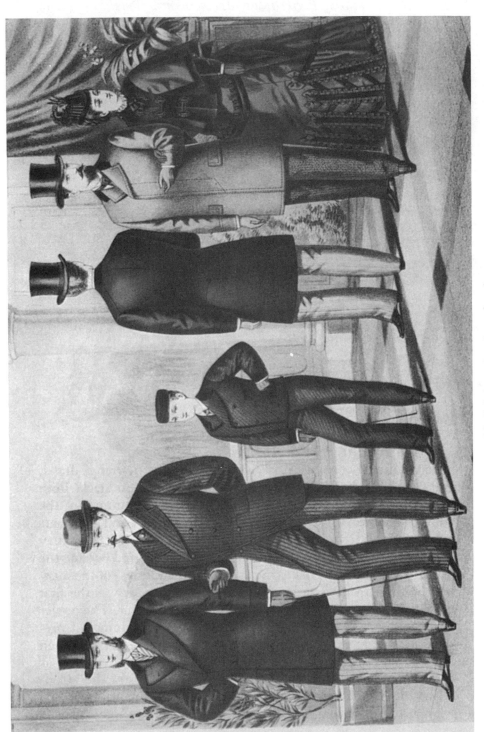

15. Fashionable Sobriety: An 1872 advertisement.

in inferior ready-made copies, the business suit became the dress of many working-class men as well, forming another specific instance of the cultural hegemony of the bourgeoisie.[17]

Other aspects of the exemplary gentleman's public appearance furthered this image of undemonstrative sobriety. Not only did he wear a heavy, dark overcoat in cold weather; by 1890 one adviser reported, "In large cities, men rarely walk in the street in their dress-suits without wearing a very thin overcoat, even in summer. This is to avoid being conspicuous." The gentleman carried a walking stick or, during business hours, a rolled umbrella—which became virtually the emblem of bourgeois circumspection. The fashion for full beards and mustaches that swept the United States as well as Europe in the second half of the nineteenth century added to the sense of weight, maturity—and illegibility—in the face.[18]

For a lady the standards of street dress were even more exacting, since her very respectability and physical safety might depend upon the signs she communicated through her appearance. Writing in 1837, Eliza Ware Farrar sounded the theme that numerous other advisers would elaborate when she stressed: "singularity is to be avoided, and she is best dressed whose costume presents an agreeable whole, without anything that can be remarked." In practice, of course, women did not always attain this ideal—or wish to—at least in a traveler's eyes. Surveying with amusement women's bright array on Broadway during his 1841–42 American tour, Charles Dickens exclaimed: "What various parasols! what rainbow silks and satins! what pinking of thin stockings, and pinching of thin shoes, and fluttering of ribbons and silk tassels, and display of rich cloaks with gaudy hoods and linings!" Nonetheless, approved fashions in women's street clothes, as in men's, steadily darkened over the course of the century. By 1890 one writer urged basic black with unassailable logic: "Black is becoming to every woman, but as she does not dress to be seen when walking, it would be well to wear it, even if she thought it not becoming." A lady was encouraged to attend scrupulously to all aspects of her costume, avoiding overly rich materials, excessive displays of jewelry, heavy perfumes, and frayed or muddy skirt edges. Such details, she was warned, would be pitilessly examined, and her status as a true lady or vulgar pretender judged accordingly.[19]

Garbed, then, with impeccable inexpressivity, the lady and gentleman ventured forth. In deportment as in dress, each aimed

16. Subdued "Walking Costumes": An 1885 advertisement.

17. Sidewalk Swaggerers: The Bowery boy and the Broadway swell.

to offer nothing to arouse strangers' notice or clues to seize upon, remembering the injunction "A lady or gentleman should conduct herself or himself on the street so as to escape all observation." Through strict bodily control each sought to create "a symbolic shield of privacy," which permitted one to move through a public space while keeping aloof from engagement.[20]

Take the apparently simple act of walking in the street. Among men, a figure such as the Bowery tough or the fashionable "sport" called attention to himself by "swagger[ing] along the street, shouting and laughing with his companions, his hat on one side, a cigar between his fingers. . . ." The dandy, "glorifying in his appearance," affected a slouching posture and "mincing" step. Meanwhile, the greenhorn loped along with a ludicrous "swinging gait," and the "impolite man of humble life" shuffled with downcast eyes. The physiognomic vision of etiquette manuals approached Poe's manic student of the crowd in its gradations of social types and the walks characteristic of each. "Not only is a man's walk an index of his character and of the grade of his culture," proclaimed *The Mentor*, "but it is also an index of the frame of mind he is in. There is the thoughtful walk and the thoughtless walk, the responsible walk and the careless walk, the worker's walk and the idler's walk, the ingenuous walk and the insidious walk, and so on." To walk like a gentleman, then, one had to *be* a gentleman both habitually and at the very moment in question. He proceeded attentively but unselfconsciously to his duties, neither hurrying nor sauntering, with a strength of self-discipline so practiced as to be "natural."[21]

For a lady walking on the street, the demands were even higher: "every passer-by will look at her, if it is only for one glance; every unlady-like action will be marked." She was admonished by numerous authorities throughout the nineteenth century to walk slowly, in "a modest and measured gait," turning her head neither right nor left. She did not "eye another lady's dress, as if studying its very texture," and she scrupulously avoided "any gesture or word" that might attract attention, especially from men.[22] "Loud talking and laughing in the street" not only were "excessively vulgar," an adviser warned darkly, but exposed her to "the most severe misconstruction." If possible, she tried not to stop on the street for any reason. If she wished to speak to a gentleman she knew, she allowed him to accompany her briefly; in the case of another lady, instead of exposing her "to the jostlings of dirty boys, and the pelting of mud from carriage-wheels," the two walked together during their conversation. In either case she took care "not to utter their names loudly."[23]

Such bodily controls by both men and women exemplified what the anthropologist Mary Douglas has called "the purity rule": "The more the social situation exerts pressure on persons involved in it, the more the social demand for conformity tends to be expressed by a demand for physical control. . . . A natural way of investing a social occasion with dignity is to hide organic processes." Through attentive and disciplined body management, an individual both paid deference to the social situation of which one was a part and guarded against any weakening of controls, either one's own or another's.[24]

In public especially, but also in private, one sought particularly to stifle all activities that might draw attention to the internal workings of the body, such as coughing, sneezing, yawning, scratching, tooth picking, throat clearing, and nose blowing. More intimate functions were generally beneath discussion. Occasionally, however, warnings such as this one against nose blowing and rubbing evince displacement of deeper anxieties (including that great nineteenth-century bugaboo, masturbation):

> The nose is the most prominent and noticeable feature of the face, and, as its functions are not all of the noblest kind, it especially behooves people who desire to be nice to avoid drawing attention to them. Consequently, all its requirements

18. How Not to Cough.

should be attended to in the quietest and most private manner possible. It should never be fondled before company, or, in fact, touched at any time, unless absolutely necessary. The nose, like all other organs, augments in size by frequent handling, so we recommend every person to keep his own fingers, as well as those of his friends or enemies away from it.[25]

Etiquette advisers prohibited chewing gum or eating on the street. They censured males smoking in public, particularly in the presence of ladies, and anywhere on the street, helping to make it illegal in Boston in the mid-nineteenth century. They were forced to moderate their positions slightly toward the end of the century, however, when such laws were long since repealed—and respectable women were themselves beginning to smoke in private. But they saved their most fervid denunciations for the national male pastime that so offended Frances Trollope, Charles Dickens, and other European visitors: tobacco chewing and spitting. Through the mid-nineteenth century, tobacco spit flew without restraint in places frequented by men: in railroad cars, stages, and steamers, saloons, hotels, and theaters, hospitals, colleges, and churches,

shops, offices, private houses, post offices, courtrooms, state legislatures, the halls of Congress, and even the White House. Etiquette authorities helped turn the face of respectability against
tobacco chewing, limiting its scope by the late nineteenth century.
As one writer bluntly declared, spit "is an excrement of the body,
and should be disposed of as privately and carefully as any other."[26]

All the little gestures of bodily adjustment and self-engrossment
similarly demanded precise regulation. "Boring the ears with the
fingers, chafing the limbs . . . and even a too fond and ceaseless
caressing of the moustache are in bad taste. Everything connected
with *personal* discomfort, with the mere physique, should be as
unobtrusively attended to as possible." Forms of self-involvement
that obtruded upon the attention of others aroused special ire—
irrepressible noisemaking, for instance. "Don't beat a tattoo with
your foot in company or anywhere, to the annoyance of others,"
scolded one adviser. "Don't drum with your fingers on chair, table,
or window-pane. Don't hum a tune. The instinct for making noise
is a survival of savagery." The man who habitually went around
"singing, humming, or whistling," a second writer concurred, "has
the manners of a boor, and deserves the calaboose for disorderly
conduct."[27]

Just as etiquette writers warned against gestures of self-engrossment, so, too, they cautioned their readers against *overinvolvement*
in the affairs of others. In this respect, they especially emphasized
disciplining the eye in social encounters, avoiding the "extremes of
shyness and boldness." The stares of the idle, with no business of
their own to mind, outraged them. They advocated that delicate
modulation of vision that Erving Goffman has called "civil inattention," by which one notes another's presence and makes appropriate
adjustments without unduly altering one's demeanor either by a
fearful, downcast look or a bold stare. Because eye contact often
served as a pathway to a social overture, etiquette writers decried
its abuse. Statements with the eyes demanded as strict a censuring
as speech: "Under any ordinary circumstances, it is not allowable
to leer, to wink, or to say anything with the eyes which it would
not be entirely proper to say in so many plain words." Propriety
depended upon both forswearing visual intrusion upon another and
refusing to collaborate in another's self-exposure: "The rule is im-
perative, that no one should see, or, if that is impossible, should
seem to see, or to have seen, anything that another person would

choose to have concealed; unless indeed it is your business to watch for some misdemeanor." Municipal police and detectives properly assumed this business—significantly, Pinkerton made the symbol of his detective agency an unsleeping eye, from which the phrase "private eye" originated. But the urban bourgeoisie was taught to *overlook* as much as to look and to read the city at a glance.[28]

The force of such rules is clear from the scorn heaped upon those who broke them. Offenders took a number of forms. In New York and other cities in the early nineteenth century, for example, the "bloods" hung out on street corners, appraising the passing women, and remarking for all to hear, "An Angel, by H——s!" "Dam'd fine girl, by g—d!" "Where do you lodge, my dear?" But perhaps the most flagrant culprit was the dandy who emerged by the mid-nineteenth century. The dandy flouted the code of civil inattention by both making a spectacle of himself and brazenly making others, especially women, objects of his scrutiny. A comic valentine of the period taunted:

> Put by your glass, you quizzing elf,
> Or in it view your foolish self,
> With cane so smart hung on your arm,
> No doubt you think the ladies charm.
> But instead of that you are disgusting,
> You are getting old and somewhat rusting,
> So go your way you ugly beast,
> Made up of mischief not the least.[29]

The dandy's mischief was still harder to bear when his quarry could not easily escape his gaze. At a concert, complained one writer, he "amuses himself by scanning the faces of performers and persons near him," then, at the intermission, trained his *lorgnette* upon a lady from an adjacent seat. Fellow dandies imitated his rudeness, until the unwilling cynosure withered under the rapt, even lascivious gaze of fifty opera glasses.[30] To stare at a woman in such a way was to violate her modesty and assault her honor, even to group her with the prostitutes and painted women of the city. "Such "jackanapes" and "cads," apostles of gentility agreed, deserved to be hissed down, thrown out, or even arrested.[31]

19. A Valentine for a Dandy.

Women in Public

Middle-class women, of course, were admonished not to respond to such ogling and to make their own eyes behave. An 1880 manual sternly warned coquettes against "the bold free eye, which speaks what the lips would not dare to utter" as they flirted with strangers on the street. A few years later another adviser reiterated firmly, "A lady never seeks to attract the attention of the other sex or form their acquaintance on the street. To do so would forfeit all claims to consideration as a lady, and would justify a suspicion of her virtue." Etiquette advisers defended a feminine ideal of uncompromising modesty, particularly in public. Once breached, descent was swift and sure: "familiarity leads to disrespect, disrespect to vulgarity, vulgarity or indecency to vice, and vice to misery."[32]

Under such exacting standards, the growing polarization between "public" and "private" bore down upon women with special intensity. When middle-class women left the confines of their home to venture out in public, they entered a realm in which they felt—or were expected to feel—particularly vulnerable. Possibilities for in-

20. Under the Relentless Male Gaze.

trusion and symbolic violation abounded. From an impertinent glance, an unwelcome compliment, the scale of improprieties rose through a series of gradations to the ultimate violation in rape. According to many etiquette writers, a properly behaved woman would escape all rudeness. But this superficial assurance concealed a less pleasant implication: Any disrespect a woman *did* encounter she must have deserved. As a number of etiquette writers were fond of declaring, "The true lady walks the street, wrapped in a mantle of proper reserve, so impenetrable that insult and coarse familiarity shrink from her. . . . By her pre-occupation [she] is secure from any annoyance to which a person of less perfect breeding might be subjected."[33]

To preserve a woman's privacy in public, nineteenth-century etiquette authorities coached her thoroughly in the key principles of bodily management that sociologist Lyn Lofland has found to be vital and enduring strategies in the twentieth-century city. She minimized her own expressivity in dress and deportment. She minimized body contact, keeping herself to herself and remaining alert to other pedestrians' movements. She minimized eye contact with all but her acquaintances. She dealt with potential offenses by studiously ignoring them if possible, "hearing nothing that she ought not to hear, and seeing nothing that she ought not to see," or, "having unmistakably heard, she did not understand." At times she might have to resort to considerable theatrics of her own to protect herself in the streets. One young woman reportedly dealt with a man's persistent overtures by pretending not to understand simple English, finally turning with an air of resignation and giving him a dime as if he were a beggar, saying in French that it was all she could afford. If all else failed, a woman "hastened her steps" and fled the scene or appealed to a policeman, while endeavoring to keep her composure intact.[34]

But what if some women welcomed such attention? Then they were not respectable—according to the dictates of middle-class gentility. Even more than their male counterparts, the dandy and the ruffian, they were objects of scorn. Indeed, what most distinguished a prostitute was the way she attracted male attention by brightly colored attire, her notable omission of a hat that might shield her face, and her searching gaze. Fashionable working women also defied genteel norms of dress and demeanor, as in the case of New York's "Bowery Gals," who emerged as a characteristic metropolitan "type" in the 1840s. In contrast to the inconspicuous passage of the proper lady, the Bowery Gal's "very walk . . . [had] a wink of mischief and defiance in it, and the tones of her voice . . . [were] loud, hearty and free." Disdaining the muted colors of respectable middle-class women, she delighted in startling contrasts, "a light pink contrasting with a deep blue, a bright yellow with a brighter red, and a green with a dashing purple or maroon." She, too, rejected the lady's bonnet or veil in favor of ostentatious hats that left her "face entirely exposed, and the eyes at full liberty to see what is going on in every direction." A rebel against both middle-class respectability and her own family's supervision, she moved freely about the city, linked easily with strangers, and, in some cases, made casual prostitution an important part of the working-class female economy.[35]

Such liberties were in marked contrast to those of middle-class women, although in the course of the nineteenth century they also increasingly enjoyed a freedom of movement in public far greater than that of their counterparts abroad, for all its constrictions. By the end of the century there is evidence that a sexual revolution was beginning, in which middle-class women moved about with fewer constraints, encouraged by the development of the growing consumer economy, in which they played such an indispensable role. Department stores and other shops helped to create new metropolitan spaces, like New York's "Ladies' Mile" along Broadway from Fourteenth to Twenty-third Street, in which middle-class women were encouraged not to proceed as inconspicuously as possible but with a new sense of entitlement. Significantly, while an 1866 etiquette manual warned women against stopping on the street at shopwindows, especially when alone, by 1891 another guide confidently reversed this judgment.[36] New urban entertainments, from vaudeville theaters to amusement parks, proclaimed their respectability in hopes of attracting women and families as well as men, but at the same time promised a new sense of vitality and freedom distinctly different from prevailing Victorian propriety.

Theodore Dreiser, who portrayed Carrie Meeber suffering the public gaze as she began looking for work in Chicago, also depicted her experiencing for the first time the anxious pleasures of the urban promenade. Here, with her new friend Mrs. Vance, Carrie joins in the afternoon parade of fashionables down New York's Broadway from Thirty-fourth to Fourteenth Street past the fine shops and theaters:

> In all her stay in the city, Carrie had never heard of this showy parade, had never even been on Broadway when it was taking place. On the other hand, it was a familiar thing to Mrs. Vance, who not only knew of it as an entity, but had often been in it, going purposely to see and be seen, to create a stir with her beauty and dispel any tendency to fall short in dressiness by contrasting herself with the beauty and fashion of the town.
>
> Carrie stepped along easily enough after they got out of the car at 34th Street, but soon fixed her eyes upon the lovely company which swarmed by and with her as they proceeded.

She noticed of a sudden that Mrs. Vance's manner had rather stiffened under the gaze of handsome men and elegantly dressed ladies, whose glances were not modified by any rule of propriety. *To stare seemed the proper and natural thing* [italics added].[37]

Male Aid and Female Dependence

By the strict standards of propriety, however, much of urban male etiquette toward women, in turn, constituted an elaborate form of protection and reassurance that violations would not occur; yet the price of such courtesies was dependence upon male good faith and a severe restriction upon female freedom to move about the city at will and to feel at ease in public. Although female readers of etiquette books were frequently congratulated on the comparative freedom they enjoyed in America to venture forth in the city without male escorts, increasingly toward the end of the century they were warned "not to abuse it," and to "err on the side of caution rather than . . . of boldness." In general, respectable women were told "not to venture out upon the street alone after dark," particularly in large cities, but to rely ideally upon a male relative, or else their host or his servant to escort them. They learned to assume an air of apology befitting dependents. "If the host wishes to accompany you himself, you must excuse yourself politely for giving him so much trouble," Emily Thornwell advised her readers in 1856, "but finish, however, by accepting." Otherwise, women might expect rudeness and gossip. In an extremity a married woman might return home alone; an unmarried one, never. Women were assured they could "lunch or breakfast [dinner was evidently another matter] without gentlemen in respectable public restaurants, *but* two ladies should if possible be together rather than one . . . alone [italics added]." Two women might "attend, with perfect propriety, a place of amusement without an escort"—*but* they need to be, "under the circumstances, exceptionally quiet in their manners and their dress."[38]

The reputation of young ladies was particularly vulnerable, and by the close of the nineteenth century etiquette advisers disputed

among themselves about the necessity of a strict system of chaper-
onage, day and night. Many books flatly restricted to fiancés and
near relations the men with whom a young woman might properly
walk in the evening—a stance the humorist James Thurber would
later parody in his mother's apocryphal exclamation: "Why, when
I was a girl, you didn't dare walk with a man after sunset, unless
he was your husband, and even then there was talk." The entire
ritual structuring of urban life, although performed in the name of
honoring women, assumed and encouraged their subservience to
men.[39]

Contemporary magazine illustrations depicting women on the
streets of New York support this point in interesting ways. A
prominent theme is the courteous aid women receive from male
protectors, both personal escorts and especially policemen, who use
their power, vigilance, and authority on women's behalf.[40] Such
courtesies, however, ritualize women's subordination to men. Perhaps the mildest example shows a couple crossing Brooklyn Bridge
during a rainstorm, the woman holding her escort's arm as he carries
her package and shelters her with an umbrella—here both a practical
device and a symbol of his solicitude. In accepting his protection
she also subtly yields to his direction and constraint. To the left,
an imperturbable policeman in an oilskin coat stands guard, further
relieving the woman from any necessity of vigilance on her own
behalf.

Two other illustrations depict young women more decisively
surrendering to male control as they accept aid from the gallant
police officers of New York's "Broadway Squad." *Harper's Weekly*
described these men as "all over six feet high," "well-proportioned,"
"generally handsome," and "always polite—to the ladies, especially
to those who are young and pretty." In one instance a massive
policeman confidently escorts two young ladies through the melee
of traffic (leaving, the magazine writer slyly noted, an old lady to
fend for herself) as others are intimidated by the passing horses.
In the second case, with one arm an officer carries a young lady
over the winter slush to a horsecar as a parent might a child.[41]

Another drawing takes this theme a step further. During an 1881
"hot wave" (as the phrase was then) in which, *Frank Leslie's Illustrated
Newspaper* reported, many people collapsed, both male and female,
strong and weak, the weekly's illustrator sidestepped the spectacle

21. Under Male Protection: "A Wet Day on the East River Bridge" (1887).

22. A Chivalrous Escort: "Crossing Broadway" (1870). In the crush of horses and pedestrians, the woman at the extreme right drops her packages. On the left another horse nibbles on an old man's jacket.

23. A Strong Right Arm: "A Broadway Scene in a February Thaw" (1872).

24. Exposed and Defenseless: "A Hot Wave in New York City—a Fair Pedestrian Overcome by the Heat on Broadway" (1881).

of a prostrate "lusty stevedore" in favor of a subject that neatly fit within the gender ideals of male courtesy and female subordination: "beauty in distress." In his drawing a pretty young woman has fainted on the street and lies exposed to the stares of passersby. Through no fault of her own, she has lost all the bodily control, self-possession, and inconspicuousness on which women especially were taught to depend in public. Only "the vigorous buffetings of a stalwart officer" keep the crush of the curious from her—helping both to revive her and to repair her lost dignity. Such male attentions had become paradigmatic images of urban civility, protecting women against the severities of both nature and the crowd. They were ostensibly reassuring images, but they came at a high price: women remained in the position of wards to their male guardians.[42] Significantly, one of the most common and scathing ways of caricaturing women's-rights advocates in the nineteenth century (and into the twentieth) was to reverse the gender roles of male dominance and female subordination.

25. Women on Top: A satirical view of "The Triumphs of Womans Rights" by Currier & Ives (1869). As "Miss Hang Man" and "Susan Sharp-Tongue" run for office, mannishly dressed women cluster around the ballot box. A hapless male is saddled with the care of an infant by a menacing woman at right.

Greetings in Public: How to Tip a Hat and Other Lost Arts

The intricacies of movement in public were compounded in the conduct of greetings. Of all everyday social rituals on the street, perhaps this one most exquisitely tested an individual's ability to maintain a dignified reserve, protect gender ideals, and exert bodily management. To allow anyone access on any terms meant to surrender all rights of privacy and open oneself to all claimants and counterfeits. But precisely *whom* to greet and *when* and *how* to do it raised fundamental issues concerning the terms of social recognition and deference in a liberal capitalist democracy.

Older courtesy guides placed great stress on the different greetings owed to social superiors, equals, and inferiors. For example, the French courtesy book of 1595 later dutifully copied by young George Washington showed a keen sensitivity to social rank. "In Speaking to men of Quality," it advised, "do not lean nor Look them full in the Face, nor approach too near them[;] at lest Keep a full Pace from them." Social subordinates were to know their place and wait for the cues of their acknowledged betters. This power to give or withhold access was extremely important in societies where patronage was crucial to advancement. In seventeenth-century France, for instance, King Louis XIII and his son tightened their power over courtiers by holding them in suspense, conferring or denying the royal presence, gaze, and ear at their pleasure, raising one by singling him out for a greeting while leaving others in darkness.[43]

In the sprawling capitalist society of nineteenth-century America, however, the hierarchies of social position grew much less distinct. Great divisions of class and power assuredly remained—indeed, new ones came into being—but they did not command the same personal acknowledgment as before. European travelers in particular frequently complained about the coarse familiarity and egalitarianism they experienced, which confounded all traditional notions of rank and deference. Frances Trollope observed tartly that among her neighbors in Cincinnati she was generally known as "the English old woman" and her husband as "the old man," while the same people customarily spoke of "the lady over the way what takes in washing," and "draymen, butchers' boys, and the labourers on the canal were invariably denominated 'them gentlemen.'" Similarly and with like amused contempt, the English writer Frederick Marryat reported in 1839: "One of the most singular points about the lower classes in America is that they will call themselves ladies and gentlemen and yet refuse their title to their superiors." One would ask, "'Are you the *man* who bought the newspaper?' 'Yes,' replied I. 'The young *gentleman* who sold it to you has sent me to pay you four cents.'" Half a century later in 1889 another British novelist, the young Rudyard Kipling, sarcastically observed that when a hotel clerk in San Francisco "stoops to attend to your wants, he does so whistling or humming, or picking his teeth, or pausing to converse with some one he knows. These performances, I gather, are to impress upon you that he is a free man and your equal. From his general appearance and the size of his diamonds he ought to be your superior."[44]

The logic of the capitalist metropolis, if taken to its extreme, encouraged the clerk to flaunt his diamonds, for it reduced all questions of status and social worth to questions of market value. The society such logic creates was portrayed by Theodore Dreiser in *Sister Carrie*, where individuals learn to appraise one another and to estimate themselves as they do objects for sale. Throughout the novel he emphasized the telling shadings of greetings that declare an individual's relative standing as exactly and pitilessly as the quotations of the stock market. Here is how he described the man who becomes Carrie's lover, George Hurstwood, in his position as manager of a prominent Chicago saloon:

> He knew by name and could greet personally with a "Well, old fellow," hundreds of actors, merchants, politicians and the general run of successful characters about town, and it was a part of his success to do so. He had a finely graduated scale of informality and friendship, which improved from the "How do you do," addressed to the fifteen-dollars-a-week clerks and office attachés who by long frequenting of the place became aware of his position, to the "Why, old man, how are you," which he addressed to those noted or rich individuals who knew him and were inclined to be friendly. There was a class, however, too rich, too famous, or too successful, with whom he could not attempt any familiarity of address, and with these he was professionally tactful, assuming a grave and dignified attitude, paying them the deference which would win their good feeling without in the least compromising his own bearing and opinions. There were, in the last place, a few good followers, neither rich nor poor, famous nor yet remarkably successful, with whom he was friendly on the score of good fellowship.[45]

In the course of the novel, Dreiser stressed how quickly such greetings could alter with a turn of fortune's wheel. After Hurstwood steals from his employers and flees Chicago, his inexorable decline is charted by the painful, humiliating greetings he receives from erstwhile acquaintances on the street. Finally, he is reduced to beggary, in which no greeting is given him at all. With no role in the marketplace, he is socially obliterated—and it is but a short while before he commits suicide. Carrie's rising prosperity is registered in similar terms. When, for example, she is promoted from the chorus line to a position as a leading actress and first receives her new salary from the cashier, "it was accompanied by a smile and a salutation. . . . Right after came one of the insignificant members of the company, and she heard the changed tone of address. 'How much?' said the same cashier sharply."[46]

Such estimates of face value, of course, were not confined to the city. Walter Wyckoff had graduated from Princeton and begun to study for the ministry when he broke off his training in order to

discover American society at first hand. Although most disguised their identities to climb upward, Wyckoff was part of a pioneering generation of investigative reporters and sociologists who adopted new identities temporarily to plunge downward into the lives of the poor and oppressed. For two years, from 1891 to 1893, he conducted what he called "an experiment in reality," working as a common laborer from coast to coast. Almost immediately he met a reception different from anything he had known. In his first venture, around Highland Falls, New York, "my good-morning was not infrequently met by a vacant stare." He asked the way of the keeper of a country store only to receive a long look, "a spurt of tobacco-juice, which stirred the dust between my feet, and, finally, a caustic sentence to the effect that he 'did not much know, and did not care a damn.' "[47]

American etiquette manuals were less concerned with the gradations of professional and social standing than their European counterparts, but they were hardly oblivious to them. Throughout the nineteenth century some books urged special deference toward social superiors, while leaving vague just who these superiors were. Others struck a more democratic note—though they could not always hold it. "We allow precedence to but two classes:—to women and the aged," declared one adviser, then added, "—or at least we do in theory; but considerations of station, culture, and, we are sorry to say, even wealth are largely recognized." Another book, published in 1891, swept aside the issue of superiors in terms less egalitarian than imperious: "Always be polite to your inferiors, and it naturally follows that you will be politeness itself with your equals. A gentleman has no superior."[48]

Perhaps not surprisingly, etiquette writers offered much more detailed instruction on how to greet inferiors than superiors. Most of them emulated the spirit of Lord Chesterfield when he wrote: "I am more upon my guard as to my behaviour to my servants and others who are called my inferiors, than I am towards my equals; for fear of being suspected of that mean and ungenerous sentiment, of desiring to make others feel that difference, which fortune has, and, perhaps, too undeservedly, made between us." Yet both the excesses that advisers warned against as well as the snobbery they often betrayed give abundant evidence of the limits of egalitarian sentiment in the nineteenth-century metropolis. "Avoid condescending bows to your friends and equals," an 1836 guide admonished readers. But it immediately added, "If you meet a rich *parvenu*, whose consequence you wish to reprove, you may salute him in a very patronizing manner: or else, in acknowledging his bow, look somewhat surprised and say, 'Mister—eh—eh?' " Later in the century, other writers reproved snubbing social inferiors of any sort, suggesting that this was itself the practice of *parvenus* and those anxious about their own position.[49]

Etiquette authorities urged readers not to scruple to acknowledge servants, milliners, seamstresses, and the like in the street, though they split in recommending whether to bow or simply to "salute them in a kindly voice." A kindly or at least civil voice was especially urged in place of the kicks, growls, and curses some men thought just replies to newsboys, fruit sellers, and bootblacks.[50] Advisers similarly chastised those who shunned their country friends in the city "on account of their rustic or unfashionable dress." Reasoned Eliza Leslie in *Miss Leslie's Behaviour Book* of 1859, "There is no danger of plain country-people being mistaken for vulgar city people. . . . Those to be avoided are such as wear tawdry finery, paint their faces, and leer out of the corners of their eyes, *looking* disreputably, even if they are not disreputable in reality."[51]

Beginning in the 1850s and continuing throughout the rest of the century, etiquette writers told and retold an anecdote that epitomized their advice on greetings to inferiors—and its tensions. The story is deeply distasteful to modern readers in its racism and self-regarding condescension, but its very remoteness from current attitudes illuminates how differently nineteenth-century advisers viewed social relations. For them it was a model account of gentlemanly deportment and *noblesse oblige*. George Washington was walking with a friend when an old black man bowed deeply to him. Washington returned the bow fully, whereupon his friend asked in astonishment, "What! Do you recognize Negroes?" Washington supposedly replied, "Would you have me outdone by a Negro in politeness?" There were a number of variations in the story. Sometimes the black man becomes a black woman, in one version a wounded black soldier, in another a hod carrier. Although Washington is the hero of the anecdote in at least eight versions, in five others it is told not about him but about Henry Clay, and in two from the 1880s, about Daniel Webster. But the moral of the tale always remains the same: In the last analysis one is polite to inferiors not for their sake but for one's own; the manners of a gentleman—

or a lady—are the final proof of his social superiority and hence not to be eclipsed by anyone.[52]

Although etiquette advisers applauded such courtesies, they sought to check familiarities in greeting at every opportunity. They generally shared Frederick Marryat's distaste of Americans' incessant handshaking. "You go on shaking hands here, there, and everywhere, and with everybody," he moaned, "for it is impossible to know who is who, in this land of equality." Declared Robert De Valcourt in *The Illustrated Manners Book* of 1855: "I may have much respect for a man, and yet not wish to touch him. What a barbarity, then, are these universal hand-shakings, and how utterly meaningless they become!" Another etiquette adviser, writing in 1870, denounced the public receptions in which a political leader or visiting dignitary was obliged to shake the hands of all comers as "democratic intrusiveness" carried to excruciating lengths. Nonetheless, the ritual continued from the days of Lafayette's American tour and Andrew Jackson's election in the 1820s throughout the nineteenth century, reaching a climax when on New Year's Day, 1907, President Theodore Roosevelt shook hands with an estimated 8,150 people. Yet secretly Roosevelt agreed with the ritual's critics. "Ugh! Ugh!" he grunted after a similar occasion. "Shaking hands with a thousand people! What a lot of bugs I have on my hands, and how dirty, filthy I am!" He immediately washed himself thoroughly, then announced, "Now I am clean. I always do this after a reception. You should remember it. It may save your life some time!"[53]

Etiquette advisers much preferred a simple bow to passing acquaintances to handshakes and undue familiarity. As one writer complained, "I have often been amazed by being stopped in the street, and held by the hand by a person of whom I had no recollection whatever." Even bows were not to be given promiscuously. Although writers admitted that in small towns it was customary through the nineteenth century to bow to everyone, the metropolis demanded much greater discretion and reserve. Various shadings to a bow might express the warmth of a relationship: "It may be coolly civil, respectful, cordial, familiar, or affectionate." A respectful bow, however, was never to be returned at a discount, in a "condescending or patronizing" manner. Advisers were fond of quoting the maxim of La Fontaine: "The bow is a note drawn at sight; if you acknowledge it, you must immediately pay the full amount."[54]

One principle in greetings upon which all authorities agreed was the special deference owed to women. Because their honor was more fragile than men's, women were granted exceptional privileges and protections. When, for example, a woman met a male acquaintance on the street, particularly one who was not a close friend, many etiquette writers insisted it was her prerogative to greet him first. This rule followed English custom but departed from Continental practice, and American etiquette commended it because it gave to the woman the active choice whether to acknowledge an acquaintance. If she greeted him, it was his duty to respond in kind; if she passed him by, he had no appeal.[55]

By scrupulously observing prescribed forms, men and women signified to one another their self-command, "good-breeding," and honorable regard. A slight smile and graceful nod were the most effusive expressions permitted to a lady. A gentleman responded by demonstrating his mastery of the now all but forgotten art of hat-tipping. Consider these four passages from late-nineteenth-century etiquette books, when instructions were often especially precise:

> A gentleman when bowing should lift his hat slightly from his head. To merely touch the rim of his hat, or make a gesture toward it, is not the correct form. But while the hat should be lifted slightly it should not be carried away from the head with an ostentatious flourish. A slight inclination of the head at the time the hat is lifted should occur, but the body need not be bent.[56]

> A gentleman should remove his hat from his head with the hand farthest from the person saluted. This turns the hat from instead of toward them. If you see that the person saluted is going to stop to shake hands, use the left in order to leave the right free.[57]

> Gentlemen should not recognize ladies by removing their hats and describing a gymnastic curve with them. A bow proper consists in simply lifting the hat so as to permit the inclination of the head. Observe how many idiots clutch the hat, describe a half circle with a radius equal to the length of the arms, and then gravely restore their head covering.[58]

26. The Lost Art of Hat-Tipping: A gentleman meeting a lady.

As haste is incompatible with grace, and as there is an old pantomimic law that "every picture must be held" for a longer or shorter time, the jerk-and-sling manner of removing the hat in salutation, is not to be commended. The *empressement* a man puts into his salutation is graduated by circumstances, the most deferential manner being to carry the hat down the full length of the arm, keeping it there until the person saluted has passed.[59]

During this procedure the man's most expressive features—his eyes, mouth, and hands—required precise governance. He exerted this ceremonious control on behalf of all women of his acquaintance (if they acknowledged him), no matter whether they were social antagonists, at one extreme, or intimate relatives, at the other. He honored each as a woman without making his expression of honor in public specific to her as an individual. He paid attentive deference without subjecting her to pointed scrutiny. He aimed to make all his gestures consistent, fluid, intelligible, and easily read without being eccentrically conspicuous. Throughout, he testified to his own self-control and ritual competence.

There were even further refinements. A gentleman also lifted his hat to any lady whom an acquaintance walking with him saluted, even if a stranger to him personally. Eyes were then especially controlled on all sides: "He does not look at [her] . . . neither does he seem to avoid meeting her gaze, which it is safe to say in the brief flash of recognition permitted by a street bow is directed wholly toward his friend."[60]

Much of greeting was conducted in this mute pantomime. To speak was to risk being overheard. Readers were enjoined not to make introductions on the street[61] or even to use names in greeting where strangers might hear.[62] Using first names or nicknames was even worse. Although we now live in a time when even upon first meeting, adults are routinely greeted with their given names by salespeople, physicians, politicians, children, and virtually all Californians, nineteenth-century etiquette advisers were suspicious of instant intimacy. Putting the rule most strictly, an 1839 guide admonished readers "never to lay aside the habit of addressing your friend as 'Mr. so-and-so,' and never to permit it to be laid aside by him. It will temper at all times the warmth of undue approach, and will enable you to check an occasional freedom by the immediate interposition of a shield." For a man to address by her first name a woman who was not his kinswoman, fiancée, or servant was regarded as a particular impertinence.[63]

Just as hat-tipping is a lost art, so, too, is the art of "cutting," or snubbing, an acquaintance on the street. Cutting reversed rituals of greeting to signify unmistakably the end of all bonds of fellowship, and etiquette authorities debated its propriety. The most pointed rejection possible was the "cut direct" in which one met another's bow with a stony stare. Some advisers ruled flatly that this was never permissible. It was, one writer sniffed, "a vulgarity of which none but a plebeian nature would be guilty." Others, however, saw it as a form of banishment justifiable in extremities of "inexcusable rudeness" or "some grave misdeed."[64] When, for example, a lady discovered she had been deceived by "a liar, a cheat or an adventurer," one writer exhorted, "let no half courtesy continue, but break at once." A gentleman was never to cut a lady, but, "when a woman makes herself conspicuous by rough cheeks, blackened eyelids, enamelled complexion, or vulgarities in dress or conduct," male readers were advised, "one may surely be excused from persisting in not meeting her eyes." Ordinarily, however, authorities recommended dropping an acquaintance by degrees, first returning a bow with cold civility and then avoiding eye contact on future meetings. The tides of metropolitan life could be expected to do the rest and absorb erstwhile friends back into the sea of strangers. Thus in rejection as in greeting, individual reserve, bodily management, and gender ideals were all scrupulously observed. Affections and enmities were equally disciplined.[65]

Clearly, the achievement of proper deportment in public was by no means simple. Emotional displays had to be practiced as thoroughly as social gestures: a proper smile cultivated as surely as a proper walk, an angry frown curbed as completely as a roving eye. Ultimately, the ability to present an accomplished social self in public through disciplined bodily management could not be separated from the management of feeling and from private life.

CHAPTER FIVE

Emotional Control

The physical control and self-discipline demanded by nineteenth-century etiquette were supported by equally exacting standards of emotional control. These "feeling rules" formed a still-deeper level of etiquette governing social relations among the middle classes.[1] Even though, inevitably, people did not always live up to these norms, they were judged—and often judged themselves—by them. Such rules extended the demands of the public realm and the special tensions of class and gender in nineteenth-century urban America deep into the texture of everyday life, both public and private, and into the individual personality. The segmentation of society was mirrored by a segmentation of self.

As Norbert Elias first observed a half century ago, a rising standard of emotional control is one of the most striking, if hitherto neglected, historical developments in modern northern European (and later, American) society. Before the seventeenth and eighteenth centuries, extremes of jubilant laughter, passionate weeping, and violent rage were indulged with a freedom that in later centuries would not be permitted even to children.[2] Emerging out of a complex intersection of causes, as we have seen in Chapter 1, there appeared in the eighteenth century a decisive shift in notions of appropriate behavior, including a new stress upon emotional control that was profoundly extended in the course of the nineteenth century with the development of an urban-industrial capitalist society. The feeling rules of the eighteenth-century gentleman, like other popularized elements of etiquette, proved to have (in Max Weber's phrase) an "elective affinity" with the demands of nineteenth-century urban bourgeois life. Nineteenth-century readers were taught, in the spirit of Franklin, to hold themselves to strict account in the management of their emotions while they attended to the feelings of others. Ward McAllister, Mrs. William Astor's minion and the arbiter of New York's fashionable elite in the late nineteenth century, encapsulated this ideal when he declared, "The highest cultivation in social manners enables a person to conceal from the world his real feelings." So concealed, fragmented, and denied, the "reality" of these feelings became problematic. The tension between feeling and feigning could exact a heavy toll. It was but a short step from McAllister's stern teaching to the emotional dissonance of Madeleine Lee, the sensitive heroine of Henry Adams's novel of American society and politics, *Democracy* (1880):

> Madeleine dissected her own feelings and was always wondering whether they were real or not; she had a habit of taking off her mental clothing, as she might take off a dress, and looking at it as though it belonged to someone else, and as though sensations were manufactured like clothes.[3]

The pressures and paradoxes of such a situation, as we shall see, reflected essential tensions in the culture of the urban marketplace.

"Command Yourself"

To conceal feelings meant to discipline them, and etiquette manuals praised such discipline as fundamental to politeness. "A sure mark of good breeding," a typical passage ran, "is the suppression of any undue emotion, such as anger, mortification, laughter, or any form of selfishness." "Good-breeding," philosophized another writer, "is like religion; it is sanctioned, but not suggested by nature. The promptings of nature are all selfish; the principles of good-breeding are founded in generosity." Through will and practice an individual could learn to contain eruptions of feeling just as one learned to stifle a yawn. "Command yourself," *The Illustrated Manners Book* enjoined its male readers in 1855. "The man who is liable to fits of passion; who cannot control his temper, but is subject to ungovernable excitements of any kind, is always in danger. The first element of a gentlemanly dignity is self-control. . . . This quality is to be acquired when it is wanting; and it may be, to an extraordinary degree, by a steady effort to bear up against small annoyances."⁴

The pursuit of emotional self-control raised the question of the relation of inner feeling to physical expression. One important response lay in the physiognomic assumptions of the nineteenth century, which held that to gain control over one's features and capacity for emotional display was to gain mastery over the feelings themselves. The implications of this doctrine were breathtaking. One popular author of both physiognomic and etiquette manuals explained:

> As we look, so we feel, so we act, and so we are. But we may *direct* and *control* even our *thoughts*, our *feelings*, and our *acts*, and thus, to some extent—by the aid of grace—become what we will. We can be temperate or intemperate; virtuous or vicious; hopeful or desponding; generous or selfish; believing or skeptical; prayerful or profane. We are free to choose what course we will pursue, and our bodies, our brains, and our features readily adapt themselves and clearly indicate the lives we lead and the characters we form.⁵

In this description, despite the quick nod to divine grace, the possibilities of self-help were virtually unlimited. Sensations indeed appeared to be, in Henry Adams's phrase, "manufactured like clothes." But unlike Adams's heroine Madeleine Lee, popular writers never doubted the reality of these feelings. To put on a smile stimulated cheerfulness, which made the smile genuine. The put-on-a-happy-face formula for positive thinking that Dale Carnegie, Norman Vincent Peale, and countless other preachers and salesmen would extol in the twentieth century was already well developed in the nineteenth. By disciplining the features, one could create the feelings one wished.

Other popular writers arrived at the same conclusion, although sometimes by more tortuous routes. An 1839 etiquette manual, *Advice to a Young Gentleman*, began by asserting that since feeling flowed from within, "the only mode of controlling the face is to control the feeling. If an emotion be dwelling in the heart, agitating and disturbing it, it is physically impossible that it should not be visible in the features." But almost immediately the writer began to turn from this rocky road of emotional necessity toward the grassy slopes of emotional manipulation. "Although," he reasoned, "what is suffered within, must be exhibited without," a man might gain "a great command of countenance" by acquiring "a great command of passion." In advising how to acquire this, the author calmly reversed his original premise, declaring that if the only way of controlling the face was to control the feeling, one might also control feeling by controlling the face:

> An admirable method of controlling feeling is to maintain by effort, the serenity and suavity of the countenance. It is impossible for a man to have rage in his breast who has a smile on his countenance. . . . The best resource to a man who knows himself liable to frequent and sudden irritation is to fasten an amiable expression upon the lip and eye, with a resolution to maintain it; for as long as it is maintained there is no danger of an explosion.

The determined smile of sociability thus faced two ways: outward to placate others and inward to grin down the rage in the breast.[6]

Emotions and Heredity

Yet even as self-help advisers placed new stress upon the power of the will to shape and master feeling, the age's leading thinkers on the subject, Charles Darwin and William James, challenged conventional wisdom in key respects. In his classic study *The Expression of the Emotions in Man and Animals* (1872), Darwin boldly declared: "Most of our emotions are so closely connected with their expression, that they hardly exist if the body remains passive."[7] Darwin concentrated, therefore, on these expressive aspects, arguing that they were the products—in some cases the vestiges—of habits and actions dating back to primordial times. Such expressions, in his view, worked according to three principles. Some, like the baring of the teeth in anger which once led to biting, originated as "serviceable associated habits" even though in civilized life they might be useless. As certain states of mind became associated with these habits, antithetical gestures developed to signify opposite emotions—Darwin's second principle. Hence dogs stiffen and bristle with hostility (a serviceable associated habit—to prepare for attack), but bow and wag with affection (an antithetical gesture). Finally, Darwin described a class of gestures that sprang directly from excitement of the nervous system, such as trembling in fear, anger, or great joy.

Drawing upon a wide array of observations of infants and children (including his own), the insane, people of various races and cultures, and animals, Darwin argued that these principles and the basic emotional vocabulary they generated were universally shared among human beings and related in many respects to animal gestures as well, thus supporting his theory of evolution and of a common human descent. Contrary to those who believed that human beings might control their gestures and feelings by force of will alone, Darwin asserted that "the chief expressive actions, exhibited by man and by the lower animals, are now innate or inherited,—that is, have not been learned by the individual." Over the course of evolutionary development, actions that were originally voluntary "became habitual, and at last hereditary, and may then be performed even in opposition to the will." The will itself Darwin regarded as the accumulation of countervailing habits through which humankind has acquired the ability to resist carrying many gestures to their original conclusions.[8]

Emotional Control and Its Limits

William James treated in much greater detail than did Darwin the role of the will and of habit in emotional life; yet his interpretation also contained disturbing implications about the limits of individual coherence and self-determination. He presented his arguments in the two-volume *Principles of Psychology* (1890) and the condensed, reworked version for classroom use, *Psychology: The Briefer Course* (1892). James admitted in a letter that *The Briefer Course* was "unsystematic and loose," but added he preferred it so, since "a terrible flavor of humbug" affected the work of any psychologist who pretended to consistency and exactitude.[9] Not only *The Briefer Course* but its parent volume reveal much of this looseness, including shifting emphases and assumptions that are telling both about the nascent discipline of psychology (which James insisted was only

27. Expressions of Hostility and Affection: Two drawings from Darwin's *Expression of the Emotions*.

28. The Face of Terror: Illustration from Darwin.

beginning to be a science) and the larger intellectual and cultural climate of late-nineteenth-century America. James struck at many points eminently Victorian notes on the importance of habit, training, and the centrality of character, while at others he anticipated much of twentieth-century psychology and social thought. Stressing the need for order both in individual psychology and civilized life as a whole, he nonetheless acknowledged elements of disorder, of fragmentation and multiplicity, of the role of the passions—indeed, the undesirability of a perfectly ordered and passionless world.

Like Darwin, James insisted that emotions did not exist apart from bodily processes, but he focused on the role of the brain in reacting to instinctual visceral changes. His theory of the emotions directly challenged conventional understandings of their workings. Our commonsense understanding of an emotion is that it begins with a mental perception of some fact exciting, say, grief, fear, rage, or love, which in turn triggers a bodily expression. Declared James:

> My theory, on the contrary is that *the bodily changes follow directly the perception of the exciting fact, and that our feeling of the same changes as they occur* IS *the emotion.* Common-sense says, we lose our fortune, are sorry and weep; we meet a bear, are frightened and run; we are insulted by a rival, are angry and strike. The hypothesis here to be defended says that this order of sequence is incorrect, that the one mental state is not immediately induced by the other, that the bodily manifestations must first be interposed between, and that the more rational statement is that we feel sorry because we cry, angry because we strike, afraid because we tremble. . . . Without the bodily states following on the perception, the latter would be purely cognitive in form, pale, colorless, destitute of emotional warmth.[10]

But if emotion depended upon bodily feeling, this did not mean that individuals could not exert any conscious control over their bodily processes. To avoid any such misunderstanding, in *The Briefer Course* James added a "corollary" to his theory that brought him surprisingly close to the advice on emotional control of etiquette writers and other popularizers. If the springs of each emotion lay in its characteristic bodily processes, then, James reasoned, that emotion could be aroused or suppressed in a "voluntary and cold-blooded" fashion by working directly on its bodily manifestations. Starting off assaulting conventional wisdom, James looped around to support it with a volley of maxims and advice:

> Refuse to express a passion, and it dies. Count ten before venting your anger, and its occasion seems ridiculous. Whistling to keep up courage is no mere figure of speech. On the other hand, sit all day in a moping posture, sigh, and reply to everything with a dismal voice, and your melancholy lingers. There is no more valuable precept in moral education than this, as all who have experience know: if we wish to conquer undesirable emotional tendencies in ourselves, we must assiduously, and in the first instance cold-bloodedly, go through the *outward movements* of those contrary dispositions which we prefer to cultivate. The reward of persistency will infallibly come, in the fading out of the sullenness or depression, and the advent of real cheerfulness and kindliness in their stead. Smooth the brow, brighten the eye, contract the dorsal rather than the ventral aspect of the frame, and speak in a major key, pass the genial compliment, and your heart must be frigid indeed if it do not gradually thaw![11]

If a life without feeling would be insupportable, James suggested, a life at the mercy of the passions would be equally so. Emotions needed to be harnessed in the service of character, and a principal means to do this was through the rein of habit.

At the head of the chapter on habit in his *Briefer Course* James wrote in his own hand, "Sow an action, and you reap a habit; sow a habit and you reap a character; sow a character and you reap a destiny." A newly acquired habit, for James, was not just a familiar routine but a physiological attainment: *"a new pathway of discharge formed in the brain, by which certain incoming currents ever after tend to escape* [italics in original]." Education thus became a form of investment—the metaphor is James's—in the formation of, first, personal habits, then intellectual and professional ones: "It is to fund and capitalize our acquisitions, and live at ease upon the interest of the fund." James here sounds like those etiquette writers and advisers on success of the time, who also taught their readers to regard their character as capital. He quoted the famous remark of the Duke of Wellington, so beloved by etiquette advisers: "Habit a second nature! Habit is ten times nature!"[12]

If habit was essential to individual development, it was also crucial in the maintenance of civilization as a whole. In a remarkable passage, James grimly celebrated habit for holding people to their unequal lots in life, for resigning them to their inequitable fates. Habit became the motor of cultural hegemony:

Habit is . . . the enormous fly-wheel of society, its most precious conservative agent. It alone is what keeps us all within the bounds of ordinance, and saves the child of fortune from the envious uprisings of the poor. It alone prevents the hardest and most repulsive walks of life from being deserted by those brought up to tread therein. . . . It dooms us all to fight out the battle of life upon the lines of our nurture or our early choice, and to make the best of a pursuit that disagrees, because there is no other for which we are fitted, and it is too late to begin again. It keeps different social strata from mixing. Already at the age of twenty-five you see the professional mannerism settling down on the young commercial traveller, on the young doctor, on the young minister, on the young counsellor-at-law. You see the little lines of cleavage running through the character, the tricks of thought, the prejudices, the ways of the "shop," in a word, from which the man can by-and-by no more escape than his coat-sleeves can suddenly fall into a new set of folds. On the whole, it is best he should not escape. It is well for the world that in most of us, by the age of thirty, the character has set like plaster, and will never soften again.[13]

James went on, however, to stress, not the solidity of the self, but its fragmentary and provisional character. He emphasized, first, the multiplicity of potential selves from which we must choose in the course of our lives, if we are lucky enough to *have* a choice. In addition, he pointed repeatedly to instances that testify to unforeseen breakdowns of self-coherence: in people afflicted by multiple personalities and other mental illnesses, for example, in hallucinations, spiritualist experiences, hypnotic trances, and other psychic states he would later explore further in *The Varieties of Religious Experience* (1902).

Even among those most thoroughly rooted in the here and now, James pointed to the experiences of fragmented, multiple identity in daily modern life and to the momentary lapses that frequently resulted. Identity, he insisted, is not singular but a composite of all our relationships: "Properly speaking, *a man has as many social selves as there are individuals who recognize him* and carry an image of him in their mind." Even if many of these impressions overlapped, still, James argued, "he has as many different social selves as there are distinct *groups* of persons about whose opinion he cares." To each group he showed a different side of himself; and while this division might be a harmonious one, as when a man is tender to his children but stern to his troops, it might also be "a discordant splitting, as where one is afraid to let one set of his acquaintances know him as he is elsewhere."[14] Here James adumbrated a major theme in twentieth-century American social psychology, developed by George Herbert Mead, Charles Horton Cooley, Harry Stack Sullivan, and, emerging from a different tradition, Erving Goffman, in which identity is viewed as a social construction assembled out of the estimations of others. In a capitalist democracy where one was encouraged to manufacture a self pleasing to others and to anticipate their responses, such a conception of identity inevitably thrived. The self becomes a series of stage effects, a repertoire of social roles, without any solid and stable core of individuality. In pointing to the "discordant splittings" of the self and the fear of discovery, James suggested the deep anxieties of daily life in a complex, segmented society. Ironically, such anxieties easily led to further role-playing as a defense—as the profusion of etiquette books eloquently testifies.

Etiquette writers ignored treacherous questions of the limits of self-control and the coherence of the individual personality that in different respects both Darwin and James raised. Confident that emotional excesses could be curbed through will and habit, they urged readers to become practiced social actors and to monitor their feelings with special care. Emotional displays of all sorts were to be checked, affection and hilarity as well as anger, and advisers gave specific instructions for each.

Anger and Conflict

Shows of anger concerned writers most. Of all emotions, anger most violently betrayed a loss of self-possession and irreparably shattered the spirit of civility. To abandon oneself to a fit of temper, however righteous, was strenuously to be avoided by both men and women. Yet in more detailed instructions on the avoidance of anger and the handling of disputes, questions of gender and status quickly came into play.

In addressing men, advisers earnestly aimed to supplant traditional notions of manly honor with the control of temper and avoidance of disputes. They defended the ideal of the gentleman summarized by John Henry Newman as "one who never inflicts pain"—"unintentionally," mocked some wits.[15] Although, particularly in the antebellum period, many Southern and some Northern males' sense of honor, once offended, demanded satisfaction in a duel or assault, only one etiquette book supported such conduct. Even combativeness and violence should be conducted without any "blustering, bullying, or any exhibition of anger," *The Illustrated Manners Book* argued. "You meet your adversary, you fight, you kill or are killed; and all without one word or act, which is not characterized by the most gentlemanly politeness." Typically, however, antebellum etiquette advisers condemned duels altogether. In an 1847 manual Timothy S. Arthur told the story of two young men who became embroiled in a challenge to duel at, of all places, a lecture on proper conduct, after one felt insulted by the other's declining of his offer of a seat. Numb to the farcical aspects of his anecdote, Arthur went on to denounce the practice of dueling as, above all else, "a narrow and blinding" act of egotism, and a "trampling under foot of the noble and manly spirit of forgiveness. Self, and only self, rules." Another mid-century etiquette book exhorted readers to obey the precepts of manly Christian courtesy rather than traditional codes of honor: "When his enemy smites him on one cheek, meekness requires [the Christian] to turn the other, also, and for personal abuse to return acts of kindness."[16]

Late-nineteenth-century advisers continued to stress avoidance of conflict but often showed themselves much more willing to accept actual violence if it did not involve displays of anger. In *Every-Day*

Etiquette Louise Bryson emphasized, "Constant exercise in social amenities helps to overcome the brute that is in us." At the same time, she added, "We must have the courage of our convictions, the courage of principle. Thus violence, even, may become good form. It is possible in a perfectly well-bred way, to tell a man that he is a liar, or to turn another out of the house when his conduct merits it." A manual titled (with unintentional irony) *The Manners That Win* declared simply: "No gentleman brooks an insult, and the only effective answer to some insults is a blow." But another book, *The Mentor*, suggested a more politic course: "If a man boasts that he could worst you in a set-to, answer that you think it very likely as you have no experience in fisticuffing; that you have never struck any one and should hardly know how to go to work to do it." If a man threatened to do you bodily harm, the adviser continued, run. "There is more glory in avoiding a *mêlée* by running away than there is in remaining and coming off the victor." But if all else failed and a fight ensued, the writer concluded, "teach him, to the best of your ability, that you are not really a poltroon, though you are quite willing that bullyism should think you one."[17]

Gentlemen as well as ladies were to avoid arguments and direct contradiction that might fan the flames of anger. In the spirit of Franklin, they were advised to cultivate the habit of modest diffidence on social occasions, particularly in mixed company:

> If a gentleman advances an opinion which is different from ideas you are known to entertain, either appear not to have heard it, or differ with him as gently as possible. You will not say, "Sir, you are mistaken!" "Sir, you are wrong!" or that you "happen to know better;" but you will rather use some such phrase as, "Pardon me—if I am not mistaken," etc. This will give him a chance to say some such civil thing as that he regrets to disagree with you; and if he has not the good manners to do it, you have, at any rate, established your own manners as those of a gentleman in the eyes of the company.[18]

Dispensing advice that dated back at least to the seventeenth century, etiquette writers stressed that religious controversy was to be shunned and the very topic of religious doctrine avoided. Politics came under a similar prohibition.[19] In social gatherings, civility supplanted substance. Substantive discussion was channeled into particular occasions and protected settings, often apart from women.[20]

Significantly, the specialized parliamentary etiquette rapidly adopted by American middle-class voluntary organizations, Henry Martyn Robert's famous *Robert's Rules of Order* (first published in 1876), sought to devise forms that permit debate while avoiding personal attacks. Robert was no doubt mindful of the inflammatory language and occasional violence that had erupted even in Congress in the antebellum period, culminating in the brutal caning of Senator Charles Sumner of Massachusetts by Congressman Preston Brooks of South Carolina. In his *Rules* Robert enjoined speakers to confine their remarks "to the question before the assembly, and avoid personalities." Whenever possible, they were not to mention opponents by name, speaking instead of "the member who spoke last" and referring to officers by their official titles. "It is not allowable," Robert cautioned, "to arraign the motives of a member, but the nature or consequences of a measure may be condemned in strong terms." To keep differing viewpoints from igniting angry confrontations remained a prime consideration.[21]

Egalitarian assumptions provided an important check to displays of anger in nineteenth-century America, as even avowed critics of democracy such as Frederick Marryat acknowledged. Impressed despite himself by Americans' "good temper" and "quiet and obliging" manner, Marryat grudgingly conceded that it appeared "one of the few virtues springing from democracy." In hierarchical societies, he reasoned, people learned to control themselves before their superiors or equals, but indulged their tempers with inferiors. In a democracy, however, "under institutions where all are equal, where no one admits the superiority of another, even if he really be so, where the man with the spade in his hand will beard the millionaire, and where you are compelled to submit to the caprice and insolence of a domestic or lose his services, it is evident that every man must from boyhood have learnt to control his temper." Without such training himself, Marryat's own patience clearly wore thin.[22]

Yet nineteenth-century Americans were hardly immune to considerations of class or to snobbery, and particularly in the late nineteenth century, when the spirit of egalitarianism among the socially privileged waned considerably, etiquette advisers revealed special sensitivity to the role of status in the display of anger and handling of disputes. While urging emotional control under all circumstances, writers expressed their awareness of the varying stakes depending upon rank. "To get angry with an inferior is degrading; with an equal, dangerous; with a superior, ridiculous," warned *The Mentor*. Addressing men, another adviser provided a slightly more flexible rule:

> To your equals a tranquil nature and manner should always be shown, no matter how trying the position. To inferiors temper should not be shown while in sight or hearing of equals, and even when alone with servants or agents only in case of breach of duty, and then should merely be shown sufficiently far to make a reprimand more severe.

As for an insult from an inferior, the same writer advised:

> Pay no attention to such, unless it is followed by violence, or when it places you in an awkward position in presence of equals, and even then, if from one decidedly inferior, or a woman, do not return it, but summon the agents of the law to rid you of the nuisance.

In a similar vein, another writer declared, "Never quarrel or discuss anything which does or does not please you, with subordinates. See the head man and make known your joy or your grievance." Implicit in all this advice was the recognition that, while the expression of anger was the prerogative of social superiors, in a heated dispute that superiority might easily be lost and participants placed on a more equal footing. Self-possession did not exert authority all by itself; rather, it allowed the authority based upon class and rank ultimately to win recognition.[23]

Far fewer instructions on the control of anger and conduct of disputes were addressed specifically to women than to men. The gap is significant: while both male and female advisers urged men to curb their tempers, they apparently assumed women had less of a temper to curb and were, both by nature and social circumstances, less disputatious. Rather, women were expected to take the lead in adapting to the constraints of nineteenth-century urban-industrial society by shedding egotism, even to some degree ego itself. Wrote Eliza Ware Farrar in *The Young Lady's Friend* in 1837: "The best way to overcome the selfishness and rudeness you sometimes meet with in public occasions is by great politeness and disinterestedness. . . . Contending for your rights stirs up the selfish feelings of others; but a readiness to yield them awakes generous sentiments." Similarly, within the home wives were urged to learn the gentle art of giving way in disputes: "There is something inexpressibly endearing in small concessions, in gracefully yielding to the will of another, and giving up a favorite opinion; and equally painful is the reverse." Such emotional pliancy was not typically demanded of men.[24]

When a man succumbed to anger, he lost dignity; when a woman succumbed, however, she betrayed her very femininity. *The Young Lady's Own Book* (1833) called "an enraged woman . . . one of the most disgusting sights in nature." *Miss Leslie's Behaviour Book* (1859) depicted such a gorgon: "When a woman abandons herself to terrible fits of anger with little or no cause, and makes herself a frightful spectacle, by turning white with rage, rolling up her eyes, drawing in her lips, gritting her teeth, clenching her hands, and stamping her feet, depend on it, she is not of a nervous, but of a furious temperament." Appealing to feminine concern for appearance as well as following popular physiognomic assumptions, Eliza Leslie recommended treating this paroxysm through its display: "A looking-glass held before her, to let her see what a shocking object she had made herself, would, we think, have an excellent effect."[25]

As for what one adviser called "little tempers," the "cool deliberate spite and secret rancor" to which women were supposedly more susceptible, these, too, could be overcome by strengthening the will. A simple means was to count to twenty-five before speaking. But if this failed, other emotional exercises lay at hand. The author of an 1881 guide, *Gems of Deportment*, reported approvingly: "A lady who was much given to hasty speaking broke herself of the habit by saying inwardly, 'What if Nellie should die?' Nellie was her only child, and lived to complete the good work." Thus guilt was the guardian of virtue.[26]

Affection and Laughter

Although the subject of anger aroused greatest concern, emotional displays of all sorts demanded constant discipline. Advisers cautioned against any demonstrations of affection in public as both an exposure of intimacy and excessive mutual engrossment.[27] They propounded myriad rules to keep courting couples from premature intimacy, declaring, for example, that on a country walk a woman's escort should always remain standing while she rested. They debated whether "the prudent and modest maiden should not even allow her lover, (even after their engagement), to kiss her." Some gave the couple guarded permission; others advised waiting till after marriage: "Engagements are often broken off and no privileges should be granted which, in case of such an occurrence, could cause the lady any regrets." Their concern was not simply with controlling sexuality but with preserving public dignity. Private relationships and feelings were to be kept private, so that even husband and wife ideally held themselves aloof from one another in public. "In society," one writer suggested, "we ought, above every thing, to avoid being personal; for a husband or a wife is another self; and we must forget that self." A second adviser declared: "There can be no better rule for the manners of a husband and wife, than that they should treat each other, in all outward forms, and in all true respect and courtesy, as if they were not married." Etiquette authorities generally regarded kissing in greeting, even between relatives or women, as "a reprehensible custom," and toward the end of the century hopefully predicted it would soon fade away. "Happily," one adviser wrote, the distasteful European customs of "kissing and embracing among men are never seen in this country." A 1905 book of etiquette for young people summarized the bulk of generations of advice when it firmly declared: "It is not well-bred to kiss any one on the street, even a baby." Some mid-century advisers justified their distaste by claiming that kissing in greeting led to hypocrisy, "compel[ling] us to give an expression of tenderness to indifferent or even repulsive persons." Later in the century, as the cult of sincerity waned, writers seized upon germ theory to make hygienic appeals against promiscuous kissing: "Disease may be introduced in this way that many years would fail to eradicate."[28]

Laughter demanded, if anything, even greater regulation. In the Anglo-American tradition, an effort to restrain laughter in favor of gravity clearly emerged as early as the Tudor-Stuart period as part of the growing emphasis on bodily controls of all sorts. Figures in authority revived classical teachings that if great men laughed at all, they should do so sparingly and decorously. Loud, unrestrained laughter was as vulgar as uncontrolled coughing or sneezing. By the eighteenth century, English courtesy books had thoroughly absorbed these injunctions, and members of the ruling elite taught them to their posterity, most famously in Lord Chesterfield's letter to his son in 1748:

> Frequent and loud laughter, is the characteristic of folly and ill manners: it is the manner in which the mob express their silly joy, at silly things; and they call it being merry. In my mind, there is nothing so illiberal, and so ill bred, as audible laughter. True wit, or sense, never yet made any body laugh; they are above it: they please the mind, and give a cheerfulness to the countenance.[29]

Chesterfield's stricture set the tone for much of nineteenth-century American advice; indeed, it was sometimes cribbed directly. Although occasionally an etiquette adviser praised laughter's effects, more typically writers uneasily considered its excesses. Laughing or smiling too much, too loudly, or inappropriately all showed a lack of self-control. "Be very careful to guard against over much laughing," warned one adviser. "Nothing gives a sillier appearance than spasms of laughter upon the slightest provocation. It soon grows into a very disagreeable habit."[30]

Both women's need to remain inconspicuous and the narrower emotional range permitted them meant that they especially needed to discipline their mirth, particularly where they might be overheard by strangers. Warned one adviser: "Few things are more distasteful than a party of young women making themselves conspicuous in public places by loud talk and laughter. If they are careless enough to attract attention in this way they must not be surprised if they bring upon themselves rude notions from some of the other sex." For a woman to laugh immoderately was to risk losing the protections due to a lady.[31]

Proper forms of laughter were self-consciously taught. In *How to Teach Manners in the School-Room* (1888) Julia M. Dewey rebuked giggling, smirking, and guffawing even among the young: "Incessant smiling or laughing is silly and disagreeable. Smiling or laughing is allowable when there is something to laugh at. Giggling is unpardonable. Hearty laughter is allowable in some places, but boisterous laughter never." In the same spirit, an 1891 guide instructed men on the proper way to laugh at a joke:

Laughter should never be forced; if you are not amused, merely smile. When laughing at a small matter do so in a light sincere way; when amused by some good joke or occurrence, laugh heartily but not too loudly; merely convey the fact that the joke or event is appreciated. This rule should apply at all times when ladies are present.[32]

Telling a joke was much more risky than responding to one, and some advisers declared flatly, "Do not indulge in a joke in society," since it might easily misfire.[33] Joking survived, of course; but even as gifted a storyteller as Mark Twain, for whom the subject of genteel propriety provided such a broad target, occasionally had a joke blow up in his face when he aimed at cherished figures and institutions. For example, at an 1877 dinner for the contributors to the *Atlantic Monthly* celebrating the twentieth anniversary of that magazine as well as the seventieth birthday of poet John Greenleaf Whittier, Mark Twain offered a comic spoof. Three rogues pretending to be Ralph Waldo Emerson, Henry Wadsworth Longfellow, and Oliver Wendell Holmes—literary eminences all present at the dinner—take over a Sierra miner's cabin, drink up his whiskey, cheat at cards, and steal his boots. All the while they quote to the befuddled miner outrageous pastiches of these and other New England worthies' verse. Exasperated, the miner announces he is going to move: "I ain't suited to the littery atmosphere." In cloyingly genteel diction, Mark Twain demurs, " 'Why my dear sir, *these* were not the gracious singers to whom we & the world pay loving reverence & homage: these were impostors.' The miner investigated me with a calm eye for a while, then said he, 'Ah—impostors, were they? are *you*?' " The story fell flat, was castigated as in "exceedingly bad taste" by much of the press, and threw Mark Twain into an agony of apology mixed with self-justification from which he never totally recovered. For the joke to have worked, his audience and readers had to be willing to enjoy the absurdity of their genteel literary culture brought low, the high-mindedness of their "gracious singers" (as the poets are piously called in the story) reduced to conniving gamblers. They would have had to acknowledge—if only for an instant—the arbitrariness of their own literary and social situation by recognizing in a laugh how it might appear if comically inverted. In Freud's terms, they would have had momentarily to relax conscious control in favor of the subconscious. The efforts of etiquette advisers all pushed the other way, toward a firmer tightening of controls, a greater self-awareness, and a refusal to confound the refined and the vulgar.[34]

Hence their discomfort with jokes and laughter. At best an imperfectly controlled act, laughter broke through the system of bodily restraints that bourgeois culture prized and propagated. As a social response, laughter frequently pointed to "areas of structural ambiguity in society itself." Thus, both in ritual and in social terms, laughter was potentially subversive. It might topple the carefully constructed public persona that the individual had erected. It broke, if only momentarily, formality and social distance. It threatened to overturn the social hierarchy and to "rechannel all subsequent exchanges into a different set of pathways." The ritual order of etiquette, by sternly guarding against slips in bodily and emotional control, assured the individual's deferential participation in the dominant social order. Instead of allowing any outward relaxation, bourgeois etiquette drove the tensions back within the individual self, providing ritual support for the psychological defense mechanisms of repression, displacement, and denial necessary to cope with the anxieties of the urban capitalist order.[35]

"You Are Never Alone"

These tensions emerge clearly in the assiduous private efforts middle-class families were encouraged to make to acquire the emotional discipline that public life demanded. The home, of course, offered a much more protected setting for personal expression, relaxation, and social interaction; and it was enshrined by a host of nineteenth-century popular writers as a sanctuary of purity, harmony, and affection from the demands of the outside world. But the home was also a place of preparation and social performance, where the principal inhabitants rehearsed the roles they would perform in public life. Modifying the famous assertion often attributed to Thomas Jefferson, "Eternal vigilance is the price of liberty," nineteenth-century advisers taught a distinctly less radical message. "Constant practice, eternal vigilance, is the price of good manners," an 1890 guide declared. ". . . The surest way of doing a thing right is to have the habit of doing it right on all occasions, in private as well as in public. . . . Good manners must be worn all the time, when in the presence of others and when alone, like shoes and stockings." As this language suggests, individuals were encouraged to dress and groom themselves emotionally as well as physically while in private, so as to be fully prepared for public social performances.[36]

Material household furnishings offer important evidence in these matters. The increased prominence of mirrors in particular is indicative of the habitual self-regard and preparation for public roles that etiquette advisers demanded. Before the nineteenth century, studies of household inventories reveal, most families who owned a looking glass at all had only one, and it usually hung in the parlor. By the mid-nineteenth century, however, mirrors were a standard feature of middle-class homes, spreading in many cases to virtually every room. On walls, over mantels, on hallstands, sideboards, and cabinets, mirrors of varying size and expense ornamented the best rooms, adding depth and light and reflecting prized objects as well as occupants. Other mirrors appeared on bedroom and dressing room walls, wardrobes, dressing tables, and chests of drawers. Such mirrors, one may speculate, played an important role in heightening a theatrical sense of the self. They were not only an indispensable aid to new standards of grooming. They taught users to appraise their images and the emotions they expressed frequently and searchingly, anticipating the gaze of others. In *Miss Leslie's Behaviour Book* of 1859, Eliza Leslie advised that when a caller arrived for tea, the hostess should immediately have her shown upstairs to a vacant room, there to be left alone to prepare for her appearance in the parlor: "The toilet-table should be always furnished with a clean hair-brush and a nice comb. We recommend those hair-brushes that have a mirror on the back, so as to afford the lady a glimpse of the back of her head and neck. Better still, as an appendage to a dressing-table, is a regular hand-mirror, of sufficient size to allow a really *satisfactory* view. These hand-mirrors are very convenient, to be used in conjunction with the large dressing-glass. Their cost is but trifling." By so cultivating in private a sense of the self as a social actor, readers might acquire a habitual ease and feeling of entitlement necessary for social success. A passage from the 1896 manual *Social Etiquette* by Maude Cooke (who was, significantly, also an actress) captures this process of self-appraisal and the ends it served:

your face will freeze that way!

Indulge in no facial contortions, as they rapidly become habits difficult to break and usually leave their traces on the face in lines impossible to efface. Lifting the eyebrows, rolling the eyes, opening them very widely, twisting the mouth and opening it so as to show the tongue in talking, are all disagreeable habits, that, once acquired, can only be broken by ceaseless vigilance. Practice talking without moving the facial muscles but slightly. *Do this before your mirror daily, if necessary, and before the same faithful mentor* learn to open the eyes less widely, parting the lids only just so far as to show the colored iris without a glimpse of the white portion, or cornea, of the eye above or below it. The time thus spent will result in a change most gratifying to yourself and friends [italics added].[37]

Such training, advisers recognized, was most easily acquired when young, and they particularly emphasized the importance of habitual self-control and proper emotional display in etiquette manuals for children. Instruction could not begin too early. Etiquette advisers delighted in telling the story in which a respected authority (in different versions a clergyman, a physician, a lawyer, a respected family friend) was asked by a mother when she should begin teaching her child manners. "How old is the child?" inquired the friend. "Three years," the mother replied. "Then," declared the friend gravely, "you have already lost three years."[38] Particularly toward the latter part of the nineteenth century, writers bore down equally hard on children's emotional expressions as on their actions: "Self-repression [used here in a pre-Freudian sense] is second only to self-control in children's training," declared one author. "Impatience, yawning, indifference, when another is trying to amuse or entertain, are habits that should not be tolerated for a moment." In the same vein, a second adviser wrote: "Politeness requires that young folks shall learn to express the better emotions in their faces, and, above all, that they shall not frown or scorn, grin or simper, and thus give the impression to strangers that they are habitually cross or silly." Girls especially were urged to "cultivate kindly feelings." Enthused one writer: "A girl who is a little reserved, and never rude, who says pleasant and does kindly things, who is not always thinking first of herself—what is more charming!"[39] *a boy who does so?*

Nineteenth-century advisers' stress upon gently nurturing inner emotional control from infancy represented an important departure from earlier generations' insistence upon breaking truculent spirits and gaining external obedience at once. A passage from one of the first children's books reprinted in the American colonies, *A Little Pretty Pocket-Book* by the eighteenth-century English writer John Newberry, offers a telling contrast. Faced with an angry son, Newberry recommended what he considered "Reasoning and mild Discipline" instead of fierce denunciation or whipping. But by the standards of the nineteenth century, Newberry's approach was harsh indeed:

> I should take him aside, and point out to him the Evils that attend passionate Men; tell him, that my Love for him would make me overlook many Faults, but that this was of so heinous a Nature, that I could not bear the Sight of him while he continued so wicked; that he should not see his Mother, nor any of his Play-mates, till he had sufficiently repented of that Crime: Upon which, I would immediately order him (in a very calm Manner) to be shut up from any Company for five or six Hours, and then, upon his Confession of the Fault, asking Pardon on his Knees, and promising Amendment for the future, I would forgive him. This Method, regularly pursued, would soon break his Passion of Resentment, and subdue it to Reason.[40]

Yet if late-nineteenth-century authorities advised gentler means of moral suasion, they aimed for much more than the filial submission Newberry gained: a total victory over the private passions. Two model dialogues between instructors and pupils from the 1890s make this ambition clear. In the first, a teacher has just admonished a student to learn to sit properly:

> *B.* Well, I'm glad I'm not obliged to be in company all of the time!
> *Teacher.* You are never alone.

A second manual pressed the point further in a colloquy between a girl named Rosalie and her mentor Miss Fitts. Confessing the difficulty of exerting constant control, Rosalie speaks of "the lurking savage in us" that "likes to get the upper hand sometimes." Miss

Fitts's response is firm. "In our new ideal American civilization," she replies, "we are not going to veneer the savage, or gild him, or hide him; we are going to exterminate him." There would be no sanctioned spaces or occasions for regression. Ideally, children would absorb a thoroughly "civilized" conscience at a tender age so that no emotion or impulse escaped its discipline.[41]

Refinement and Specialization in the Home

Yet it would be entirely mistaken to suggest that nineteenth-century bourgeois culture sought to stifle all personal expression. What is striking is the extent to which expression was displaced from the exhibition of individual attributes and actions in the public realm to domestic objects and rituals and also—as we shall see in a later chapter—to public performers. As the expressive possibilities of everyday public life grew more constricted and its meanings more unstable, the importance of emotional expression in the domestic realm expanded proportionately. Similarly, as individuals sought to guard the unintentional meanings they revealed in their personal appearance and deportment, they projected those meanings upon the objects and rituals of their domestic routine. The equation of personal character with the sum total of personal choices, preferences, and objects of daily association was a maxim repeatedly coined and widely circulated in the nineteenth century. John Ruskin, who was enormously influential in the United States as well as in Britain, put the claim most sweepingly: "Taste is not only a part and an index of morality;—it is the ONLY morality. . . . Tell me what you like, and I'll tell you what you are." Private tastes, rather than public actions, became the crucial indicator of sincerity and authenticity. Given such convictions, it was easy to endow the home with special significance as the center of private life and the domain most expressive of personal preference and practice. "Much of the character of every man may be read in his house," declared the influential American landscape architect Andrew Jackson Downing, and countless others uttered the same conviction, though usually less memorably.[42]

As a result, the house itself and its objects assumed heightened importance as ritual adjuncts in the effort to stabilize social meanings and social relationships.[43] In the course of the nineteenth century the middle-class home was reshaped in accordance with rising standards of middle-class gentility. The cause of refinement and the need to play more exacting social roles demanded highly differentiated spaces, each with its specific furnishings and function. Beds, for example, which vanished from the parlors of wealthy households in the second half of the eighteenth century, lingered in less stylish houses well into the nineteenth. But by the latter part of the nineteenth century, middle-class houses and apartments were characteristically divided into major zones of society, privacy, and service, and each zone further subdivided into rooms with specialized functions. These zones assumed a hierarchical relationship. The places of most formal social ceremony, the front hall, parlor, and dining room, properly stood in constant readiness to receive guests; and more prosperous middle-class families who could afford a separate living room might avoid the use of the parlor entirely when not entertaining. Other more informal and intimate spaces remained sheltered from most visitors; these included bedrooms, dressing rooms, bathrooms (not common to middle-class homes until the 1870s), and children's playroom, as well as the necessary but lowly service areas: kitchen, pantry, laundry room, back stairway, and servants' quarters.

Each space carried its own specific requirements of self-discipline and emotional management in accordance with the activities and roles to be performed, the intimate no less than the social. The new circumspection in the use of beds offers one example. The nineteenth-century urban middle classes were certainly not the unrelenting enemies of conjugal sexual pleasure of popular stereotype. Indeed, it is arguable that they cultivated such pleasure beyond the experience of previous generations. But they pursued sexuality within a context of moderation, self-control, and, above all, privacy.[44] Parents increasingly slept apart from children (and children were themselves segregated by sex) in bedrooms divided by hallways, so that privacy could be protected.

The defense of personal privacy (and with it, of role segregation) within the home extended far beyond bodily exposure and sexual intimacy. "The right of privacy is sacred, and should always be respected," family members and friends alike were sternly admonished. "It is exceedingly improper to enter a private room anywhere without knocking. No relation, however intimate, will justify an abrupt intrusion upon a private apartment. So the trunk, boxes, packets, papers, and letters of every individual, locked or unlocked, sealed or unsealed, are sacred." Another adviser, Eliza Leslie, worried particularly about the risks of excessive intimacy between women friends. She regarded the *entrée*—the privilege of entering a friend's room unbidden—with particular uneasiness as a practice often abused and rarely to be extended. The woman who entered a house and went directly to her friend's chamber and bolted into her room risked catching her out of character and unprepared to play her proper social role: "You may find her washing, or dressing, or in bed, or even engaged in repairing clothes,—or the room may be in great disorder, or the chambermaid in the act of cleaning it." More darkly, she warned, "friendships are not always lasting—particularly those that become inordinately violent, and where both parties, by their excessive intimacy, put themselves too much into each other's power. Very mortifying disclosures are sometimes made after a quarrel, between two Hermias and Helenas, when recriminations begin to come, and mutual enmity takes the place of mutual kindness."[45]

Relations with servants posed dilemmas that were less easily resolved. Much of middle-class gentility depended upon servants, both to do the daily labors of household cleaning, washing, ironing, cooking, and tending children, and also to assist in the performance of various social rituals such as receiving guests and serving meals. They stood in an ambiguous position as essential actors of the household who, nonetheless, were not members of the family, figures to be relied upon but "nonpersons" to be socially ignored. Servants were overwhelmingly women and disproportionately foreign-born or black. Throughout the nineteenth century and up to the time of the First World War, most lived with their employers. Nonetheless, books of etiquette and household and architectural advice, as well as interior photographs of the nineteenth century, ignored their living quarters almost entirely. Although some families might provide a maid's room next to the kitchen, many relegated servants to often squalid conditions in attics and basements. In their waking hours, however, servants' duties carried them from the utilitarian zone of kitchen and laundry to their employers' most intimate spaces.[46]

This proximate dependency created great uneasiness. "Servants are a necessary evil," an 1836 manual, *The Laws of Etiquette*, bluntly declared. ". . . They are domestic spies, who continually embarrass the intercourse of the members of a family, or possess themselves of private information that renders their presence hateful, and their absence dangerous. It is a rare thing to see persons who are not controlled by their servants." The anxieties of embarrassment and betrayal, so vibrant on city streets, extended into the very haven of domestic life. The "servant problem" was compounded, some advisers suggested, because many domestics were drawn from "the ill-trained, incapable, and vicious peasantry of Europe" and further corrupted by the popular American democratic ethic to believe that they were " 'as good as anybody.' " As a result, they were incompetent and disrespectful workers, who soon moved on to other jobs, taking their knowledge of the family with them.[47]

As with all other relationships, the ways in which master and mistress dealt with their servants tested their own emotional control and character. "There is no surer sign of ill breeding and ill feeling than the rude treatment of dependents," warned Robert Tomes in his influential *Bazar Book of Decorum* (1870), and others developed the theme. Speaking to males in *The Complete Bachelor* (1896), an adviser cautioned: "In the treatment of servants a man must exercise an iron will. He can be kind and considerate, but he must never descend to disputes with one, and certainly not swear at him. To be on familiar terms with one's servants shows the cloven foot of vulgarity."[48]

Such advice placed special tensions upon the middle-class mistress, who was enjoined to be a model of angelic sweetness and graceful concession with family members, yet a commanding military officer with servants. She gained their respect by her dignity, firmness, and self-control. Anything less invited familiarity, insolence, and household anarchy. Here the imperatives of emotional management were tightened another notch: "The mistress must not lose her temper. She must be calm, imperturbable, and dignified always. If she gives an order, she must insist, at whatever personal cost, that it shall be obeyed. Pertinacity and inflexibility on this point are well bestowed."[49]

All such discussions, of course, reflected the perspective and self-interest of the employer. Servants had their own complaints about lack of privacy and undue familiarity, as well as the stigma of social inferiority their work carried. "Whatever you do, don't go into service," one woman advised. "You'll always be prisoners and always looked down on." Another, who worked as a chambermaid for a cotton-mill owner, reported: "My trouble was I hadn't any place that I could be alone a minute. . . . In that splendid big house the servants' room was over the kitchen,—hot and close in summer, and cold in winter, and four beds in it. We five had to live there together, with only two bureaus and a bit of a closet, and one washstand for all. There was no chance to keep clean or your things in nice order, or anything by yourself, and I gave up." A third servant complained that though she was generally well treated, her employers freely entered her personal quarters adjoining their own rooms: "I do not know what minute one or the other member of the family may pop in, & the door between the rooms does not lock." Here was an abuse of the *entrée* no etiquette adviser considered.[50]

Genteel Performance in Hall and Parlor

Of the three major areas of the home, the demands of polished performance and emotional self-control were most exacting in the social zone. Typically, a visitor entered this area through a series of ceremonial frames: past a fence or hedge and along a walkway that allowed one to feel the full impact of the house's architectural façade, up the front steps, across a porch and through a framed doorway, and into a front entrance hall (preceded, in more elaborate houses, by a vestibule). Ideally, the visitor would be met by a servant. If the desired member of the house was "not at home" (either absent or simply not wishing to receive the caller), the genteel visitor left an engraved calling card. Leaving cards embroiled visitors in one of the most intricate social codes of late-nineteenth-century etiquette. Consider only one aspect, folding the corners. Each corner of the card assumed a distinct meaning when turned down: the upper right-hand corner signified a personal visit; the upper left, congratulations; the lower right, a formal leave-taking when departing the community for some time; the lower left, condolence. Bending the entire left-side end of the card denoted a call upon the family at large. Now virtually forgotten, this elaborate system might be suspected to have been rarely practiced; yet extensive collections of card receivers and calling cards from the period testify to its strict observance not only in major cities but in small towns throughout the country from the mid-nineteenth century well into the twentieth.[51]

If the object of the visitor's call was indeed present and willing to receive the caller, other discriminations came into play. The hall functioned both as a corridor to the more specialized "public" rooms of the house, such as the parlor, library, and dining room, and also as a reception area in which visitors could be appraised and treated accordingly. Social inferiors such as "messenger-boys, book-agents, the census-man, and the bereaved lady who offers us soap . . . with the story of her woes thrown in," were kept waiting in the hall. There they sat on serviceable, hard chairs (since it was thought comfort would be wasted on them) and were further humbled by the imposing presence of a massive hallstand that clutched umbrellas in its crook-shaped paws, reared up to a height between six and a half and eight feet, and glowered like a Cyclops with its massive mirrored eye.[52] Social equals and superiors might leave their hats, coats, and umbrellas and be conducted to the parlor to await a family member.

The parlor or drawing room was the setting for a variety of social functions: formal calls and visits from friends, teas, small concerts, theatricals, receptions, and other entertainments, as well as many key family ceremonies, including holiday celebrations, baptisms, engagement parties, weddings, and funeral receptions. Some etiquette advisers urged readers to reserve a special room for guests if they could afford one,[53] but for most middle-class families the parlor doubled as the family sitting room. Nonetheless, they furnished it as a carefully elaborated social statement with their most treasured objects and best furniture. After the mid-nineteenth century such statements drew upon a well-established vocabulary of furnishings that offered a number of rhetorical possibilities.

This rhetoric depended heavily upon three principles of decoration as ways of heightening refinement. The first was specialization. Even within the parlor, a room with a highly specialized function, families employed increasingly specialized seating with "gentlemen's parlor arm chairs," smaller "ladies' parlor chairs" (often without arms), upholstered children's chairs, side chairs, "window chairs," "reception chairs," "parlor rockers," "nursing rockers," "tête-à-têtes" (small sofas), settees, sofas, lounges, and ottomans. A second strategy was softening, cushioning, and harmonizing the parlor through the profuse use of fabrics—a material

29. Tasteful Consumption: "A Parlor View in a New York Dwelling House" (1854). The accompanying article described this room as "a fitting abode of a man of refinement" and a place "where a lady of elegant manners and educated taste might appropriately receive her guests."

analogy to the role of etiquette in smoothing away potential rudeness and angularity. Not only did upholstery become steadily more prominent in parlor seating; the use of fabrics spread throughout the room until by the late nineteenth century some parlors became virtual cocoons of gentility. Families covered the floor with carpets, shrouded the windows with thick draperies, hung curtains called portières across the entrance, swathed center tables, mantel tops, and pianos with hangings and skirts; they erected mountains of decorated sofa pillows and scattered throws and tidies. A third major principle was the artful display of objects of cultural attainment and personal association. These objects included a piano or parlor organ, well-stocked bookcases, homemade artworks such as needlepoint and painted china, and personal collections of photographs, engravings, and souvenirs of travel, exhibited on walls, parlor tables, étagères, hanging shelves, mantelpieces, and art corners. The parlor became a kind of "memory palace" of culture, a miniature museum thick with meaning, an artful declaration of its owners' sensibility. In the words of an influential adviser on household decoration, Clarence Cook, this "room ought to represent the culture of the family,—what is their taste, what feeling they have for art; it should represent themselves, and not other people; and the troublesome fact is, that it will and must represent them, whether its owners would let it or not."[54]

This last statement, with its "troublesome fact" that the parlor willy-nilly constituted a family's major act of self-representation, caught middle-class families between conflicting ideals and demands. How indeed were they to represent themselves? As cultivated and fashionable members of society? Or as sincere and comfortable people who refused to put on a special public face? A number of etiquette advisers stressed the theatricality and artifice the parlor demanded. It was, as one writer put it, "a stage upon which parts are performed before a public, that applauds or hisses, according to the merits of the actor. It is necessary to watch one's self as well as others, and to maintain a deportment and language adapted to that locality."[55] Readers were coached in how to enter the room gracefully, how to stand and sit properly, how and what to talk about, how and when to leave, and how to achieve proper emotional control throughout the performance. Nevertheless, many popular advisers often professed disdain for the affectations of the fashion-conscious and extolled virtuous simplicity as most appropriate in republican America. How to reconcile the requirements of middle-class gentility with sincerity in the home was a vexing issue.[56] Even one of the most ardent apostles of the guileless Christian home, Harriet Beecher Stowe, recognized how subtly the demands of genteel social performance could insinuate themselves.

Stowe dramatized this process in "The Ravages of a Carpet" (1864), a sketch in which Christopher Crowfield, a frank, genial man with simple, old-fashioned tastes, contends with the modish desires of his wife and daughters. The story begins as Crowfield's wife urges that they buy a gorgeously patterned and wondrously inexpensive Brussels carpet to replace the old, worn one in their parlor. This parlor had been the center of family activities as well as of easygoing sociability with friends. There by an open hearth Mr. Crowfield customarily spread out his books and papers and worked at a writing table while his wife sat on an old-fashioned

30. "Ungraceful Positions": An inventory of errors from *Hill's Manual of Social and Business Forms*. No. 1 stands with arms akimbo; no. 2 sits with elbows on knees; no. 3 wears his hat and sits astride the chair; no. 4 stands with legs crossed, soils the wallpaper with his hand, and heedlessly eats an apple; no. 5 puts his foot on the chair cushion; no. 6 teeters in his chair, soils the wall with his head, and smokes in the presence of ladies. Note the spittoon at lower right. Courtesy of the Margaret Woodbury Strong Museum, Rochester, New York.

31. "Gentility in the Parlor" shows all these errors mended as each figure assumes "an easy, genteel attitude" while strictly observing the "laws of etiquette." But not simply posture has changed. All the furnishings have been transformed in accordance with the rhetoric of refinement and the inhabitants have adopted tasteful dress, grooming, and demeanor. Courtesy of the Margaret Woodbury Strong Museum, Rochester, New York.

lounge with her clothes-making and mending. There, too, in preference to the nursery, the Crowfield children had played with their
toys while growing up, and a small menagerie of dogs and canaries
basked by their owners. Friends dropped by without ceremony,
attracted to the warmth of the family circle.

As soon as the new carpet is laid, however, it begins to transform
the parlor and the life Mr. Crowfield prizes. To protect the carpet
from fading or soiling, the family must have new blinds, the large
open hearth must be converted to a closed iron grate, and pets
and plants be banished. The old, worn parlor furniture suddenly
looks shabby, and Mr. Crowfield's writing materials and his wife's
old-fashioned lounge and work basket appear out of place. The
daughters, on the threshold of adulthood and keenly attuned to the
fashions of their neighbors, argue that the parlor is no longer appropriate for daily family use. " 'We don't have any parlor,' " the
youngest complains. " 'Our parlor has always been a sort of log-
cabin,—library, study, nursery, greenhouse, all combined. We
never have had things like other people.' " Within a year of the
fateful purchase of the new carpet, the Crowfields have "a parlor
with two lounges in decorous recesses, a fashionable sofa, and six
chairs and a looking-glass, and a grate always shut up, . . . and
great, heavy curtains that kept out all the light that was not already
excluded by the green shades." Mr. Crowfield pronounces it "as
proper and orderly a parlor as those of our most fashionable neighbors"—but neither the family nor their best friends truly use it.
Instead they all retreat to a large back room that the exiled Mr.
Crowfield has claimed as his study, and there they find the old
parlor reassembled. Here was "where we all sat, where the old
carpet was down, where the sun shone in at the great window,
where my wife's plants flourished and the canary-bird sang, and
my wife had her sofa in the corner, and the old brass andirons
glistened and the wood-fire crackled"—here, in short, was the room
to which the soul of the household had fled.[57] Significantly, however, the story does not end with the Crowfields reclaiming the
front parlor of old. Although Mr. Crowfield struggled against the
tide of fashion, he could not resist it altogether.

Nor could Harriet Beecher Stowe herself. In 1873, a few years
after she wrote "The Ravages of a Carpet," she and her husband,
Calvin Stowe, bought a recently built house in the small community
of Nook Farm on the western edge of Hartford, Connecticut. Its

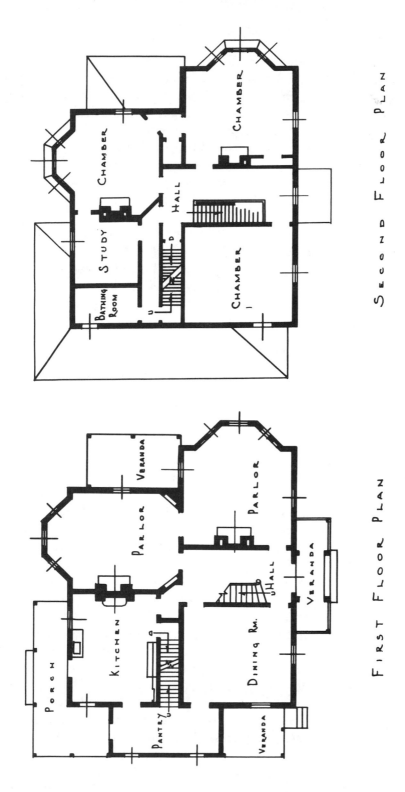

FIRST FLOOR PLAN   SECOND FLOOR PLAN

32. Floor Plan, Stowe House, Nook Farm, Hartford.

organization epitomizes the division between the domestic and the social realms that had become commonplace with her generation. The ground floor included a large entrance hall furnished with fashionable Gothic side chairs, a dining room off to the left, and, to the right, a front and back parlor. Although Stowe spurned heavy draperies in favor of plants around the windows, she followed genteel conventions in furnishing the front parlor elegantly as a social stage for entertaining guests, with stylish furniture and carpeting, paintings and souvenirs from her European travels, photographs and bric-a-brac. As in the Crowfield household, the Stowes' rear parlor was the family retreat where members could shed their social roles to read, play hymns on the piano, and sing. The arrangements of the rest of the house further preserved conventional role segregation. Front and back staircases divided formal and service traffic to the second story. An upstairs hallway made possible private entry into each bedroom. The Stowe twin daughters, Hattie and Eliza, who never married, shared the chamber over the dining room. Calvin used the other front bedroom, on the right, and Harriet took the back bedroom, with an adjoining study. The elder Stowes' rooms also permitted private communication through a shared closet. Throughout the house, as in middle-class urban culture as a whole, the segmentation of space acknowledged and preserved the multiplicity of roles its owners played even within the domestic circle and channeled into "appropriate" forms the behavior and feeling that would transpire in each part.[58]

The management of emotions is a requisite task of all societies, but the terms on which each achieves it are varied and illuminating. The standards propounded by nineteenth-century American etiquette books were part of an increasingly instrumental stance toward feelings, an effort to manipulate them in both private and public contexts in order to create the desired social effects. Etiquette advisers joined numerous other figures in urging a kind of "deep acting" based upon habitual emotional management to achieve polished social performances. Increasingly, middle-class men and women would raise their children for and themselves inhabit a world in which the control and appropriate regard of feelings would be critical. Females would be confined to a significantly more restricted range of emotional expression than males and given special responsibility to provide "altruistic" charm and comfort as part of the price of their subordination. Meanwhile, servants, other social inferiors, and the working classes generally would learn early that their own personal feelings received scant regard, and that they were judged to a much greater extent on their behavior, observance of the lines of authority, and emotional deference to superiors. In this way the realm of emotional management extended the "hidden injuries" of both gender and class in a putatively democratic capitalist society. These would assume various new forms within the service economy of advanced capitalism in our own time, when the manipulation of feelings has been still more thoroughly subsumed within a commercial setting. As Arlie Hochschild's brilliant study *The Managed Heart* has suggested, an increasing number of jobs centrally involve *emotional* labor, in which a supervised worker seeks to elicit a desired emotional response from a customer: reassurance through a (characteristically female) flight attendant's smile; intimidation through a (male) bill collector's gruffly insistent voice. But the foundations for our current situation, with all its accompanying opportunities and persistent inequities, were laid in the nineteenth century.[59]

Some of the deeper implications of the effort to achieve a new standard of civility with special demands for bodily and emotional management will be considered in the next two chapters. In both public and private life, as we shall see, these demands powerfully reinforced class distinctions while transposing them to the plane of "refinement." The first of these chapters concerns the single most important and elaborated social ritual of the home: the act of dining. The second takes up a critical aspect of social gathering in public: the expressive role of audiences in artistic performances.

CHAPTER SIX

Table Manners and
the Control of Appetites

Bodily management and emotional control merged in their most exquisite social test in the act of eating. Gastronomes, etiquette authorities, and anthropologists of the day agreed: "Brutes feed. The best barbarian only eats. Only the cultured man can dine."[1] Modern social scientists, of course, are more wary of facile claims of evolutionary cultural progress. Instead, they would emphasize that eating is a ritual activity, invested with special meaning, in all cultures. Such a primary bodily act, with all its attendant vulnerability, requires "protective symbolic covering."[2] The distinctive ways in which different peoples eat express their attitudes toward their physical bodies, their social relationships, and their sense of the larger cultural order. In uncovering those meanings, we may reveal aspects of a culture that are in other respects less obvious. At the same time we must not claim too much. No single ritual or set of rituals, particularly in a pluralistic culture such as that of nineteenth-century America, can provide a skeleton key that unlocks the innermost meanings of a people. Instead, what secular as well as religious rituals characteristically do is to mediate between ambiguous and frequently contending realms of value. They allow participants to negotiate between various aspects of their experience and often to articulate in heightened form elements that are to some degree embattled or suppressed in everyday life.[3]

Anyone contemplating the history of table manners, as with other changes we have been considering, cannot help but be struck by the extraordinary transformation in notions of propriety and refinement from the late Middle Ages to the late nineteenth century.

Although the twentieth century has witnessed a growing informality in many respects—with each parental generation newly bemoaning the decay of manners—we are still far closer in our attitudes to our ancestors of the past century than to those who came before.

Consider, for example, the courtly manners of the late Middle Ages. Although medieval courtiers sneered at the table manners of peasants, by later standards they themselves revealed astonishing crudity in their display of bodily processes and mutual contact in dining. Feudal lords owned opulent knives and spoons and other table decorations. Yet they simply felt no need for the refined practices or proliferation of utensils of later centuries. Not only did they eat with their hands, slurp soups and sauces directly off their plates, and lift dishes to their mouths; they also dipped their fingers freely into common bowls and drank from a common goblet. Often two diners would eat from the same board. The courtesy books of the day offered advice that in later periods would be regarded as too elementary even for children (and sometimes too indelicate to mention at all): don't place half-eaten food in the serving dish; don't blow your nose on the tablecloth (use your fingers instead); don't spit on the table but underneath; and the like.[4]

A painting by the early-sixteenth-century German artist Jörg Ratgeb depicts the Last Supper conducted according to the prevailing standards of etiquette of his day. As Jesus extends a sop to Judas, one apostle courteously turns from the table to blow his nose with the fingers of his left hand, saving his right to serve himself from common dishes.[5] Another drinks from a wine bottle; a third clasps his neighbor's shoulder; and the rest assume various postures of repose that would have been startlingly rude to later generations. Only the sleeping St. John on Jesus' bosom expresses an iconographic tradition (based on the account in John 13:23) of man's trust in Christ rather than normal practice.[6]

Erasmus's enormously popular book on the subject, *De civilitate morum puerilium* (*On Good Manners for Boys*), which first appeared in 1530, represented a modest tightening of standards, but certainly not a radical departure. "It is rude to offer someone what you have half eaten yourself . . . just as it is disgusting to spit out chewed food and put it on your plate," Erasmus advised readers. "If you happen to have eaten something that cannot be swal-

33. *Last Supper*, painting by Jörg Ratgeb.

lowed, you should discreetly turn away and toss it somewhere."[7]

Beginning in the sixteenth century and continuing through the nineteenth, however, Europe saw an extraordinary elaboration in table manners, first among the nobility and then among the middle classes. Individual plates and goblets replaced communal ones, and the use of forks gradually superseded fingers in polite society and narrowed the scope of the knife. Diners confronted a proliferating array of specialized utensils and rules for their use. Dining no longer took place in a vast kitchen or hall, but in its own distinct room, apart from the butchering, cooking, and, on the European continent, even the carving of the meat.

The Transformation of American Dining

Americans saw a similar transformation in dining, though perhaps lagging slightly behind Europe. In the seventeenth century two people typically still shared a single wooden trencher and drank from a common vessel. Only the very best houses in Plymouth Colony, for example, boasted individual plates, trenchers, cups, and mugs. Early colonists ate with their fingers, supplemented by communal knives and spoons. In 1633 an English friend sent Massachusetts Bay's Governor John Winthrop a "case containing an Irish skeayne or knife, a bodekyn & a forke for the useful application of which I leave to your discretion." This appears to have been the first table fork in the English colonies—and one may fairly wonder if Winthrop ever used it.[8]

Over the course of the eighteenth century in America, individual table settings and more elaborate furnishings became more prevalent, and by the early nineteenth century the early ways of dining had become a sign of poverty, rusticity, and even indecency. Daniel Drake, a physician born and raised in frontier Kentucky at the end of the eighteenth century, later recalled with amusement a childhood neighbor, "Old Billy Johnson," who epitomized the boorish customs of a bygone era: "He and his sons would frequently breakfast in common on mush and milk out of a huge buckeye bowl, each one dipping in his spoon. When the old gentleman happened to be in a hurry and wished to have them all in the field as quick as possible, he would eat in the manner of the rest, till they came towards the bottom, then throw down his spoon, pick up the bowl with both hands, drink off the remainder, jump up, and saying they had all 'eat enough,' start away."[9]

How rising standards of refinement were felt even on the frontier may be measured by an incident in the life of the celebrated preacher Peter Cartwright a quarter century later. As a circuit rider along the Illinois prairie in the 1820s, Cartwright was shocked to discover the meagerness of a household in which he held a Methodist meeting. It had a deeply worn earthen hearth for cooking, a single broken chair, a crudely fashioned half-log of a table, "wooden trenchers for plates, sharp-pointed pieces of cane for forks, . . . tin cups for cups and saucers," and only "one knife besides a butcher's knife, and that had the handle off." The rest of the house was just as meanly furnished. It was not the destitute setting alone that aroused Cartwright's ire, but that he knew the family could afford far better. A rugged spokesman for plain habits and simple worship who sneered at genteel refinement, Cartwright nonetheless found himself urging the virtues of domestic comfort to the head of the household: "Now, brother, . . . do fill up this hole in the hearth, and go to town and get you a set of chairs, knives and forks, cups and saucers, and get you a couple of plain bedsteads and bed-cords. . . . Give your wife and daughters a chance." The man protested, but ultimately did as Cartwright exhorted and joined the ranks of domestic respectability.[10]

Yet the transformation in dining did not occur all at once. Older, less refined habits of eating persisted in many cases even though new table furnishings were adopted. In the antebellum period especially, foreign travelers frequently remarked upon the speed, silence, and slovenliness with which Americans ate—especially the men, who still dominated public gatherings and often held dinners from which women were excluded. British visitors, suspicious of American cultural pretensions, were particularly acerbic. Dining at a Nashville inn in 1831, the army officer James Edward Alexander reported:

> No ceremony was used; each man helped himself with his own knife and fork, and reached across his neighbour to secure a fancied *morceau*. Bones were picked with both hands; knives were drawn through the teeth with the edge to the lips; the scalding mocha and souchong were poured into saucers to expedite the cooling. . . . Beefsteaks, apple tart, and fish, were seen on the same plate the one moment, and had disappeared the next!

Diners bolted their food "as if it were their last meal," then arose from the table, and "wiping their mouths with the heel of their hand," strode into the bar for a drink and a plug of chewing tobacco.[11] "Nobody says anything, at any meal, to anybody," added Charles Dickens, reporting a similar scene on a canal boat. ". . . Every man sits down, dull and languid; swallows his fare as if breakfasts, dinners, and suppers, were necessities of nature never to be coupled with recreation or enjoyment; and having bolted his food in a gloomy silence, bolts himself in the same state."[12] Writing privately to her sister in England in 1827, Margaret Hunter Hall expressed her disgust even more forcefully: "They helped themselves to butter, stewed onions, salt, or potatoes, all with their own nasty knives, with which the moment before they had been eating, and spit to the right and left during their meal. They are a nasty people, the Americans, at table; there is no denying that fact."[13]

The transformation in the conduct of dining was especially sweeping among American middle-class households in the course of the nineteenth century. Although separate dining rooms were common in the homes of the wealthiest Americans by the time of the Revolution, they were acquired by most of the urban middle class probably about the mid-nineteenth century, and they often doubled as family sitting rooms. Quickly, architectural writers, family reformers, and other advisers on the home enshrined the dining room as a central element of refined living. Urging the appropriateness of a dining room in even the simplest farmhouse, the plan-book writer and landscape architect Calvert Vaux sighed, "It is the custom with some farmers to make a constant practice of taking all meals in the kitchen; but this habit marks a low state of civilization."[14]

A book published in 1867, *Six Hundred Dollars a Year*, showed housewives how to furnish a separate dining room on the modest income even an office or shop clerk, mechanic, or skilled laborer might command. Taking her own experience as an example, the author allotted:

Twenty yards Carpet, at $0.75	$15.00
A Good Second-Hand Table	5.00
Six Cane-Seat Chairs, at $1.50	9.00
Cutlery	10.00
Stone-China Dinner Set	10.00
Tea Set, white French China	5.00
Window-Shades	1.00
Total,	$55.00

Like most middle-class dining rooms before the 1880s, this one was intended primarily for family use rather than entertaining. When a friend did join the family for a meal, the author served their "usual fare," but "set the table with greater care, and display[ed] my nicest dishes and finest table-linen." Even on a budget of $600 a year, she insisted on a servant, allowing in her weekly budget $1.50 for "girl's wages."[15]

Beginning at this time, more affluent middle-class families might boast a sideboard as well, either built-in or free-standing. Though a sideboard cost more than a dining table (and might even be the most expensive single item in the house), it allowed the family to store and display the expanding array of silver and dishes; often it included a mirror to enhance the splendor.[16]

Such furnishings became tokens of status and refinement to strive for by those on the lower rungs of the middle class. The story of Walter Teller Post is instructive in this regard. A young junior clerk for the Northern Pacific Railway in St. Paul, Minnesota, Post married in 1894 and with his new wife, Lillie, rented a six-room house. He spent $150 at a local department store for furnishings, putting $100 down and pledging the balance in sixty days. The furniture for the dining room was the most expensive in the entire house: $13.50 for "one dining table . . . solid quarter sawed oak. 1 side board $19.50, 4 dining chairs $5.00." No doubt the sideboard held many of the couple's wedding presents, which included six Haviland China plates, six glasses, six silver fruit knives, six oyster forks, six silver teaspoons "from home," a gravy ladle, a carving set, and four sugar bowls and creamers. Sadly, Post's reach for the trappings of gentility exceeded his grasp. He failed to pay the money he owed for the furniture, and he and his wife soon moved out of their house and into a less expensive apartment.[17]

The availability of table settings themselves also changed dramatically in the course of the nineteenth century. Early on, pewter, glassware, and china dishes began to supplant wooden trenchers and tankards. By mid-century, machine-pressed glassware, transfer-printed earthenware, bone china, Britannia metal (an improved form of pewter), and electroplated silver cutlery were transforming middle-class tables. The glass, ceramic, and silver industries all expanded enormously during the second half of the nineteenth century by appealing to a wide variety of tastes and budgets. Beginning in the 1850s, even country storekeepers could easily supply customers with silver tableware by ordering from manufacturers' price lists. As silver prices dropped and companies began developing their distinctive patented patterns in the late 1860s, catalogues grew much more elaborate. The elegant, heavy silver plate tableware that more affluent travelers encountered at leading hotels, restaurants, steamships, and railroad dining cars also shaped domestic tastes. In such places many first used specialized pieces such as oyster forks and demitasse spoons. In the closing decades of the century, silver makers expanded their offerings immensely. By the 1880s a host of serving pieces achieved popularity for the household, including sugar tongs, salt spoons, butter knives, and lemon forks. Much more specialized pieces proliferated. To speak only of forks, they included separate serving forks, often in two sizes, for beef, cold meat, fish, salmon, sardines, vegetables, spinach, tomatoes, salad, chicken salad, pickles, chowchow, olives, asparagus, bread, toast, melon, strawberries, and pastry. For individual place settings, distinct varieties of forks were available for dinner, fish, oysters, lobster, terrapin, salad, lettuce, berries, mango, fruit, dessert, pie, even ice cream. Already by 1880 Reed and Barton offered four grades of flatware in over a dozen patterns, most of them including ten different kinds of knives, twelve different forks, and twenty different spoons, plus tongs, servers, and other pieces. No one would be expected to buy the complete inventory of any one pattern, of course; but the extreme specialization of function revealed the extent to which bourgeois households mirrored the increasing specialization of the workplace. By 1897 even Sears, Roebuck displayed in its catalogue page after page of such pieces, including a bonbon serving spoon, "solid silver, with gold plated bowl" for $1.15. The late nineteenth century also saw silver-plated tableware offered as "premiums" for buying specified amounts of cereal, soup, or other household staples. In a relatively short time silver flatware had gone from being a luxury associated with the nobility to a ubiquitous necessity among the middle class.[18]

Epitomizing the new refinement was the changing use of the fork. Through the first half of the nineteenth century most table forks were made of iron or steel with two sharp prongs.[19] One held such a fork in the left hand and, after cutting a piece of food, raised the morsel upward with the fork still in the left, then used the flat, rounded blade of the knife in one's right to put the food in one's mouth.[20] But as the two-tined fork yielded to forks with three, then four tines (and often of silver), the cumbersome and characteristically American practice developed, whereby one transferred the fork from left to right after cutting a piece of food, and only then raised it to one's mouth.[21]

34. A Fork for Every Purpose: Place forks for individual service. Where size or design varied in different patterns, several examples are shown. *Top row (l. to r.):* medium or dinner fork, dessert fork, pie fork, fish fork, salad fork, pastry fork, oyster fork, lobster fork, terrapin fork, ice cream fork, berry fork, mango fork. *Middle row (l. to r.):* oyster cocktail fork, fish fork, lobster fork, terrapin fork, fruit fork (hollow handle), oyster cocktail fork, oyster fork, lobster fork, child's fork, salad fork (small), salad fork (large). *Bottom row (l. to r.):* ramekin fork, lettuce fork, terrapin fork, berry forks (four styles), oyster forks (four styles), oyster fork-spoon.

With the rise of the new fork, as early as the 1830s, both the older style of eating with the knife and the two-pronged fork itself became marks of rusticity and vulgarity. Caught in the transition, President Andrew Jackson reportedly provided dinner guests with two forks, one of silver, the other of steel—his personal preference.[22] Meanwhile, an apostle of the new refinement, the cultivated Philadelphian Sidney Fisher noted in his diary his disgust when a man he respected "ate with his knife, smacked his lips, [and] wiped his face & mouth with a red silk handkerchief instead of a napkin."[23] Such clashes between rusticity and refinement abounded in comic possibilities. Traveling up the Mississippi River from New Orleans in the early 1830s, an Eastern general spurned the "haymakers," or two-pronged forks, in favor of his own three-pronged silver one. But what was only proper among fashionable Easterners smacked of affectation on Western riverboats; and "a backwoods passenger incensed at the refinement of the General, one day made himself a huge wooden fork, and when the General called for his silver one at dinner, Kentuck produced his wooden one, and ate with it, in derision, immediately opposite the man of war."[24]

At the same time and in a similar spirit, D. C. Johnston satirized a farmer's son who had left home and turned into a dandy, returning to his parents' house and swooning at the sight of a two-pronged iron fork. The dialogue reads:

[Dandy:] "O! dear! remove that horrible vulgar looking two pronged iron fork from my plate or it will be the death of me"

[Father:] "Well I wonder now if this is really my son Bob that used to eat his pork & beans in the fields with the dung-fork across his lap"

[Mother:] "Dear! dear! what a thing it is to travel to foreign parts and get polished!"[25]

Yet dandies often had the last laugh. Another polished visitor from foreign parts, Charles Dickens, marveled during his tour of the United States in 1842 how Americans "thrust the broad-bladed knives and the two-pronged forks further down their throats than I ever saw the same weapons go before, except in the hands of a skilled juggler."[26]

Etiquette books charted the ascendancy of the fork over the knife.

35. "The Farmers [sic] Son Metamorphosed into a Finished Exquisite" by D. C. Johnston (1835).

Writing in the mid-1830s, Eliza Farrar defended the old practice of eating with a knife despite cosmopolitans' sneers:

> If you wish to imitate the French or English, you will put every mouthful into your mouth with your fork; but if you think, as I do, that Americans have as good a right to their own fashions as the inhabitants of any other country, you may choose the convenience of feeding yourself with your right hand, armed with a steel blade; and provided you do it neatly, and do not put in large mouthfuls, or close your lips tightly over the blade, you ought not to be considered as eating ungenteelly.[27]

Eight years later, in 1845, an etiquette adviser barely condoned the practice: "If possible, the knife should never be put in the mouth at all, and if at all, let the edge be turned downward."[28] By the next decade knife wielders had clearly lost the battle of fashion: "Eat always with a fork or a spoon—unless, indeed, in those old-

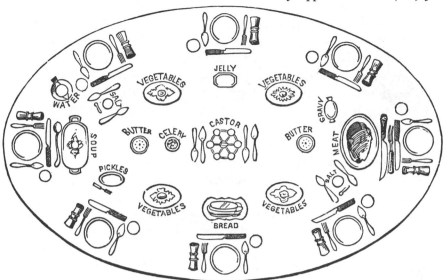

36. How to Set a Table—a Mid-Nineteenth-Century Version.

fashioned houses, where there are only *two*-pronged forks, you are obliged to use your knife."[29] Reflecting the declining importance of the knife, mid-century guides often recommended putting the dinner knife across the top of each place setting instead of to the right of the plate.[30] Opponents of the new fashion might grumble that eating peas with a fork was like "eating soup with a knitting needle," but to no avail.[31] The rise of the fork in the cause of refinement was irresistible. So modish did it become that one social wit proclaimed he took everything with his fork except afternoon tea.[32] By the time Grover Cleveland ran for President in 1884, an editor's gibe that he ate with his knife rankled so deeply that even after his victory Cleveland refused to shake hands with such a gross slanderer.[33] Not "You are *what* you eat," but "You are *how* you eat," became in effect the maxim of the refined.[34]

Table Manners Begin at Home

Instruction in middle-class table manners properly began at home. Etiquette writers advised families to conduct their daily meals as an unceasing rehearsal for company. Slovenliness at home would lead to awkwardness when dining out, as well as embarrassment if guests arrived suddenly at a family dinner. "The table should be made as tasteful and attractive as possible." In the well-ordered household, meals were served according to a regular schedule, and family members came to them punctually, carefully groomed and dressed, even at breakfast.[35] Family members learned to regard their individual plate, cup, glass, knife, fork, spoon, and other items as their "own private property" during the course of the meal, not to be used by others or to be extended into common serving dishes.[36] Even within the family, the lessons of individual control and self-consciousness in anticipation of the larger public world were strictly enforced.

By rigorously observing the niceties of the table on a daily basis, parents would provide a crucial element in their children's education. Nineteenth-century etiquette writers knew as well as any parent today how tortuously children mastered the rigors of table etiquette. Where these writers especially differed from most modern parents was in the depths of their conviction that children retraced the slow, ascending steps of Western civilization as a whole from savagery to refinement. From infancy onward, in the manner in which one ate, one gradually imbibed the lessons of modern civilization: to discipline the cravings of the stomach and the "lower" body by force of intellect, will, and habit. With self-discipline rather than self-gratification the goal, advisers held up austere standards. The author of *The Young Folks' Book of Etiquette* savored how "a certain private school" taught an important lesson in table manners at lunch each day with soda crackers:

> The crackers are passed to the children, and as each receives his, he holds it in his hand until all have been served. Then all break their biscuit open, taking especial care not to scatter crumbs. Bites are taken from one piece until it is gone, then the other is eaten. It is considered a disgrace to drop a crumb upon the floor. If you could see that schoolroom after lunchtime you would know that even so crumbly an article of food as a cracker may be eaten without any disorder.[37]

In learning proper, middle-class table manners, children thus learned the qualities necessary to take their places in the larger society: to subject their least wants and most trivial actions to rule; to value propriety over immediate pleasure. And as they learned to anticipate their adult roles at table, so they learned to defer their own desires until their elders' were satisfied. "Children should not be brought to table till they are able to feed themselves, first with a spoon, and next with a fork," declared Eliza Leslie. "And not then, unless they can be depended on to keep quiet, and not talk."[38] In *The American Woman's Home*, Catharine Beecher and Harriet Beecher Stowe also urged children to keep a respectful silence, adding, "They should always be required, too, to wait in silence, till all the older persons are helped.[39]

Such instructions on children's table manners illuminate the Victorian prudery that governed dining as well as sexuality. Denying the sexual impulses of the child, authorities nonetheless sought to contain them. The lessons of repression and sublimation, once learned at the table, could be carried to the bedroom and to the world at large.

Appetite and the Social Body

The bodily symbolism involved in Victorian table manners had broader social dimensions as well. As the anthropologist Mary Douglas has argued, the rituals that different cultures assign to the human body allow it to serve as a symbol for society at large. The ways people feed their physical bodies express larger concerns about the needs and perils of the *social* body. The bourgeois ideal enshrined a highly articulated body with all its parts functioning in harmony, controlled by the "higher" faculties of reason, "taste," refinement, spirit, and, by analogy, the "higher" authorities and social classes, especially the bourgeoisie itself. Yet the rapid social and economic growth of later-nineteenth-century America raised disturbing questions about the interrelationship of society's members and of how they would be incorporated—that is to say, embodied. What would occur if the "higher" faculties were overwhelmed by the "lower"? Instead of a body of classical proportions and dignity, the result would be a grotesque body driven by base desires and impure appetites.[40]

Cartoonists brilliantly explored the possibilities of such excess. A prominent image of unrestrained greed was a banquet party with bulging stomachs, aghast at the presence of a ragged intruder, with whom they would not think of dining. Here was the story of the

37. "The Political Poor Relation."

rich man Dives in the biblical parable, who refused poor Lazarus even the crumbs under his table, told in modern dress.[41] For example, an 1891 cartoon by C. Jay Taylor entitled "The Political Poor Relation" depicted a thin and ragged American farmer supplicating a group of tariff-gorged industrialists. While the farmer's plight goes unattended, congressional waiters, including the great champion of the cause of protectionism in Congress, William McKinley, offer the banqueters free whiskey and tobacco. Other congressional musicians play the "High Tariff Kinder Sinfonie." Meanwhile, the scent of a war tariff wafts in from the congressional kitchen.[42] The cartoonist Joseph Keppler drew a related image in 1889 when he protested the dominance of the U.S. Senate by the trusts, here depicted as monstrously bloated moneybags. A sign on the wall bluntly declares: "This is a Senate of the Monopolists, by the Monopolists and for the Monopolists!" and the people's entrance is marked "Closed."

Another, even more grotesque, image of loss of control was a devouring figure, swallowing everything in reach, however gross and unpalatable. In some depictions, such a figure lost all sense of restraint and turned social cannibal. The fervently Republican cartoonist Thomas Nast used such an image to devastating effect in 1872 in caricaturing the ability of a motley coalition of Democrats

38. "The Bosses of the Senate."

(whom Nast portrayed as a low-browed figure in convict stripes, with a pistol tucked into his Tammany Hall–Ku Klux Klan belt) and Liberal Republican Horace Greeley to swallow each other's positions whole and unite behind Greeley's candidacy. An even more abusive contemporary cartoon, "The Great Fear of the Period," expressed nativists' alarm over foreign immigration by sketching an Irishman from the shores of the Atlantic and a Chinese from the Pacific consuming Uncle Sam from either end simultaneously, then the Chinese swallowing the Irish in the next gulp.

By cultivating practices of refined dining, holders of industrial and commercial wealth protected themselves against such grotesque caricatures. In the disciplined way they satisfied the primal need for food, they presented an alternative model of social incorporation and growth. According to this model, diners might properly enjoy abundance and, if their means allowed, even luxury, but their appetites were appeased in a quiet and orderly way, and the control of mind and will never faltered for an instant. The ritual structure of Victorian table manners mediated between contending needs that were central to the maintenance of social order: between individual appetite and communal order, bodily satisfaction and social modesty, egalitarianism and hierarchy, public and private.

Table manners thus played an essential part in the alchemy that converted economic capital into social and cultural capital. Taste in food and "tasteful" forms of dining are, of course, creations of

39. Voracious Politics: Greeley and the Democrats swallow one another.

class and culture. Not only are the delights of wealthy epicures and their elaborate dining service beyond a working-class family's means; such luxuries are often unpalatable and their trappings and procedures clumsy to this family compared to eating a sandwich with two hands and drinking beer from a mug or a bottle. Yet because such tastes and practices are so habitual and because they are literally embodied in the individuals who share them, they take on the character of *natural* categories. It becomes easy for the socially privileged to regard their class position and prestige as the *product* of their natural attributes, including their superior "taste" and "breeding," rather than the *cause*, and for those lower on the social scale to accept their domination and to see the rich (in Scott Fitzgerald's famous phrase) as "different from you and me," set apart by nature rather than class and culture.[43]

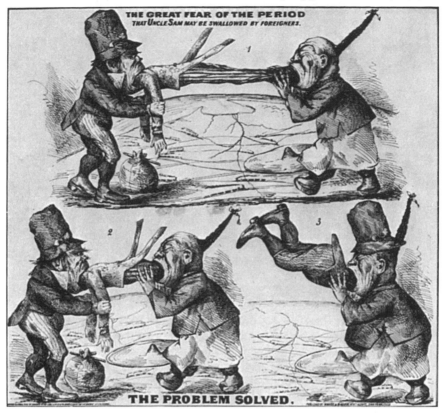

40. "The Great Fear of the Period."

Because the act of dining bore such high ritual stakes among the middle classes, it needed to be performed in protected circumstances. One etiquette manual declared: "Eating is so entirely a sensual, animal gratification, that unless it is conducted with much delicacy, it becomes unpleasant to others."[44] Etiquette advisers warned against eating in public, whether on the street, in a public place of amusement, or in a railroad coach. Groaned one writer, "The pleasure of travelling is often greatly marred by the needless spectacle of others eating."[45] Among proponents of refinement, to eat or be forced to see another eat promiscuously or immodestly was a kind of social obscenity. Just as inviting someone to dine formed a social bond, so eating, if only by necessity, in another's company joined the diners in an ambiguous act of social incorporation. Social conservatives encouraged the increased segmentation

41. "Gentility in the Dining-Room," as depicted in *Hill's Manual of Social and Business Forms*. The accompanying caption insisted that this scene depended not upon wealth but upon "good taste," "self-possession," and practice in "the usages of polite society." Ladies and gentlemen dress fashionably and sit in a room of "refined" furnishings. They are attended by a servant. Courtesy of the Margaret Woodbury Strong Museum, Rochester, New York.

of dining practices in the second half of the nineteenth century. They applauded the growing tendency among middle-class Americans to live in private houses or apartments rather than in boardinghouses, and, although they encouraged families to invite others to dinner, they extolled such an invitation as "the highest social compliment" and one not to be extended lightly.

Table manners emerged as the supreme test of refinement, character, and (to use the catchall term so dear to the hearts of nineteenth-century advisers) "good-breeding." In fashionable society, proper deportment at table was the great initiation ritual. The vulgar and inept, the thoughtless and greedy, as well as parvenus and social counterfeits—all risked "instant detection"[46] and exposure in any of the myriad possible violations of proper etiquette in the course of a meal. Even if they avoided an actual misstep, the very pains they would have to devote to their conduct would betray them.

42. "Bad Manners at the Table": An Inventory of Errors. No. 1 tips his chair; no. 2 eats with his mouth full; no. 3 feeds a dog; no. 4 holds his knife improperly; no. 5 engages in a violent argument; no. 6 lounges on the table; no. 7 brings a cross child to the table; no. 8 drinks from the saucer; no. 9 sits in his shirt sleeves and puts his feet beside his chair; no. 10 picks his teeth with his fingers; no. 11 scratches her head and arises unnecessarily. The room is meanly furnished and the diners are casually dressed. Courtesy of the Margaret Woodbury Strong Museum, Rochester, New York.

Invitation to a Formal Dinner

A simple invitation to dinner might thus pose a challenge for the social novice, but not all got off so easily. That great institution of the late nineteenth century the formal dinner loomed before the socially insecure as an excruciating ordeal by fork, "the great trial"[47] on which one's social reputation depended. Increasingly in the later nineteenth century, families of great wealth tried to consolidate their social positions as an untitled American nobility by the sort of "conspicuous consumption" that the social theorist Thorstein Veblen analyzed to devastating effect in his *Theory of the Leisure Class*

(1899). A favorite means was to hold dinners of unprecedented elaboration and luxury, at times reaching such heights of excess as the dinner hosted by the banker Henry Lukemeyer in 1872, which had as its centerpiece an oval pond thirty feet long with four swans. One dinner began with each guest discovering "in one of his oysters a magnificent black pearl"; another ended with the passing of cigarettes, each rolled in a hundred-dollar bill.[48] Clearly, such entertainments lay beyond the means of all but the very rich. Most middle-class families after the Civil War entertained at a considerably reduced—yet still impressive—scale. For example, to judge from inventories of household possessions, itemized lists of wedding gifts, and invoices from glass, ceramic, and silver manufacturers, they could set a table for six to twelve people.[49] Etiquette advisers (as well as the manufacturers themselves) held up *haut-bourgeois* standards to middle-class readers even as they urged those of modest means to give simpler dinners. "Each owes it to society and to himself, for the cultivation of his better nature, to give as many and as good entertainments as is possible."[50] Advisers reassured potential hosts that a simple dinner might surpass in enjoyment a state banquet, but occasionally a daunting series of qualifications and a patronizing tone undercut such advice and reminded readers of the economic position, as well as cultural competence, necessary to succeed in holding a dinner party. A popular 1897 manual, for example, condescendingly urged "young couples with small means" that they could achieve "a perfect little dinner"—then launched into an intimidating list of prerequisites:

Given, first, a knowledge of *how to do it*; a good cook (not a *cordon bleu*); a neat maid-servant in cap and apron—if the lady can carve (which all ladies should know how to do); if the gentleman has a good bottle of claret, and another of champagne—or neither, if he disapproves of them; if the house is neatly and quietly furnished, with the late magazines on the table; if the welcome is cordial, and there is no noise, no fussy pretence—these little dinners are very enjoyable, and every one is anxious to be invited.[51]

She then offered a sample menu:

Sherry.	Oysters on the half-shell. Soupe à la Reine. Blue-fish, broiled. Filet de Boeuf aux Champignons.	Chablis, Hock, Champagne.

Or,

	Roast Beef or Mutton, Roast Partridges. Salad of Tomatoes. Cheese.	Claret, Burgundy, or Sherry.

Ices, Jellies, Fruit, Coffee, Liqueurs.[52]

If this was a simple little dinner, what in the name of Escoffier did a more formal dinner party entail? Let us consider what late-nineteenth-century etiquette books advised on the subject, beginning with the reception of the invitation.

As a private and honorific request to a private gathering, such an invitation normally came not by post but by personal messenger. Guests were expected to respond punctually—"a delay is unpardonable"—by messenger in return. Once accepted, a dinner invitation was to be honored as "a sacred obligation" lest the hostess's plans be thrown awry. "If you die before the dinner takes place," the arbiter of fashion Ward McAllister declared with mock solemnity, "your executor must attend the dinner."[53] Guests did not know precisely who else would attend, but, in the language of one manual, since at dinner people come into "closer contact than at a dance, or any other kind of a party," one had the assurance that all would be "of the same standing in society as ourselves."[54]

All the rituals comprising the formal dinner demanded attentive and disciplined participation among hosts, guests, and servants. Guests arrived promptly in ceremonial garb, ladies in full dress costumes, gentlemen in evening dress with tails. Advisers castigated those miscreants who were not strictly punctual in their appearance. Arriving early could discommode one's hosts, who might be dressing themselves and making last-minute preparations.[55] In addition, warned one author, "you might excite the suspicion that you came so early to make sure of the feast—a certain sign of greediness."[56] Fifteen minutes was the most a host need allow a tardy guest. Then, in this era before cocktails, the butler entered the drawing room and quietly announced dinner; or, "better still," he silently caught the eye of the hostess and bowed. Then, even among supposed social equals, there followed a brief ritual of precedence. The host led the way, escorting the lady most honored on his left arm. The other gentlemen followed with their assigned dinner partners, with younger members of the dinner party giving way to their elders, and the hostess came last with the gentleman of honor, who sat at her right.[57]

Our social novice gives a sigh of relief and thinks now at last he can relax and eat. He is wrong. It was precisely at the table that the rituals of self-control and polished social performance grew most exacting.

Even so simple an act as seating oneself posed perils. "Be seated with ease," advised one writer, "without rattling your chair; not so far from the table as to endanger your dress in taking food or drink, nor so near as to press against the table and shake it at every movement of your body. Unfold your napkin and lay it across your knees, never pinning it over your breast like an alderman [whom the genteel regarded as virtually synonymous with saloonkeepers] or a slobbering infant."[58]

Once seated, the guest might scan a handwritten menu listing a meal of monumental proportions, yet so carefully orchestrated as to avoid any suggestion of grossness.[59] It began, typically, with raw oysters and champagne. Then waiters offered a choice of a white or a brown soup and poured sherry. Next came fish with Chablis. There followed an *entrée*, such as asparagus or sweet corn. Then a slice of the roast (with claret or champagne). Now perhaps some Roman punch (a watery ice made of lemon juice, sugar, beaten egg whites, and rum) to freshen the palate for the courses still to come: game such as canvasback duck (with Madeira or port), salad, cheese, pastry or pudding, ices and sweet dishes. *Then* liqueurs. *Then* fruit such as grapes, peaches, pears, accompanied by sherry or claret. *And then* waiters passed nuts, raisins, sugar plums, and candied ginger.

At the end of the meal the hostess silently bowed to the lady at the right of the host, and all rose. Gentlemen sometimes remained by themselves at the table for a quarter hour with their wine and cigars, liqueurs and cognac. Finally they joined the ladies in the drawing room for demitasse, bonbons and other dainties, and brandy.

Advisers recommended a well-modulated pace. They allowed a maximum of two hours even for a formal dinner, and recommended an hour or ninety minutes as preferable.[60] (It is perhaps fair to note parenthetically that the ideal body types of the period were decidedly fuller than in our own time.)

This extended presentation of courses marked a significant departure from the conduct of meals until the 1830s even among wealthy cosmopolitans and at fashionable hotels. Before this, guests arrived at a table already laden with dishes: soup, fish, roasts, pies, game, fowl, vegetables, stews, puddings, and so forth. The host assumed a dominant position as carver, server, and dispenser of hospitality. A figure such as the eighteenth-century Virginia planter Robert Carter III played this role even among members of his own household: "Sir—This is a fine Sheep-Head [fish], Mr Stadly [the music master] shall I help you?—Or would you prefer a *Bass* or a *Perch?*—Or perhaps you will rather help yourself to some picked *Crab*—It is all extremely fine, Sir, I'll help myself."[61] At larger meals those who sat near a roast, game, or fowl were expected to carve and serve it to whoever passed a plate, while fellow diners helped dispense other dishes. Often, at more lavish occasions, a second service followed the first, with at least an equal number of dishes, including different meats and vegetables, and, in lieu of additional soup and fish, a sweet pudding and possibly a tart, cream, or custard. An elegant dinner party might include a further dessert of whole fresh fruits and nuts.[62] Foreign travelers (whose own countries had only recently broken with the older custom of displaying all of the dinner in one or two services) were often struck by this gastronomic egalitarianism. An English visitor to the house of ex-President John Adams in Quincy, Massachusetts, in 1817 described in detail their Sunday dinner: "first course, a pudding made of Indian corn, molasses and butter;—second, veal, bacon, neck of mutton, potatoes, cabbages, carrots, and Indian beans; Madeira wine, of which each drank two glasses."[63]

However, this style, sometimes referred to as the Old English plan, was supplanted by a new fashion of service *à la Russe*—so called because it was supposedly introduced by the Russian ambassador to France in 1810, a doubly exotic provenance that may have added to its appeal.[64] No longer were guests called upon to carve and ladle foods or forced to signal waiters in order to have their plates passed and filled with the dishes of their choosing. The new fashion drew a sharp line between diners and servants. (Advisers recommended one servant for every three guests—while acknowledging fewer might do.)[65] Carving and serving took place out of sight, so that diners were spared the communal labors of service and the passing of plates, as well as the sight of leftovers. Instead of covering the table with a promiscuous abundance of dishes and urging diners to choose among them, dinner followed a distinct order of courses, arranged in harmonious sequence, each consisting of one central dish, served with its complementary wine.[66]

The popular American writer Catharine Sedgwick was delighted by this style of presentation when she first encountered it in Frankfurt in 1839. She arrived at a table decorated with "fruits and flowers, instead of being stupefied with the fumes of meat. There was no bustle of changing dishes, no thrusting in of servant's arms. The meat was carved and brought from an adjoining room." Upon Sedgwick's return to America, she discovered that the same fashion was rapidly being adopted in New York.[67]

But not everyone was similarly captivated. The urbane and socially prominent Philip Hone, onetime mayor of New York, first experienced this innovation at a dinner party in January 1838. He did not like it:

> The dishes were all handed round; in my opinion a most unsatisfactory mode of proceeding in relation to this important part of the business of a man's life. One does not know how to choose, because you are ignorant of what is coming next, or whether anything more is coming. Your conversation is interrupted every minute by greasy dishes thrust between your head and that of your next neighbor, and it is more expensive than the old mode of shewing a handsome dinner to your guests and leaving them free to choose. It will not do. This French influence must be resisted.[68]

Despite Hone's grumblings, the influence spread. Although holders of family dinners and informal meals clung to the old ways, hosts of formal dinners, especially after the Civil War, increasingly followed the Franco-Russian mode, further refining it to minimize the handling of "greasy dishes." The Old English style emphasized the display of plenty rather than order. Although soup and dessert marked the meal's beginning and end, the interim was relatively unstructured; diners simply followed their appetites in choosing what to eat. This freedom, however, became redefined as disorder, even slovenliness, according to the rising standards of middle-class refinement. Appetites were no longer to be freely satisfied, but to be disciplined in accordance with sanctioned notions of taste and ceremonial forms and rhythms. In dining *à la Russe* the meal assumed a dignified and stately progression, a drama in which guests were recipients rather than actors and in which even host and hostess assumed roles as understated as possible. Gone was the host's central part in serving food to his guests. The courtliness of an earlier day would have seemed far too obtrusive. Waiters served as silently as possible. Courses mounted in scale and importance from the relatively simple, light, and uncooked to the richer and more lavishly prepared, ending with a series of sweets. Each of the dramatic succession of courses demanded its special *mise-en-scène*: china, stemware, cutlery—so that a formal dinner *à la Russe* required an enormous proliferation in table service. In casting the meal as an aesthetic and ethical drama, governed by harmony, restraint, and propriety, in which diners never helped themselves or voiced their desires but only declined what they did not want, hosts and guests showed their easeful superiority to bodily necessities. They denied the "low," elemental need for food that they shared with all humanity and animals and transmuted eating into high art. The elaboration of structure and the celebration of hierarchy in the meal itself certified the diners' own place in the larger social hierarchy.[69]

Rituals of Refinement

During the entire course of the dinner, whether at a simple meal or a stupendous feast, diners sought to cloak their bodily needs and invest the occasion with dignity by distancing themselves from organic processes. Symbolic demonstrations of bodily control testified to their commitment to social order and constraint.[70] Such controls took a number of ritual expressions. First, diners avoided commenting on the food before them, even in praise. Such remarks would be too naked an expression of "animal and sensual gratification" over mankind's "intellect . . . and . . . moral nature."[71] According to these rituals, eating was such a private act that it was possible to do with others only if one pretended to ignore it.

Similarly, diners minimized their own appetites and sought to avoid any hint of greediness. Etiquette authorities warned them not to eat hastily, take large mouthfuls, tilt a soup plate for the last spoonful, "scrape the last morsel of food from your plate," or attempt to drain the last drop from a glass.[72]

Polite dining also meant that one's food was touched as little as possible. No matter how much handling might be involved in the meal's preparation, in the dining room servants and guests participated in elaborate rituals of purity. Although neither group generally wore gloves (men and women alike removed theirs as they sat down), each waiter wrapped a napkin around the thumb in serving so that a hand never touched the surface of plates or dishes. Some advisers applauded the custom of having servants pass dishes to and from guests on little silver or brass trays instead of with their hands.[73]

Observing the hierarchy of cutlery that had developed, etiquette advisers reminded their readers not only to keep their knife blades out of their mouths but to minimize the knife's use in general. One used the fork, the utensil of greatest refinement, whenever possible, and resorted to fingers only in a very few cases. In eating fruit, for example, one book noted: "It is always better to use a fork, even at the peril of seeming affected, than to offend the taste of another by making a mess with the fingers, as some careless people often do."[74] The sight of teeth marks on a partially eaten piece of bread, fruit, or an ear of corn filled etiquette authorities with special disgust. Such an unmistakable imprint of bodily processes undercut all the elaborate rituals designed to keep them at a distance.

An equally offensive and naked act of ingestion was eating or drinking noisily. A lapse of this sort was taken to betray an almost hopelessly coarse and inconsiderate nature. For such offenders, the "laws" of etiquette were necessary to provide the social discipline that the "well-bred" possessed instinctively. With withering contempt, one writer denounced these boors:

No sensitive person can hear any one taking his soup, coffee, or other liquid, without positive annoyance. Yet, those who would be very unwilling to consider themselves ill-bred are constantly guilty of such breach of politeness. The defect is that they are not so sensitive as those with whom they come in contact. They would not be disturbed by the offense; they never imagine, therefore, that any one else can be. It is for them that rules of etiquette are particularly designed. Were their instinct correct, they would not need the rule, which, from the absence of instinct, appears to them irrational, purely arbitrary.[75]

All the little gestures of bodily adjustment and self-engrossment that were to be avoided in polite society demanded especially precise regulation at the table. Diners were admonished not to scratch their heads, to pick their teeth, or to make similar gestures, and indeed they were advised sternly to "keep the hands below the table when unoccupied."[76]

Refined diners sought here above all else to stifle all signs of the internal bodily processes, such as coughing, sneezing, and nose blowing. "Never if possible, cough or sneeze at the table," one writer declared. "If you feel the paroxysm coming on, leave the room."[77]

More generally, diners were expected to demonstrate their own refinement, self-control, and subordination to the social gathering by guarding against disruptions of all sorts. They regulated emotional displays as rigorously as they did their bodies, avoiding both extremes of sadness and boisterous laughter. As one adviser declared, "Moods should be our own secrets."[78] Diners were encouraged not simply to fall silent but to engage in conversation while eating, keeping the table talk light and steering away from "heated discussions" and "heavy or abstruse topics."[79]

Here is a model conversation between two guests, as supplied by one authority on manners:

Having seated themselves, and exchanged a few comments (of course flattering), on the table decorations, the lady, wishing to ascertain whether her companion was one of the silent diners-out, might say:

"Some people do not care to eat and talk at the same time, but prefer to let what few comments they make come in between the courses."

[He:] "A man must be a dull fellow who cannot do both, with satisfaction to his neighbor if not to himself."

[She:] "Then I may talk to you without fear of interrupting your enjoyment of your dinner? But you speak as though it were easier to please your neighbor than yourself."

[He:] "Set down that speech to my gallantry. Ladies are so

good natured that they take the will for the deed, while my modesty precludes my taking credit for any efforts of mine."[80]

The prospect of such repartee perhaps also consoled the uninvited.

If despite all one's efforts at grace and refinement, an accident occurred—a spilled wineglass, an upset plate—what then? "Do not appear disconcerted, nor apologize while at the table," etiquette authorities advised. Calmness and self-composure should reign above all.[81] Part of the hostess's duty in such minor emergencies was to aid the hapless guest by standing as "a model of serenity, tact, and self-possession. . . . If her precious china and her rare glass are broken before her eyes, she must seem to take but little or no notice of it."[82]

Once the meal had concluded, guests were expected to remain and talk for an hour or so. Leaving too soon might suggest that one came merely for the food and not for the company.[83] Similarly, when the time came to depart, profuse expressions of gratitude were frowned upon. As one adviser wrote, "guests may express the pleasure the occasion has afforded them, but further thanks are now considered old fashioned."[84] Recipients of invitations, whether they actually attended the dinner or not, were also expected to make a brief formal call upon the host within ten days after the occasion. And ultimately, of course, they were obliged to repay the "debt" of hospitality.

The Force of Ceremony

What may we conclude from such dining rituals? The life of all communities is dialectical in nature, and no ritual may be said wholly to epitomize a society's concerns. Nonetheless, the ceremonial forms that govern a given occasion shape its content and possibilities in profound ways, whether its participants are aware of it or not. They provide devices that frame, channel, and control experience, admitting certain possibilities, foreclosing others.[85]

The rituals of polite Victorian dining sought to elevate and protect the individual dignity and self-possession of all participants. They demanded, above all, the virtues of mutual respect, tact, and self-possession. Adopting and further refining the ceremonial forms of the nobility, advocates of polite dining insisted upon their special relevance in a democracy. Here, if each individual was to be masterless, it was all the more essential that he be master of himself. In Victorian table manners and especially in the conduct of the formal dinner, one may see a great effort to maintain social order, hierarchy, and individuation through the very ritual structure of dining.

As we have seen, an important element in these table manners was a recognition that the process of eating might reduce all involved to an animal level of appetite and competition, a Hobbesian "war of all against all." In a period of American history when economic competition was at its fiercest, rituals of refined dining guarded against the spread of such struggles into the private realm of friendship and family. Nature, and even business, might be "red in tooth and claw," but the domestic circle could provide a refuge of sympathy, harmony, and refinement.

This tightening of controls also guarded, less clearly but equally effectively, against a stripping away of social distinctions and the achievement of a celebratory human bondedness, what the anthropologist Victor Turner has called "communitas."[86] In all societies, as Turner has observed, "a contrast is posited between the notion of society as a differentiated, segmented system of structured positions . . . and society as a homogeneous, undifferentiated *whole*."[87] Segmentation had become one of the great principles of refinement as well as an increasingly important aspect of American society as a whole. Advocates of civility and refinement may well have sensed that the act of sharing a meal might subvert that segmentation, in favor, not of barbarism, but of some radical sort of leveling. Potentially, dining might usher in a new kind of fellowship: a melting of individual reserve and a breakdown of social norms into a changed collectivity.

A Genteel Last Supper?

Such a fellowship might take many forms, but to indicate how such possibilities were held in check, let us touch briefly on the dining ritual of fellowship and transformation most familiar to late-nineteenth-century Americans: the Last Supper. Etiquette advisers never tired of insisting that the basis of all politeness was the Golden Rule, and that the epitome of the gentleman was Jesus. But the

Last Supper was sentimentalized and trivialized to a remarkable degree in this period. No artist attempted to paint a genteel Victorian Last Supper, as Jörg Ratgeb presented an early-sixteenth-century version. Lifeless copies of Leonardo's famous depiction, some doubtless hung in family dining rooms, froze the event in the popular imagination, so that Mark Twain could with justice say, "Perhaps no living man has ever known an attempt to paint the Lord's Supper differently." At the same time, liberal Protestants severely reduced the importance of the Lord's Supper in public worship, usually according it only memorial significance.[88] Neither is surprising. For a Last Supper conducted according to the etiquette of a late-nineteenth-century dinner party would have been impossible. The rituals of polite dining simply would not have permitted it. Such a departure would have threatened to forge participants into a new kind of communion that would subvert the established order.[89] The point of comparing the two is neither to accuse advocates of refined dining of hypocrisy nor to make light of the Gospels. It is rather to offer one final illustration of the larger stakes that rituals of dining contain in their conduct and their symbolism, and, more specifically, to underscore the profound conservatism implicit in late-nineteenth-century table manners.

A genteel Victorian Last Supper would have been impossible, first, because it is ludicrous to imagine Jesus and his apostles donning formal dress and participating in the ceremonies of private ownership and display. Their radical insistence upon poverty and acceptance of the lowly would have subverted the genteel concern with the maintenance of status and the enshrinement of private goods.

In addition, the Victorian emphasis upon prescribed social forms and procedures would have amounted to pharisaism, a strict insistence upon the letter of social ritual in such a way as to kill the spirit. As a recent commentator has emphasized, Jesus' gatherings at table with his followers provoked scandal in his own day—and surely would have in nineteenth-century fashionable society—because he excluded no one, even open sinners, from table fellowship or, by extension, from kinship with God and heavenly salvation.[90] And surely Jesus' warning that one would betray him would have violated the host's pose of bland good humor. Instead of introducing profound and abstruse matters, advisers might object, He above all should steer conversation toward light chitchat.

43. A Mid-Nineteenth-Century Lithograph of Leonardo da Vinci's *Last Supper*—in Mark Twain's words, "the picture from which all engravings and all copies have been made for three centuries." Courtesy of the Margaret Woodbury Strong Museum, Rochester, New York.

More fundamentally, Jesus' insistence that the shared bread and wine be regarded as His body and blood in holy communion would have struck Victorians as a revolting analogy. They located threats to purity without, in the objects one ate and the way one ate them. He insisted that the great threats to purity lay within.[91] He offered salvation through Grace; they sought distinction through the social graces.

Finally, Jesus' washing of the disciples' feet after supper would have thrown etiquette advisers into consternation. In Victorian dining practices, each individual tended to his own ritual cleansing, and any suggestion that it required another would have been an affront. In addition, Jesus' act would have appeared both unseemly bodily contact and a shocking loss of dignity on the part of the host in stooping to the task of a servant.

In short, Victorian table manners were designed to set careful limits upon the possibilities of social interaction and communion, to reinforce and justify existing social relationships rather than to change them. They checked any sort of deviation from the paths of social propriety, whether it led in the direction of individual assertion or of communal transformation.

CHAPTER SEVEN

The Disciplining of Spectatorship

The new, more exacting terms of sociability, emotional expression, and the control of impulse, epitomized within the realm of private life in the act of dining and the evolution of table manners, dramatically transformed public life as well. The dynamic character of social relationships in the rapidly industrializing economy led to a more specialized and segmented civic order. From the Jacksonian era to the late nineteenth century, both the physical settings and the social expectations supporting public gatherings among the urban middle classes changed profoundly. The expressive, often rowdy, male-dominated assemblies that played so conspicuous a part in the first half of the century were increasingly challenged by disciplined, passive, and segmented gatherings in which middle-class women figured prominently. A new bourgeois ideal was inscribed upon the city: orderly, regulated, learned, prosperous, "civilized." Its monuments included fashionable residential enclaves, well-policed boulevards, genteel public parks, revitalized shopping districts such as New York's "Ladies' Mile," elegant department stores, magnificent libraries and museums, imposing governmental buildings, substantial public schools, and often opulent theaters, concert halls, and opera houses.

Institutions of the performing arts, in particular, provide a telling index of how the terms of social interchange in public were transformed. Here one can study at close range critical changes in the character of theatrical and musical performances and the relationship between performers and their audiences. Here, too, one sees the larger cultural stakes involved in issues of manners and deportment and how the genteel ideals of public deportment urged by etiquette advisers fit within an important larger history. Rising demands upon audience behavior, far from trivial, were intimately connected to fundamental transformations in the character of America's cultural life and the definition of the public realm.

The history of the performing arts in this period is a complex one, but its outlines may be very briefly sketched. In an astonishingly short time, from roughly the end of the Civil War to the early twentieth century, there arose many of the nation's most renowned institutions of art, theater, and music, as well as many of its most vital popular amusements. Equally important but often overlooked, with this growth and specialization emerged an increasingly hierarchical conception of the performing arts. On one side stood "high" or "refined" art (opera, particularly Wagner; symphonies, particularly Beethoven; the "legitimate" theater, particularly Shakespeare—once he had been redefined into a "classic").[1] On the other side lay "popular," "light," or, more pejoratively and lower in the scale, "cheap" and "vulgar" "amusement"—no longer to be accorded the dignity of Art. The increased professionalization of the performing arts and this hierarchical conception had profound implications for the intended audiences. The largely male audience drawn from a variety of classes that interacted freely with performers in a shared public culture up to the mid-nineteenth century would be opened to admit women on a more equal footing, but it would also increasingly be divided and disciplined to accept a passive role. As auditors mounted the artistic scale to "high" or "refined" art (with its obvious class implications), they were expected to behave in a more "refined" manner themselves. Many of the institutions, physical settings, and dominant conventions of artistic performance established during this time still prevail today. More subtly and ambiguously, the specialization of artistic activities, their cultivation of authority, their injunctions to disciplined passivity, their emphasis upon spectacle, and the kinds of audiences they helped create all marked a move toward a more segmented, privatized society in which divisions of "taste" and deportment masked and reinforced divisions of class.

Antebellum Artistic Performance and Audiences

The changing character of American entertainment and artistic performance in the later nineteenth century emerges most sharply when contrasted with the antebellum period. Although during this earlier time distinctions between levels of cultural activity can assuredly be made, what struck many contemporary observers, especially visitors from abroad, and what still strikes historians today, is the way in which boundaries between different forms of art, entertainment, and performance in American cities were not neatly fixed or sharply delineated.

The term "opera," for example, was applied to almost any kind of musical performance, with or without dialogue, from Italian operas to outrageous burlesques, from melodramas to musical farces, from curtain raisers to afterpieces, from opera-ballets to horse operas (or hippodramas) and blackface Ethiopian operas that prepared the way for the wildly popular minstrel shows.[2] Often operas were stitched together from several works, sometimes from different composers, and even the most respected opera companies occasionally substituted popular songs for certain arias.

"Museum" proved an equally elastic category. From the opening of the nation's first museum by Charles Willson Peale in Philadelphia in 1784, American museums had a distinctly eclectic character. Peale's own assemblage of curiosities at points strained his ideal of "rational amusement" and the orderly reflection of the great Book of Nature. His numerous successors broke with this ideal altogether and aggressively emphasized the bizarre, freakish, and fraudulent, even adding a motley series of performers in a crude precursor to vaudeville. The most famous and successful of these impresarios, P. T. Barnum, acquired his first museum in New York in 1841. It was then a dismal collection of oddities and a lackluster succession of presentations, including a contortionist, O'Connell the Tattooed Man, a painting of Rheims Cathedral, and an exhibition of the effect of laughing gas. Barnum tirelessly scoured the nation for new attractions and promoted them with unrivaled brilliance, moving in quick succession from the outrageous hoax of the "Fejee Mermaid" to the midget Tom Thumb to the phenomenally successful 1850–52 tour of the "Swedish Nightingale," the great soprano Jenny Lind. Confounding fixed categories of taste, he established his museum as a national institution and drew to it a vast new audience hungry for morally upright entertainments.[3]

Just as opera and museum provided broad, flexible rubrics for a variety of entertainments, so, too, did the theater. Programs ranged from romantic melodramas and native comedies, often augmented by musical entertainments, to Shakespeare, who was overwhelmingly the most popular and frequently performed playwright in America, in both major cities and small towns across the country. Much more telling than mere frequency, however, was the *way* Shakespeare was presented in antebellum America. As the historian Lawrence Levine has recently emphasized, "Shakespeare was performed not merely alongside popular entertainment as an elite supplement to it. . . . Shakespeare *was* popular entertainment in nineteenth-century America." His plays were "presented as part of the same milieu inhabited by magicians, dancers, singers, acrobats, minstrels, and comics." Freely adapted and bowdlerized, Shakespeare's plays were staged with none of the self-conscious reverence offered by later generations. Like other plays, they provided the centerpiece for a variety of entertainments, often including a musical overture, a variety of between-act specialties, and an afterpiece, usually a farce. *Hamlet* might be followed by *Fortune's Frolic*, *The Merchant of Venice* by *The Lottery Ticket*, *King Lear* by *Love's Laughs at Locksmiths: or, The Guardian Outwitted*; and *Romeo and Juliet* by *Did You Ever Send Your Wife to San Jose?*—often with the same actors performing in both.[4]

They played to a broad urban audience drawn from a variety of classes and tastes in the period from the 1820s to the Civil War. Up to at least the 1840s, most theaters preserved the eighteenth-century division into three major sections. In the pit directly in front of the stage clustered both men from the "middling" classes and some from the working classes. (The more respectable Northern theaters excluded women from the pit entirely.) The wealthier patrons (including many dandies as well as all women who wished to be regarded as ladies) occupied the most expensive seats in what was the largest section of the theater, the first two tiers of boxes. The "guilty third tier" of boxes (to which a bar was attached where liquor was sold) was frequented by prostitutes, on whose regular patronage many theaters depended. Above this tier rose the cheapest seats in the gallery, occupied by people of modest means, including artisans, laborers, apprentices, and servants, together with blacks (if permitted at all) and more prostitutes.[5]

Members of the audience from all three sections conducted themselves in a far different manner from that of their counterparts in later generations. Many went to the theater not to sit passively before the performers but to enjoy one another's society, to see and be seen, to talk, and often to interact freely with the players. Throughout the antebellum period, the houselights remained on during the performance—not only to permit a better view of the stage, but also to allow spectators to see one another. Attending New York's Park Theater in 1802, the youthful Washington Irving noted that those in boxes appeared to use the theater as "a coffee-house, or fashionable lounge, where . . . [they] indulge in loud conversation, without any regard for the pain it inflicts on their more attentive neighbors." The "gallery gods," meanwhile, expressed pleasure and annoyance by "stamping, hissing, roaring, whistling," and occasionally "groaning in cadence," as well as amusing themselves by throwing "apples, nuts & ginger-bread" at the stage or whoever caught their eye in the pit. The "honest folks of the pit" around Irving stood on the benches with dirty boots and commented freely on the play in front of them.[6]

When Frances Trollope surveyed American life three decades later, she marveled especially at the informality of behavior at the theater, "which seemed to disdain the restraints of civilized manners." To her horror, as she attended performances in Cincinnati, Washington, Philadelphia, and New York, she encountered "in the front row of a dress-box a lady performing the most maternal office possible," gentlemen wearing their hats but shedding their jackets and rolling up their shirt sleeves, sprawling grotesquely in their seats, throwing their legs over the boxes, reeking of onions and whiskey, chewing tobacco and spitting incessantly. One incident in Washington especially repulsed her:

> One man in the pit was seized with a violent fit of vomiting, which appeared not in the least to annoy or surprise his neighbours; and the happy coincidence of a physician being at that moment personated on the stage, was hailed by many of the audience as an excellent joke, of which the actor took advan-

44. Bad Manners at the Theater: An illustration from Trollope's *Domestic Manners of the Americans*.

tage, and elicited shouts of applause by saying, "I expect my services are wanted elsewhere."[7]

With the publication of *Domestic Manners in America*, Trollope's descriptions of the audience quickly became famous and were supported by a catalogue of theater "indecencies" in the *New-York Mirror* and, still more eloquently and persuasively, by members of the pit themselves, who took to shouting "Trollope" whenever they spotted a transgression in the boxes.[8]

This audience freedom and informality extended to the action onstage. Theatergoers occasionally joined in famous speeches and familiar songs, and they delighted in beating actors to the punch lines of old jokes.[9] Admittedly, actors then as now sometimes wished their auditors were *more* demonstrative in applauding their scenes and complained of their silence;[10] but when listeners particularly enjoyed a song, speech, or scene, mere clapping often seemed a pallid way to express their delight, and they cried aloud, stamped their feet, and often stopped the show to demand an immediate and literal encore, that is to say, a repetition of a scene, dance, or musical interlude. They demonstrated their disapproval just as forcefully, hissing, jeering, and often throwing things at the performers. They occasionally even retailored the program to suit their tastes, as when an audience at New York's Bowery Theatre in 1833 insisted that the orchestra dispense with a symphonic overture and play "Yankee Doodle" instead.[11]

Such assertive behavior and patriotic feeling sometimes moved beyond these relatively good-natured demonstrations to what was regarded as the audience's traditional prerogative of rioting on behalf of their sovereign rights as theatergoers. Viewing themselves as constituting "the public" and the theater as a "public" (albeit privately owned) gathering place for their collective amusement, rioters dispensed rough justice by chasing offenders off the stage and breaking a limited degree of property, usually within limits set by the elite.[12] In New York in the 1810s and '20s, audiences rioted against last-minute changes in the announced program, inoperative stage machinery, and a play (Gay's *Beggar's Opera*) that they regarded as lewd and immoral. In every instance, theater managers complied with the "judgement of the public."[13] More serious were the riots against British actors Edmund Kean in New York and Boston in 1825 and Joshua Anderson in New York in 1831 and 1832. Both arose from what were construed as insults to the American public in an era of intense nationalistic fervor: in Kean's case, his refusal to act before a disappointingly small audience at one performance during his previous American tour as well as his scandalous philandering; in Anderson's case, anti-American remarks he had allegedly made en route to the United States. In both instances, not only were the actors shouted down by claques within the audience, but mobs outside battered the doors and broke the windows of the theaters. Though theater managers called the police, authorities acted with notable restraint, respecting public sentiment and the rights of the audience to declare its will.[14] Other minor theater riots continued to occur in New York in the 1830s and '40s;[15] but the most serious instance of the entire century and the great watershed in attitudes toward the prerogatives of the audience was New York's Astor Place riot of 1849.

The Astor Place Riot

The Astor Place riot arose out of a dispute between partisans of the first great American tragedian Edwin Forrest and his eminent English rival William Charles Macready—a dispute that hinged upon the prerogatives of the audience.[16] Significantly, the affair originated when from his box Forrest hissed Macready's playing of Hamlet in Edinburgh in 1846. Macready was outraged; "The low-minded ruffian!" he exclaimed in his diary.[17] But Forrest publicly defended his action as a traditional, legitimate, "salutary and wholesome corrective of the abuses of the stage."[18] Nevertheless, unforgiving British reviewers castigated Forrest's own performances on his European tour, forcing him to cut it short. Forrest, who had a volatile and suspicious temperament, returned to the United States convinced that Macready himself had masterminded a conspiracy against him.

When Macready toured the United States in 1848–49, the quarrel widened from a personal dispute into an intense class and cultural conflict. Forrest had won a mass American following by his passionate, intensely physical acting, his fervent nationalism, and his exemplary rise from working-class origins to international celebrity. Macready, by contrast, wished to elevate acting as a profession. He disdained to play to the audience and keenly resented any hint of vulgarity either in his fellow actors or in the theater public. (Commenting on a performance of King Lear by Forrest in 1843, before their break, Macready wrote in his diary: "I do not think it the performance of an artist. . . . He is now only an actor for the less intelligent of the Americans.")[19] In his concern with "taste" and "refinement" Macready attracted the support of many leading literary and social figures in England and the United States. Yet as he discovered on his American tour, Macready was easily (if inaccurately)[20] cast by Forrest and his followers in the role of an effete aristocrat, a kid-gloved English snob, the darling of the "nabobs," the "upper ten," the "codfish aristocracy,"[21] and one whose very presence was an insult to democratic American values. Forrest further inflamed the rivalry by playing "against" Macready in competing productions at a number of cities on the tour, culminating in New York. In Philadelphia, Forrest's partisans first hissed and groaned at Macready's performance of Macbeth, then threw pennies and rotten eggs.[22] Afterward Macready, who had earlier contemplated retiring to the United States, bitterly confided to his diary, "I begin to think it is a land of blackguards and ruffians with a certain proportion of gentlemen obliged to live among them. . . . [A] dungeon with urbanity and decency in one's keeper would be preferable to the range (not the liberty) allowed by consorting with these ruffians."[23] In Cincinnati, while Macready played Hamlet, a man in the gallery heaved half a raw sheep's carcass onto the stage.[24] In other cities Macready's performances passed without incident. But when at last in May of 1849 he came to New York to appear at the elegant Astor Place Opera House, popular antagonisms exploded.

First opened only a year and a half earlier, in November of 1847, the Astor Place Opera House marked a decisive step in the transformation of theater patrons from the broadly inclusive and expressive public of earlier decades to a segmented and refined audience dominated by the wealthy bourgeoisie. The shift is evident in the contrast between the Opera House and the leading theater among fashionable New Yorkers prior to it, the Park Theater, which was originally built in 1798, rebuilt in 1821 after a fire, and burned again in 1848. The most splendid American theater of the early nineteenth century, the Park was nonetheless meager, cramped, and dreary by later standards. Like other New York theaters before the 1840s, it had no lobby as such. Of its seven arched doorways facing Park Row, the outer two led directly up to the third tier and gallery; the middle five conveyed patrons to the two tiers of boxes and, down a long corridor, to the pit. Except for box subscriptions, seats were not reserved, and theatergoers squeezed onto the benches in the pit and gallery or, for particularly

45. "One of the Codfish Aristocracy." This caricature of a fop holds a walking stick and monocle in his left hand, while proudly displaying his vest and rings with his right. A tailor's bill, bankruptcy papers, and a ticket to the Astor Place Opera House protrude from various pockets. Meanwhile, the riot is depicted in the background. Courtesy the New-York Historical Society, New York City.

popular performances, stood. They elbowed past one another throughout the performance for refreshments, and the houselights remained brightly lit the entire evening.

In 1882 the critic and Shakespearean scholar Richard Grant White, who had been an enthusiastic patron of the Astor Place Opera House and a key supporter of Macready in New York, mordantly recalled the physical and social discomforts of the Park Theater from the point of view of the rising standards of New York's social and cultural elite. "No public building not indecently dirty or unhealthily exposed could be less suited to the assemblage of elegant people for elegant pleasure than the Park Theater." The pit—which White approvingly noted had in modern theaters been converted into "the most desirable part of the house," the parterre or parquet—had a dirty, broken floor, furnished with "bare, backless benches." Women were never seen there, and few gentlemen who cared at all about "comfort and luxury in their amusements." Not only was "the place . . . pervaded by evil smells," but, "not uncommonly, in the midst of a performance, rats ran out of the holes in the floor and across into the orchestra." White remembered the Park's boxes as hardly more sumptuous. They resembled "pens for beasts": crudely assembled benches "covered with faded red moreen," most (though not all) equipped with a second board at shoulder height in lieu of a solid back. These boxes were attended "by a fee-expecting creature, who was always half-drunk, except when he was wholly drunk." As for the gallery above, White sneered, it was "occupied by howling roughs, who might have taken lessons in behavior from the negroes who occupied part of this tier, which was railed off for their particular use."[25]

The Astor Place Opera House heralded a new era. Following several abortive efforts to establish a permanent site for opera in New York, a group of a hundred and fifty wealthy and socially prominent subscribers built the Opera House to embody the emerging new standards of refinement—and exclusivity—that many contemporary etiquette books expressed. The vulgar pit was totally revamped, or as one commentator put it, "aristocratized."[26] Instead of promiscuous open seating on hard benches, the Opera House boasted a parquet with fixed red damask seats, sold only by subscription. Above the parquet, two tiers of splendid boxes for the wealthiest subscribers ringed the theater. Reserve seating by subscription widened the gulf between classes, giving the wealthy even

46. "The Interior of the Park Theatre, November 1822." This watercolor shows
the structure of older theaters, with its large pit, three rows of boxes, and gallery.
Artist John Searle depicted the performance of an English farce, *Monsieur Tonson*,
and included portraits of the principal actors and more than eighty of his contemporaries (including himself) in the audience. Courtesy the New-York Historical
Society, New York City.

greater prominence and pushing the less affluent to a position of social invisibility. The only seats open to general admission during the Opera House's opening season were some five hundred in the gallery, renamed the "amphitheatre," most with views obstructed by a huge chandelier. To exclude from these seats prostitutes and other women of dubious respectability, as well as the "fancy" men they attracted, the playbill on the opening night announced firmly: "No lady admitted unaccompanied by a gentleman." "Gentlemen" themselves were expected to observe a dress code stipulating "freshly shaven faces, evening dress, fresh waistcoats, and kid gloves"—a calculated slap at working- and lower-middle-class men. The Opera House, then, represented a triumphant consolidation of financial, social, and cultural capital by New York's elite, and a reordering of theatrical space that mirrored the larger redefinition of public space by these same interests in the metropolis generally. In the reminiscence in which Richard Grant White castigated the crude, dirty, and dreary Park Theater and its motley denizens, he affectionately recalled the Astor Place Opera House as "one of the most attractive theaters ever erected" and commemorated its opening-night audience as perhaps the most elegant, refined, and socially impressive ever seen in New York. "It may safely be said," he added significantly, "that there was hardly a person present who was not known, by name, at least, to a very considerable number of his or her fellow auditors." For a moment it appeared as if the bourgeois dream of reclaiming public space in the city for a society of ladies and gentleman of "taste" and "good breeding" had been achieved.[27]

When Macready performed at the Astor Place Opera House, then, he offered Forrest's militantly anti-aristocratic, working-class supporters an irresistible target, appearing as he was in the very monument to the New York elite's social and cultural pretensions. As one of Macready's American hosts, the historian William Prescott, remarked a month after the riot, "in truth the row, though set on foot probably by the followers of Forrest, was mainly directed against the Opera House which has long been odious as an exclusive, aristocratic institution—where every man must wear white gloves and dress coats!"[28] The influential journalist Nathaniel Parker Willis agreed, arguing that the Opera House itself, as well as the dress and etiquette of its patrons, constituted an ostentatious affront by a wealthy elite to traditional notions of republican simplicity in public.[29] Macready's first performance there, in *Macbeth*, was reduced to pantomime as hecklers kept up a chorus of boos, hisses, whistles, groans, and yells, including "Three groans for the codfish aristocracy!" and "Down with the English hog!" This hubbub was punctuated by the pitching of eggs, potatoes, apples, lemons, copper coins, pieces of wood, an old shoe, a reeking bottle of asafetida, and, finally, several chairs from the gallery—until at last Macready was driven from the stage.[30] He returned for a second performance of the play only at the urging of forty-seven of New York's most prominent lawyers, merchants, businessmen, physicians, editors, and writers (including Washington Irving, Herman Melville, and Richard Grant White), a powerful Whig elite joined by a few Democrats united in the determination that the mob should not prevail over the forces of refined art and public order.[31] This time, despite renewed jeers from Forrest's claque and with the aid of aggressive policemen, Macready completed the performance. Nonetheless, thousands of workingmen outside bombarded the theater with paving stones and tried to storm the entrance—whereupon the militia fired upon them. At least twenty-two people ultimately died as a result of the riot, and over one hundred fifty were wounded or injured.[32] The riot shattered the once coherent theater "public" along sharp class lines. It revealed how complete was the class and cultural rift between Forrest's "Bowery B'hoy" defenders and Macready's "nabobs," and how directly linked were the efforts to discipline audiences and the larger aim to reshape the public sphere and redefine the terms of cultural expression as a whole.

The Segmentation of the Performing Arts

One might easily conclude, prompted by Macready's shocked response and Frances Trollope's scornful amusement, that American theater audiences were uniquely violent and vulgar and that their standards of conduct at performing arts in general were uniquely debased. Both judgments would be mistaken. Although some of American audiences' sense of prerogatives undoubtedly stemmed from their broad popular character in an age of democratic self-assertion and the absence of a nobility, theatrical audiences in London, Paris, and other European cities had often been extremely

47. Clash of Mob and Militia in the Astor Place Riot.

vocal in both their approval and their criticism of performances; the chief difference may lie in the fact that European audiences grew more segmented and disciplined slightly earlier.[33] A similar tradition of audience participation prevailed in European opera and concert halls. As late as the early nineteenth century, music was often performed as an accompaniment to other social functions, including dancing, dining, conversation, and social display, so that the modern decorum of silent, sustained attention to a musical performance was a historic innovation. Indeed, vocal expressions of displeasure at concerts and operas—cries, hisses, boos, and jeers—appear to have remained more entrenched in Europe than in America.[34]

Nonetheless, on both sides of the Atlantic, these traditional audience prerogatives would be challenged. The theater, the concert hall, the opera house, and other institutions of the performing arts would become key arenas in the struggle both to reshape the character of public behavior and more generally to determine who as cultural participants the "public" was. In Europe, as well as in the United States, an aesthetic hierarchy would develop, more rigidly separating once fluid categories of performance. The split between "elite" and "popular," between exclusive and broadly accessible art forms, would transform theater and concert life. The development of institutions of the performing arts must be considered within this broader context. Then its course can be seen, not as necessary and inevitable steps toward artistic maturity (as traditionally depicted), but as a critical, problematic, and at times contested redefinition of the place of the performing arts in metropolitan life and of their proper constituency.

An important step in this redefinition in the United States was the changing organization of cultural institutions in the second half of the nineteenth century. Across the entire range of the arts, the most prestigious cultural institutions established new sources of support and direction that markedly reduced their traditional dependence upon a local constituency in which the working and lower-middle classes were well represented. Drama, for example, had at the beginning of the nineteenth century relied upon the stock company system, in which a manager owned or leased a theater, hired actors, and cast them in plays of his choosing. To attract larger audiences, however, this system increasingly yielded first to a dependency upon touring luminaries such as Forrest and Macready and then, in the post–Civil War period, to "combination companies." Here a star performed "in combination" with a full company of actors on a prearranged tour, by the late nineteenth century specializing in a single play. With this evolution, power shifted from local managers and audiences to a handful of stars, producers, and booking agents, most of whom were based in New York.[35] In contrast to the eclectic, freewheeling, and uneven theatrical offerings of the antebellum period, the most eminent productions of the later nineteenth century offered new standards of cohesive, polished performance for a more "refined" middle-class audience, including women and children. Actors, directors, and managers, whose public careers as entertainers placed them under a moral and social cloud as late as the mid-nineteenth century, demanded acknowledgment of their artistic authority and newly won social celebrity. Although wishing to entertain, they increasingly resisted any suggestion that they were servants subject to the command of a sovereign public.

New, more centralized organizations, a new stress upon professional stature, and a new middle-class audience affected many fields of the performing arts besides the "legitimate" theater, noncommercial as well as commercial. Their dynamics are perhaps most clearly expressed in the establishment of the symphony orchestra and the rise of the conductor.

Ultimately, the American symphony orchestra achieved international preeminence, but initially its situation was anything but secure. In the United States, as in the leading capitals of Europe, in the early nineteenth century, most classical music concerts presented highly varied and often quite lengthy programs to attract an audience and mollify donors. Music historians have recounted how the typical work to appear on a program in mid-nineteenth-century America was a rousing battle piece such as Kotzwara's *Battle of Prague*, or else a lively dance number such as *The Skinners' Quickstep*, *The Fireman's Quadrille* (accompanied by firemen dancing in full uniform and extinguishing a simulated fire onstage), or *The Railroad Galop* (which in one performance included a toy locomotive running onstage to the music). They have further noted how such light works and spectacular effects were frequently leavened by vocal interludes. To place such practices in context, however, one should remember that in London, Paris, and Vienna at the same time popular-music concerts considerably outnumbered performances of classical music. Moreover, when the greatest exponent of orchestral music in France, Hector Berlioz, introduced his demanding symphony *Harold in Italy* (1834) to Parisian audiences, he felt obliged to include a concert overture, two songs for soprano and orchestra, an operatic trio, a fantasy for piano and orchestra, and an excerpt from another symphony. In Europe as well as in America, most orchestras lacked a single permanent music director and held only one rehearsal for each concert. The result was, by later standards, ragged and inept performances. (A listener at London's Covent Garden in 1833 remarked that the orchestra was worst on Saturday night, because the musicians were paid that day and promptly got drunk.) Although orchestras in New York, Boston, and other cities lagged behind their European counterparts in certain respects, what has often been mistaken for American provincialism was in fact part of a common cultural condition. So, too, were the broad outlines of the transformation that followed, in which orchestras gained more stable financial footing, a more professional character and firmer management, and more segmented, disciplined, and passive audiences, dominated by members of the bourgeois elite (in Europe allied with the nobility).[36]

Where American symphonic orchestras most differed from their counterparts abroad was in institutional structure. On the European continent, concert orchestras were generally based in opera houses. Although some precedents for orchestral independence existed in England, the permanent resident symphony orchestra, with musical direction determined by a single conductor and financial authority vested in a corporate board of laymen, was a distinctively American invention. Like most inventions, it was not perfected in a flash. Rather, it took shape gradually over the course of the nineteenth century, the collaborative effort of various conductors and a wealthy business elite eager to establish its authority over the most prestigious institutions of cultural refinement.[37]

The history of the United States' first sustained symphonic orchestra, the New York Philharmonic Society, traces this process. When a group of musicians led by the visionary American violinist, conductor, and composer Ureli Corelli Hill founded the society in 1842, it was as a self-governing, cooperative body whose members elected and paid the conductor and librarian, and distributed the profits of their brief season equally. The Philharmonic Society was an avocation for its members, not a full-time position. In its first season it offered only three concerts, the next year, four, and until the very end of the century never gave more than six, in addition to public rehearsals. Gradually, however, it accepted a nonplaying associate member as president, engaged prominent soloists, and attracted wealthy supporters, for whom classical musical performances meant cultural leadership and prestige. The lifelong musical enthusiast George Templeton Strong, then a young lawyer, described the audience at the opening of the 1843 season at the Apollo Rooms as "all the aristocracy and 'gig respectability' and wealth and beauty and fashion of the city." Thirteen years later, at the opening concert at the Academy of Music, Strong marveled: "A great change from the old scene in the Apollo rooms and not wholly for the better. Nine-tenths of this assemblage cared nothing for Beethoven's music and chattered and looked about and wished it was over." To accommodate the growing appetite for symphonic music among a determined new aristocracy of culture, in 1886 the Philharmonic traveled farther uptown to the prestigious but cavernous Metropolitan Opera House (the largest in the world at that time) and finally, in 1892, to the acoustically superior Carnegie Hall. By the 1880s the Philharmonic had won a loyal group of affluent subscribers both for its Saturday evening performances and—especially popular with "Society ladies"—the Friday afternoon concerts once known as public rehearsals. At this same time its presidency also passed from prosperous music lovers such as George Templeton Strong to great corporate financiers: first the international banker Joseph W. Drexel, next corporation lawyer and philanthropist E. Francis Hyde, and, finally, in 1901, the richest man in the world, the great industrial magnate Andrew Carnegie. Yet so long as the society resisted surrendering its cooperative, democratic character to various moguls (including Carnegie, J. P. Morgan, and Joseph Pulitzer) who pressed for control by a board of trustees, it found itself overshadowed by other professional symphony orchestras that had submitted to the authority of an individual or board.[38]

In 1881 the banker Henry Lee Higginson single-handedly created the Boston Symphony Orchestra, the first permanent, full-time, fully endowed symphonic orchestra in the United States, in what a contemporary called "a *coup-d'état*, with no pretence of any *plebiscite*." It was a magnificent but dictatorial gift to the city of Boston. Higginson hired the conductor, controlled the players, supported his conductors' occasionally unpopular programs, provided his orchestra with its own concert hall, and absorbed the deficits.[39]

Ten years later, a group of wealthy Chicago businessmen established the Chicago Symphony Orchestra and initiated a corporate model of control that would soon become typical in New York and across the country. Rather than mirroring the tastes of their audiences, symphonic orchestras and allied cultural institutions sought to mold them, to embody a standard of excellence that contained an implicit class bias and led to decisive cultural realignments. To lead the Chicago Symphony in this endeavor, the trustees rallied behind a conductor for whom the cause of the symphony orchestra was a religious mission, Theodore Thomas.

The Conductor as Master

The campaign to establish professional symphony orchestras with a classical and modern repertoire and to instruct the audience in how to listen properly was waged by a host of figures in the postbellum era, but preeminently by Thomas. The story of his career dramatically captures the changing terms of American musical culture from an eclectic semi-amateurism in which audiences expressed themselves relatively freely to a disciplined professionalism in which the conductor was master. Born in northern Germany in 1835, Thomas came to New York at age ten with his family. He early plunged into the turbulent musical waters that he would later seek to channel and purify. As a youth he played the violin at dances, weddings, theaters, and even saloons, where he would pass his hat for tips. Before he was fourteen, he toured the South on his own, billing himself as "Master T. T.," taking tickets at the door, then racing backstage to change his clothes and give a concert. He played in the orchestra for Jenny Lind's concerts in New York under Barnum's auspices in 1850–51 and, as yet only seventeen years old, with Louis Antoine Jullien during the French conductor's New York appearances in 1853. Jullien was an ebullient showman and dandy, who delighted audiences with his rapturous concerts. His programs ranged from waltzes, polkas, and quadrilles—the extravagant *Fireman's Quadrille* was his conception—to symphonies by Mendelssohn and Beethoven. For the last he donned fresh white kid gloves from a silver tray and used a jeweled baton; and after

48. Theodore Thomas.

each piece he sank languorously into a gilded red-velvet throne. "The musical charlatan of all ages," Thomas would later call him; but he gave Thomas his first glimpse of what a full-scale symphony orchestra might be.[40] In the next few years Thomas became a member of the Philharmonic Society of New York, formed with pianist William Mason an acclaimed chamber music group, appeared as a violin soloist in concerts with touring virtuosos such as the pianist-composer Sigismond Thalberg (whose "matinées musicales" were billed as for "ladies of the first families of the city"),[41] and served as a member of the opera orchestra at New York's Academy of Music. He began his conducting career in 1860 at age twenty-five and worked with various orchestras for the next thirty years, much of the time concurrently conducting the New York Philharmonic, the Brooklyn Philharmonic Society, and his own full-time Theodore Thomas Orchestra, principally in New York, when not on arduous winter tours. During most of this period Thomas teetered on the brink of financial ruin, as he endeavored to carry his orchestra's expenses himself. Nonetheless, he spurned an offer by Barnum to tour under the great showman's management like, Thomas feared, some cultural freak.[42] At last a group of Chicago philanthropists offered him that for which he had waited in vain in New York: a permanent symphony orchestra whose expenses would be guaranteed. He would remain conductor of the newly established Chicago Symphony Orchestra from 1891 until his death in 1905.

One of the most distinguished conductors of the period, Thomas was also an imposing figure, "born to command."[43] Though he measured under five and a half feet, onstage he gave the impression of a giant. He acted as a stern disciplinarian and inspirer of both his orchestras and his audiences in the rigor necessary to the performance of a symphony, which was for him a religious experience. He brought his musicians from a motley assemblage of semiautonomous players to a new level of professional training, thorough preparation, and disciplined performance. He steadfastly insisted upon high standards of conduct, appearance, and propriety from his players. Restrained in his own movements as conductor, Thomas bent every effort toward a harmonious sound and orderly appearance among members of his orchestra. He introduced uniform bowing in his string sections, motivated first, no doubt, by the desire to achieve smoother phrasing, but also, one suspects, because it contributed to the orderly ensemble he was attempting to forge.[44] All preparations, including tuning, were to be completed before his players set foot onstage. Once facing the audience, they were allowed no talking, sprawling in their chairs, or any other act that might draw adverse attention.[45] Thomas placed himself under extraordinary standards of professional commitment. Priding himself on never missing a concert, he insisted on going forward with a performance even when it meant not attending the funeral of his eldest son. "I have no right to make the public mourn with me," he explained.[46] Private emotions were to be kept strictly separate from public conduct and duties.

Most demanding of himself and secondarily of his players, Thomas also insisted upon disciplined restraint on the part of his audience.[47] Although he appears never to have lost his temper in public and was in many respects the model of a musical gentleman, throughout his career as a conductor he was known for ironic rebukes of restive and noisy listeners. An early instance occurred during one of Thomas's popular summer concerts in New York's Central Park Garden, directly across from the park at Fifty-ninth

Street and Seventh Avenue. The Garden attracted visitors with its informal air of a beer hall, where they could buy drinks and ices, and men could enjoy their cigars, though it also included a music hall proper. Nonetheless, Thomas valiantly used these concerts to educate the public in orchestral music, and he demanded listeners' close attention. One evening a young man in a front seat prattled heedlessly through the second movement of Beethoven's Eighth Symphony, then noisily struck several matches in an effort to light his cigar. Exasperated, Thomas stopped the orchestra, put down his baton, and turned to the offender with "one of his sweetest and most cynical smiles," saying, " 'Go on, sir! Don't mind us! We can all wait until you light your cigar!' " The cigar was not lit, and the man remained silent the rest of the evening.[48]

Thomas was equally willing to challenge the audience as a whole. In 1867, during the first performance of Liszt's *Mephisto Waltz* at the new Steinway Hall in New York City, Thomas's orchestra had not played long before the audience responded to the piece's unconventionality by exercising its traditional prerogative with a ragged chorus of hisses, howls, and whistles. Twice Thomas stopped the music until calm resumed, and began anew. Upon the third outburst, he faced the audience, held his watch in his hand, and announced:

> I will give you five minutes to leave the hall. Then we shall play this waltz from the beginning to the end. Whoever wishes to listen without making a noise may do so. I ask all others to go out. I will carry out my purpose if I have to stand here until two o'clock in the morning. I have plenty of time.

The audience reportedly submitted to Thomas's assertion of authority and made no further disturbance.[49]

Thomas continued to challenge audience demands to dictate the terms of performances. He disliked and resisted the giving of encores in the fashion of the day—repetitions of pieces in response to the cries of the audience. Such demands, he believed, were "greedy and in bad taste," diminishing the effect of the first rendition, prolonging and disrupting the program, and often pushing tired musicians, who might then produce less than their best. When the audience pressed its demand, he sometimes calmly sat down among the members of the orchestra, "as much as to say, 'Now

clap away till you are tired, and I'll wait here till you get through.' "
In one such battle, an audience of nine thousand clamored for an
encore and "roared and stamped, and drowned him out every time
he attempted to go on with the next number." At last Thomas
called for his trumpets and drowned out the audience in return.
An admiring reporter concluded, "Thomas is always master of the
situation."[50]

Thomas held similarly uncompromising views about latecomers,
who, he contended, rudely disrupted and thoughtlesly disturbed
the audience, players, and conductor alike. He was especially ad-
amant when they disturbed what he regarded as the holy of holies:
the playing of a Beethoven symphony; and he took to distributing
appeals for punctuality to ticketholders, then locked the doors until
the symphony was completed.[51]

Above all, Thomas came to embody the belief that the best
symphonic music demanded the most cultivated sensibilities of
players and listeners alike, the conductor most of all. In this sense,
the cause of musical manners and morality were one. Central to
his "philharmonic creed," Thomas declared, was "to endeavor always to form a refined musical taste among the people by the
intelligent selection of music; to give . . . only standard works, both
of the new and old masters, and to be thus conservative and not
given to experimenting with the new musical sensations of the
hour." In this view, the concert hall was an art museum dedicated
to the most demanding standards of connoisseurship, where only
the greatest authenticated works should be displayed. Little wonder, then, that he guarded its doors so carefully. Just as advisers
on domestic furnishings declared that the parlor expressed the culture of a family, so Thomas believed that "a symphonic orchestra
shows the culture of a community. . . . The master works of
instrumental music are the language of the soul and express more
than those of any other art. Light music, 'popular' so called, is the
sensual side of the art and has more or less devil in it.' " Although
Thomas strove to bring "good music" to a variety of listeners, he
concluded, in the words of his wife, Rose Fay Thomas, that "neither
children nor what are called 'wage-workers' were sufficiently advanced intellectually to be able to appreciate the class of music
which was his specialty." As for himself, he demanded priestlike
purity. Early in his career as a conductor, a friend began an off-
color story. Thomas broke in as soon as he realized its character.

"You must not tell me stories like that," he protested. ". . . Suppose you tell me this story and to-night when I am about to conduct some work of beauty and purity I catch sight of your face in the audience. Do you not see that involuntarily my mental state is distorted from the idea of purity I ought to have, and it will not be possible for me to give to that composition the interpretation of perfect purity that it demands?" Although Thomas began his career playing in theaters and saloons, he ended it endeavoring to make the concert hall a shrine.[52]

Enforcing Audience Restraint

Thomas's long struggle in the cause of artistic authority and decorum could not have succeeded alone. Victory depended upon repeated assaults by the combined forces of refinement fighting on a number of fronts until offenders either relented or were driven from the field. An important strategic weapon in these battles was written admonitions to the audience. As early as the mid-1850s the New York Philharmonic Society distributed printed appeals for silence to its listeners, and in its 1857 annual report the governing board scolded noisy patrons at length, declaring in part:

> We must, necessarily, insist upon musical *good manners*. The inattention and heedless talking and disturbance of but a limited number of our audience are providing a serious annoyance at our Philharmonic performances. . . . If each little neighborhood would take care of itself, and promptly frown down the few chance disturbers of its pleasure, perfect order would soon be secured. . . . In foreign audiences it is ever effectually done.[53]

Yet the next year, 1858, found George Templeton Strong grumbling in his diary, "Spent half an hour last night at the Philharmonic concert, crowded and garrulous, like a square mile of tropical forest with its flocks of squalling paroquets and troops of chattering monkeys."[54] Only by the early 1870s did Strong sense that "the vile habit of talking and giggling" as well as marching in late during a concert had all declined, and attributed "the improvement . . . to our daring handbills requesting silence and to the printed notices that have been delivered with our programmes."[55]

In the years after the Civil War other institutions similarly endeavored, in Strong's phrase, to teach "audiences good manners."[56] A typical note on the program of Theodore Thomas's summer concerts in New York's Central Park Garden in the mid-1870s ran: "The audience is requested to abstain from loud talking during the performance of the music. Owing to the length of the Programmes, encores of Overtures and other long pieces cannot be complied with."[57] An 1877 program of the Mendelssohn Glee Club at the recently opened Chickering Hall in New York similarly requested no talking during the music, "complaints having been made of annoyance from this cause on former occasions." It also asked those who wished to leave early to do so between selections rather than during a piece.[58] By the 1883–84 season, the Boston Symphony Orchestra began listing the time the concert would end and instructed those departing beforehand to leave at a specified point in the program.[59] In a similar spirit, an 1876 program note for a performance of *Julius Caesar* at Booth's Theatre in New York asked the audience "to courteously remain in their places until the fall of the curtain, that ALL may have an uninterrupted view of the grand finale to the play."[60]

These salvos against rudeness were not in the least confined to the realm of high culture. On the contrary, they were discharged most steadily in the playbills of minstrel theaters in the 1850s, '60s, and '70s. In the wake of the Astor Place riot, theaters of all kinds transformed the old male precinct of the pit into the orchestra or parterre, now expressly reserved for "ladies and children," and replaced the "guilty third tier" of old with the family circle. Managers opposed boisterous behavior of all sorts. "The performance will commence at the time advertised," one notice declared; "consequently it is not necessary for boys to whistle or stamp with their feet, which will not be allowed."[61] Other notices reminded men to take off their hats during the performance, and not to "keep time with their feet" or attempt to whistle along with the music. In a mordant tone that rivaled the rebukes of Theodore Thomas, one playbill declared: "The *unmusical* portion of the audience will please avoid loud talking or moving about during the rendition of any song, as it annoys the performers, and all who have a desire to hear."[62] Numerous playbills gave notice that due to "the extreme

49. *A Genteel Family Audience Leaving a Matinée* (1866). There are no signs of rowdies or prostitutes. At the extreme left, in a gesture of liberality a well-dressed patron extends a coin to a family of beggars, who are literally confined to the margins in this picture—as they are figuratively in the society it represents. At the extreme right, stabilizing the scene of middle-class pleasure, a police officer stands guard and another attendant salutes.

length of the Entertainment, and the peculiar arrangement of the Programme," audiences could no longer demand encores of particular acts.[63] Even as the split between genteel and popular entertainments broadened, similar demands were made upon their patrons. The tumultuous cheering—and booing—that male audiences had traditionally enjoyed were increasingly relegated to saloon entertainments, burlesque, boxing matches, and similar contests.[64]

How quickly these rising standards of audience restraint became generalized may be seen from the increased asperity of contemporary etiquette books. Admittedly, some antebellum writers on manners had enjoined readers to avoid distracting their neighbors or making a spectacle of themselves at public assemblies, but toward the turn of the century etiquette advisers grew emphatic upon the subject. They articulated norms that sharply forbade once common practices. For example, James Smiley declared in his *Modern Manners and Social Forms* of 1889:

> Perfect quiet should be maintained during the performance, and the attention should be fixed on the stage. To whisper or do anything during the entertainment to disturb or distract the attention of others, is rude in the extreme. It is proper to applaud, when pleased, as that encourages and gratifies the performer, but do not stamp with the feet—to clap the hand is much better. During the intermissions it is in order to converse in a low tone, but loud talk or laughter, or displays of affection or anything to arrest the attention of others, is always in bad taste in any public place. Chewing gum, eating peanuts or anything of that kind, is very vulgar.
>
> To impudently stare at another through an opera glass is ill-bred, but a general survey of the house is proper.[65]

Several writers on etiquette specifically endorsed Theodore Thomas's reproofs of disruptive concertgoers.[66] What had earlier been customary audience behavior was now branded as a crime against decent society and against art. Etiquette advisers denounced disrupters as "thieves and robbers" who cheated performers and spectators alike,[67] persons of such monumental callousness as perhaps "to be beyond anything but the persuasion of force."[68]

Advisers did not go so far as to say readers should throttle these pleasure-robbers, but some did provide specific tactics to gain compliance with the stricter standard of audience restraint. For example, a 1913 manual spoke to the problem of how to deal with a noisy neighbor at a musical entertainment. Rather than protesting harshly, the writer suggested a rising scale of decorous appeals, beginning with a slight hushing sound. If that hint failed, then she recommended one

> lean toward the offender and say in a polite tone: *"My attention is very easily distracted by little noises, and I am going to ask you as a favor not to talk (or beat time, or rustle your programme) while the orchestra is playing."*

As a final recourse, one might appeal to an usher.[69]

The special responsibilities of audiences at classical-music concerts and operas were further discussed in magazines and newspapers in the late nineteenth century. Like the executioner Koko in *The Mikado*, each writer had his little lists of social offenders who never would be missed. The American pianist and lecturer Edward Baxter Perry, for example, itemized, among others, fashionably late arrivals and restless bolters, program-rattlers and letter-writers, idlers and nappers, talkers and whisperers of all sorts, whose heedless remarks ranged from the irrelevant ("Miss Jenks has a grey one with pink flowers") to the inane ("What a delicious melody!"). Perry insisted, "Silence is to music what light is to painting—the first absolutely essential condition, upon which all its effects and impressions depend. . . . The slightest noise, even involuntarily produced . . . blurs the outline of the work, like a shadow falling across a picture."[70]

Especially noteworthy was the way in which these standards were held up to the rich, whose presence at the opera was especially conspicuous. The opera offered an attractive forum to convert economic into cultural capital, since it combined the greatest opportunities for social display with the greatest pretensions to social and cultural exclusivity. Once broadly popular, opera came progressively under the sway of the wealthy elite in the course of the nineteenth century as a variety of barriers—including high prices, formal dress, more exacting codes of behavior, and performances in foreign languages—discouraged a broader public. Appearing in boxes visible to thousands of onlookers, occupants could feel like the Parisian banker who exulted, "All lorgnettes are turned on me and I receive an almost royal ovation." Yet the once harmonious activities of listening and socializing came increasingly into conflict. While boxholders wanted the houselights to remain on during the performance, as had traditionally been the case both in Europe and the United States, earnest musical idealists demanded they be turned down. Subscribers to boxes found their very visibility invited censure when they clearly devoted themselves to their own private gratification at the expense of the performance. Commentators complained boxholders often arrived late, left early, and chattered incessantly betweentimes. On one occasion a prominent society matron held a dinner party in her box during a performance of the Metropolitan Opera—and was publicly identified in *The New York Times*. The illustrator Charles Dana Gibson suggested, tongue in cheek, that installing plate-glass fronts to the boxes might satisfy everyone, for then occupants could be seen but not heard. With less good humor, George William Curtis, editor of "The Easy Chair" column for *Harper's Monthly* and a tireless guardian of civic values, repeatedly castigated noisy boxholders as selfish barbarians, with manners fit only for the frontier saloons of Poker Flat and Dead Man's Gulch, where, he insinuated, the family money was made. Still, a small minority rose in their defense, contending their patronage made opera possible and placed others in their debt. But most, like Curtis, would not be bought off. Together with their European counterparts, American critics generally looked balefully upon the social aspects of concert attendance unless they directly contributed to the most serious musical purposes. But what recourse did the serious listener have? Personal appeals, Curtis noted, had failed. Hissing might escalate into a war of rebukes. He applauded the example of Theodore Thomas in stopping his orchestra when, as Thomas put it, he "feared the music interfered with the conversation," and Curtis suggested opera singers might do the same. Alternatively, the offended portion of the audience might stare *en masse* at disrupters. Curtis wrestled with the difficulties that befell so many warriors in the cause of civility: How might one combat rudeness without capitulating to its methods? What leverage might the mannered use against the moneyed? One suspects part of the appeal Thomas and other commanding conductors held was that they uniquely combined musical and moral authority and were able, in Curtis's words, to do for the audience "what it has not the nerve to do for itself"—to quell disrupters and rescue meeker souls from another dilemma of civility and rudeness.[71]

Questions of enforcement apart, a few missionaries of refinement sought to raise standards of disciplined attention to new heights, curtailing or even eliminating the audience's last vestige of expressive display in applause. Within the theological vacuum of the late nineteenth century, "high art" in general and music especially were endowed with religious significance. Composers and performers were anointed as high priests, and the concert hall and opera house consecrated as churches. Symphonies and some operas (Wagner's in particular) fulfilled many listeners' longing for intense spiritual and emotional drama while sparing them questions of belief and doctrine. The analogy of a church (a genteel liberal Protestant church, at any rate) also appealed to those who wished to claim for Art a sanctified realm where one would never think of giggling, chattering, or disturbing one's neighbor. Or of applauding at all, for did one applaud in church, commentators asked rhetorically. Was it then any more appropriate in the concert hall or opera house?[72]

In the cause of the sacralization of Art and more rigorous discipline on the part of the audience, critics repeatedly invoked the pronouncements of Richard Wagner. They endorsed Wagner's dictum that to applaud singers at the end of an aria or even at the end of an act destroyed the illusion of the performance. Such curtain calls often created ludicrous contradictions in the drama, as when the dead Siegfried and Brünnhilde appeared bowing and smiling before the audience.[73]

The conduct of Wagner's own Festspielhaus (1876) by his widow and disciples in the small Bavarian town of Bayreuth offered a striking alternative to these abuses. American tourists of such varied orientations as George Gladden, son of the liberal theologian Washington Gladden and a journalist earnestly bent on a musical pilgrimage, and Mark Twain, who irreverently observed that Wagner's music is better than it sounds, agreed that what was in some respects most remarkable was not the performances but the demeanor of the audience. Operagoers at Wagner's temple assembled quietly and unostentatiously in a severely plain auditorium. Just before the overture its doors were sternly closed and the house plunged into darkness. A "misguided person nearly attempts to whisper," Gladden reported, but "is instantly hissed into silence."

The intensity of the audience's concentration profoundly struck them both. Gladden marveled, "You sit there for perhaps two hours in silence which is never broken except by the voices from the stage and the hidden orchestra. [From early in his career Wagner ridiculed those who enjoyed "*looking* at the music instead of listening to it."] No matter what your emotions are, you must not betray them by any demonstration whatever." Bodily discipline and emotional control here paid enormous spiritual dividends.[74]

Though reserving a touch of irony, Mark Twain concurred. He was familiar with the audience at New York's Metropolitan Opera who "sit in a glare, and wear their showiest harness; they hum airs, they squeak fans, they titter, and they gabble all the time." Bayreuth's audience was a revelation:

> Absolute attention and petrified retention to the end of an act of the attitude assumed at the beginning of it. You detect no movement in the solid mass of heads and shoulders. You seem to sit with the dead in the gloom of a tomb. You know that they are being stirred to their profoundest depths; that there are times when they want to rise and wave handkerchiefs and shout their approbation, and times when tears are running down their faces, and it would be a relief to free their pent emotions in sobs or screams; yet you hear not one utterance till the curtain swings together and the closing strains have slowly faded out and died.

Mark Twain, however, noted that thunderous applause did indeed come at the end. Gladden insisted he heard none whatever. Applause, he declared, was "not only unnecessary but intolerable" at Bayreuth. "Why, then," he asked, "is it necessary or even excusable elsewhere?" At "the shrine of St. Wagner," as Mark Twain called it, the *Meister*'s insistence that music was an individual, even an internal experience, was easily converted to genteel Victorian ends. The strict bodily control of intense emotion by the audience was what so impressed Gladden and both moved and unnerved Mark Twain. The duty of these worshippers was to *receive* communion, to listen intently and to mask feeling. The public as a united body of active participants had no place in the temple of Art.[75]

Refinement and the Cultivation of Spectacle

In both genteel and popular forms of entertainment in the second half of the nineteenth century, concern with refinement transformed the very setting in which spectators met. As audiences ceded much of their authority and expressiveness to conductors, managers, masters of ceremony, and performers, they were repaid by more lavish surroundings. New concert halls, opera houses, auditoriums, and theaters proliferated in the late nineteenth and early twentieth centuries, many of them on an unprecedented scale of monumental grandeur. Their construction sprang from the desire to attract and segment new audiences for the performing arts, while their often shifting uses reflected the fluidity of American artistic and cultural life.

New York's Metropolitan Opera House offers one case in point. It originated not from artistic reverence so much as social rivalry. Wealthy New York families (including the Roosevelts, Astors, Goelets, Morgans, and Vanderbilts) who desired the prestige of a box at the opera had swelled far beyond the capacities of the Academy of Music. Though the older Knickerbocker elite that dominated the Academy was willing to add an additional twenty-six boxes to the existing thirty in order to seat the newcomers, this compromise was rejected and operatic war declared. In 1883 the socially disgruntled clans built the Metropolitan with a seating capacity of over 3,600 and, more to the point, a full three tiers of boxes. The backers of the Metropolitan won this cultural competition. "I cannot fight Wall Street," the Academy of Music's manager James H. Mapleson declared; and after 1888 the Academy was given over first to vaudeville and later to the movies before it was demolished in 1926.

But the victory came at a price. The Metropolitan was designed around its boxes in ways that created intractable difficulties in staging, acoustics, and visibility in the balcony and family circles. After the first performance, the music critic Henry T. Finck prophetically declared, "From an artistic and musical point of view, the large number of boxes . . . is a decided mistake," adding with some asperity that since "the house was built avowedly for social purposes rather than artistic it is useless to complain about this or about the fact that the opportunity was not taken to make of the building itself an architectural monument of which the city might be proud."

Furthermore, the *nouveaux riches* overestimated their ability to fill the boxes. The top tier boxes were eliminated as early as 1884, and when the auditorium was further redesigned in 1893 after a fire, the baignoire boxes were also replaced with less expensive seats.[76]

The very wealthy similarly overextended themselves in the building of Madison Square Garden, which opened in 1890. Gorgeously designed by Stanford White in an eclectic idiom, part northern Italian and part Spanish, with a Giralda-inspired tower three hundred feet high capped by Saint-Gaudens's nude Diana, the Garden was an elegant palace of pleasure. It was intended as a playground for the horse shows and other entertainments of New York's cultural and financial elite, and in addition to its vast amphitheater, it included another theater, roof garden, restaurant, and various shops. But insufficient returns soon forced the management to host more popular entertainments and spectacles calculated to appeal to a broader middle-class audience desirous of splendor.[77]

The preference for lavish spectacle rather than more intimate involvement, so evident in these and numerous other auditoriums and theaters of the period, decisively transformed a variety of forms of entertainment designed to reach a broad, predominantly middle-class family audience. Where a popular impresario such as P. T. Barnum had earlier encouraged the active participation of audiences in his museum displays, his circus pageants in the later nineteenth century overawed passive spectators with their profusion of light and color, music and drama, pomp and splendor.[78] Similarly, in the late 1870s the leading minstrel entrepreneur, J. H. Haverly, transformed the minstrel show into a new kind of extravaganza, with his "United Mastodon Minstrels." Jettisoning the low comedy and raucous vulgarity that had been an essential element of minstrelsy from its beginnings in the 1840s, Haverly staged lavish production numbers that paid homage to the world of genteel art, music, and dance.[79]

But perhaps the most significant effort to offer appealing and morally inoffensive entertainment was the emergence of vaudeville in the 1880s and '90s. Vaudeville borrowed heavily from older forms of amusement, including the dime museum, the circus, and especially the variety show, but placed them in prestigious new surroundings. In New York and many other cities, variety's slapstick comics, racy songs, and broad skits played largely to working-class men who drank, smoked, and caroused in seedy "concert saloons" and music halls. In Boston, where theatrical performances of any kind in taverns were prohibited and variety shows had melded into dime museums, managers struggled to drum up interest in oddities such as Jo-Jo the dog-faced boy, the three-headed songstress, legless acrobats, and tattooed men. Vaudeville downplayed freaks and cleaned up variety acts to offer a series of fast-paced, morally inoffensive attractions, often in "continuous performance" throughout the day. A typical bill might include an opening animal act, a comic skit, a juggler or magician, a mime, an acrobatic exhibition, a singer, a dancing couple, and a one-act play. Instead of the closing burlesque piece staged by the entire troupe that had been a staple of variety shows, vaudeville reflected the desire for more segmented spectacles in a series of independent acts.

The foremost early vaudeville managers, Tony Pastor, Benjamin Franklin Keith, and Edward F. Albee, adopted the elegant decor and restrained etiquette of leading theaters and concert halls as potent additional symbols of refinement. They shrewdly sensed the allure of such trappings among the great bulk of the middle-class and wealthier working-class families who could no longer afford routinely to attend the "legitimate" theater and light opera dominated by the bourgeois elite. B. F. Keith later recalled, "In the early days of my business career, many worthy but mistaken people ridiculed the idea of a clean and respectable house and entertainment being conducted at the then price of admission (only ten cents), but I successfully demonstrated that such a thing was possible." In 1894 Keith opened the New Theatre in Boston, the first vaudeville "palace," with a richly ornamented, arched gateway, marble ticket booths with gold domes, velvet carpets, brocaded walls, and plush seats. Members of the audience now sat farther from the stage, in a cooler, more passive relationship to the entertainments.[80]

Keith and Albee together amassed an empire of theaters, twenty-nine at the time of Keith's death in 1914, including six in Manhattan, another six in Brooklyn, and two each in Boston, Jersey City, Philadelphia, and Cleveland. These theaters became known among vaudevillians as "the Sunday-school Circuit" for their insistence upon inoffensive performance. Contracts warned that management demanded "a high plane of respectability and moral cleanliness," and backstage notices banned such words as "Liar, Slob, Son-of-a-Gun, Devil, Sucker, Damn," as well as "any reference to questionable streets, resorts, localities, and bar-rooms," any double entendres, suggestive gestures, or indecent costumes.[81]

Turning their attention to the audience, Keith and Albee determinedly combated the rowdies and the heedless who threatened their success. Opening a theater in a "disreputable" neighborhood in Philadelphia, Albee marshaled the forces of middle-class refinement against the guerrilla fighters of male working-class culture. He secured a policeman to pace reassuringly outside the theater. When locals responded by spitting tobacco juice from windows on his customers, Albee hired another man to mop the streets. Clad in a white uniform, the sweeper himself proved an irresistible target. Rowdies carried the battle against gentility into the theater itself. From their traditional fortress in the gallery, they hooted at the stage acts, shouted obscenities at female performers, and did their best to break up the show. Albee fought back. He stationed bouncers in the gallery to throw disrupters out and lectured the audience at intermissions, with the rebuke, "Our theaters are for women and children and, we had hoped, gentlemen."[82]

More innocent offenders were admonished with silent courtesy. Uniformed attendants carried a variety of printed requests to distribute to errant spectators, such as:

Gentlemen will kindly avoid the stamping of feet and pounding of canes on the floor, and greatly oblige the Management. All applause is best shown by clapping of hands.

And:

Please don't talk during acts, as it annoys those about you, and prevents a perfect hearing of the entertainment.
                                                    The Management.

In accordance with genteel standards of refinement, there was even a card to correct those who laughed too loudly.[83]

The class implications of these efforts are unmistakable. Vaudeville sought to attract a diverse audience but demanded that patrons abide by the rules of middle-class gentility, now generalized as a norm of public conduct for all. From the perspective of middle-class patrons, working-class boisterousness appeared coarse and offensive at best, and potentially dangerous. Sensitive to these concerns, vaudeville managers regarded overly demonstrative behavior, whether in approval or in disapproval, as bad for business. But for members of the working class, this enforced gentility meant not only the adoption of norms of behavior that changed their relationship to the performance, but a kind of gag rule that reduced their role in a powerful arena of cultural expression to their relatively weak economic standing at the box office. Working-class customers were caught in a dilemma. To continue to cheer, boo, and call to one another from the gallery meant to stigmatize themselves as "uncivilized" boors unfit to associate with respectable families. To behave themselves meant to accede to their own marginalization.

Nonetheless, in the decades surrounding the turn of the century there still remained theaters controlled by working-class immigrants that retained the boisterous informality and conviviality that had characterized antebellum American theaters generally. The Yiddish theater of New York's Lower East Side in particular aroused intense, even fanatical involvement. Some men and women who earned only ten dollars a week in the sweatshops reportedly spent half of it on tickets, and the leading actors attracted idolatrous followers in life and gigantic funeral processions after their deaths. Like the popular theater of antebellum America, the Yiddish stage heavily emphasized melodrama and at times included jigs and songs as postludes. Yiddish theater borrowed even more freely from a variety of classical authors and traditions, particularly Shakespeare, to create stirring plays such as *The Jewish King Lear* and *The Rabbinical Student (Hamlet)*. As at the antebellum theater, too, the audience threw itself into the action, cheering wildly, crying openly, often demanding that a song be instantly repeated. Both habitués and raw newcomers could be passionately engaged. A half century earlier, Edwin Forrest's stirring portrayal of the villainous Iago in *Othello* incited a canal boatman to cry out, "You damned-lying scoundrel, I would like to get hold of you after the show and wring your infernal neck." So another actor of towering virtuosity, Jacob Adler, in the title role of *The Jewish King Lear*, stirred a man to rush down the aisle, shouting, "To hell with your stingy daughter, Yankl! She has a stone, not a heart. Spit on her, Yankl, and come home with me. My yidene [Jewish wife] will feed you. Come, Yankl, may she choke, that rotten daughter of yours."[84]

Non-Jewish, middle-class writers at the turn of the century were fascinated by the existence of such a vital theater culture untouched by the sweeping tide of refinement. In the Yiddish theater the critic Hutchins Hapgood wondrously contemplated, not an audience of isolated spectators, but an expressive, enthusiastic community of working-class men and women moved to laughter and tears by the actors. "Conversation during the play is received with strenuous hisses," he noted, "but the falling of the curtain is the signal for groups of friends to get together and gossip about the play or the affairs of the week."[85] In a more self-conscious act of aesthetic slumming, the theater critic John Corbin reported on the Italian and Yiddish theaters on New York's Lower East Side. His anti-Semitism drove him to prefer the Italian in every respect; even the Jewish babies in their mothers' arms, he complained, were far noisier than the politely nursing Italian ones. Yet in both theaters he discovered an intense commitment to art that he frankly envied. The entire audience responded passionately to the drama, laughing, murmuring, making brief remarks to neighbors, shouting with delight at the climaxes, and at the end of each act yelling "at the top of their lungs."[86] With all the gains of disciplined spectatorship, what had been lost?

The Rise of the Movies

Even as Hapgood and Corbin wrote, immigrant theater was being challenged from a different quarter. Increasingly, beginning in the 1890s, new forms of commercial entertainment would develop to tap the market of the rising middle-class, working-class, and ethnic populations. One of these, the amusement park, attracted visitors by breaking down many of the barriers that separated spectators from participants, by creating an atmosphere of festive activity in which customers could shed their workaday roles and self-consciousness.[87] But for the purposes of this discussion, the most important and certainly most widely attended new amusement, one that marks the key transition from live to recorded performance, was the movies.

Even in the dynamic context of American entertainment at the turn of the century, movies achieved a stunning rise in popularity. Beginning in "nickelodeons" in converted dance halls, shops, and restaurants in the 1890s, movies swiftly became the favorite commercial entertainment of urban working-class and immigrant populations in America. By 1910 there were ten thousand nickelodeons attracting some twenty-six million Americans every week. These included both women and children, mostly from the working class, as well as blue-collar men, even those who worked the longest days for scant wages.[88] Not only did movie houses lure patrons from vaudeville, dime museums, and ethnic theaters; they tapped an entirely new urban audience. Their attractions were many, even beyond the excitement of fast-paced one-reelers. Nickelodeons offered low ticket prices (five or ten cents), continuous shows with few language barriers, open seating, and a relaxed standard of dress and behavior. Inside the theater, members of the audience cheered the show, gossiped with one another, ate their lunches, drank in the back rows, or used the intimate darkness for lovemaking.[89] Working-class patrons brought to the early movies their recreational traditions of sociability, conviviality, and informality.

This behavior greatly alarmed many middle-class moral custodians. They feared both physical and moral contamination in dirty and dark movie houses, where working-class people promiscuously assembled to fall under the emotional sway of flickering images. At a time when reformers were declaring that the problem of the twentieth century was the problem of the proper use of leisure,[90] they targeted the storefront movie house as a social menace and demanded municipal codes and boards of censorship to regulate them.

Movie producers, exhibitors, and theater managers cheerfully capitulated. Sensing the great profits to be won, they, too, wished to make movies safe—and attractive—for the middle-class family, as vaudeville managers had earlier. By the second decade of the twentieth century, many figures in the film industry were fast adopting the strategies that other live entertainments and performing arts had developed in the late nineteenth. Led by the great director D. W. Griffith, films developed from one-reelers to dramatic features that thrilled a middle-class clientele. In the tradition of vaudeville "palaces," movie managers created luxurious new theaters to give dignity to their entertainments. In addition to creating "palaces" of their own, movie theaters marked their cultural ascendancy by taking over some of the leading vaudeville theaters, "legitimate" stage theaters, and opera houses.[91]

50. "High Class Moving Pictures": An early effort to bring gentility to the movies.

The new movie theaters of the 1910s and '20s embodied an ideal of polite order and elegant refinement significantly different from the working-class nickelodeons. The luxurious furnishings, the scheduled features, the uniformed ushers, and the introduction of differentiated pricing—all structured the experience of moviegoing in new ways, making it a more controlled and privatized act. Although theater managers sought to achieve an air of pleasurable entertainment rather than of moral uplift, they imported both the trappings and the etiquette of artistic performance that had been established by elite institutions in the later nineteenth century, and generalized it for mass audiences in the twentieth. While the era of these movie palaces quickly passed, movie theaters continued to encourage restrained, disciplined spectatorship as a basic standard of decorum.[92]

The growing professionalization of the performing arts and entertainments and the organization of their audiences had ambiguous implications for American culture in the twentieth century. The gains were enormous and incontestable. Demanding discipline and restraint from both performers and audience made new standards of artistic excellence possible. It also provided a basis for a more intense collaboration between the two, perhaps even a moment of spiritual communion in which both were enlarged. Certainly this represented the ambition of a conductor such as Theodore Thomas, and, one suspects, phrased less loftily, it was the aim of many popular entertainers and managers as well.

At the same time, the division between performers and their audience, the loss of a communal and amateur spirit of participation in which working classes played a vital role, the cultivation of spectacle, and the emphasis upon decorous, disciplined, passive receptivity all too neatly dovetailed into the terms and strategies of the modern consumer culture. Audiences increasingly viewed performers as across a gulf, and one another as strangers. The experience of attending a performance became in many respects more controlled, inexpressive, carefully structured and managed—like much of the larger society. One risk was that, despite their best intentions, artists and entertainers might become products to be passively consumed, their performances reduced to fashionable purchases. Indeed, the processes of commodification did not stop there. During the late nineteenth and early twentieth centuries, managers of entertainment grew more sophisticated in targeting the particular audiences they most wanted to reach, and appealed to them, not as members of the general public, but as a particular market. As the twentieth century progressed, audiences themselves would increasingly be treated by entertainment and media entrepreneurs as commodities, to be identified, enticed, packaged, and delivered— to various clients from advertisers to politicians.[93]

Later generations would continue to wrestle with these tensions and contradictions. But by the early decades of the twentieth century the dominant categories for the organization of many of the leading performing arts and entertainments and the terms in which audiences approached them had all been firmly established.

Epilogue

"We still . . . ask ourselves, 'Who am I?' as if the question permitted a single, neat answer," the sociologist Arlie Russell Hochschild has recently observed. "We still search for a solid, predictable core of self even though the conditions for the existence of such a self have long since vanished."[1] Our discussion would suggest that these conditions were already highly unstable in the world of the urban middle classes in the nineteenth century. The increasingly exacting rules governing social conduct and personal expression represented efforts to defend that "solid, predictable core of self"; yet, paradoxically, such rules pursued a logic that led not toward unity but toward fragmentation. The spatial and social terrain of both the city at large and the middle-class home grew progressively segmented, and so, too, did the social and psychological terrain of the individual self. The tensions inherent in the effort to maintain bourgeois class and gender ideals constantly throbbed beneath the surface of both public and private life.

Early in the twentieth century, as the consumer culture entered a new phase extending far beyond the middle classes, these tensions intensified dramatically, and the social and psychological terrain has grown inestimably more fragmented ever since. Nineteenth-century popular advisers had attempted a balancing act between the requirements of a democratic polity and the demands for social distinction within an upwardly mobile urban middle class. They further sought an equilibrium between the productive values of self-denial and disciplined acts of consumption according to canons of approved "taste." They still aimed to assemble a self out of the virtues of "character" (intimately associated with the sturdy nouns *citizenship, duty, integrity, morals,* and *manners*) rather than those of "personality" (associated with the glittering adjectives *attractive, fascinating, magnetic, forceful*) that would soon come into vogue.[2] By the decades on either side of the turn of the century, however, the possibilities of mass production and the increased application of technology to leisure-time pursuits required the development of new systems of mass consumption for their fulfillment. Building upon earlier efforts, manufacturers, entrepreneurs, and advertisers offered an ever-widening array of products and pleasures from movies to automobiles, cigarettes to household appliances, designed for the multitude. This new economy and culture conferred greater importance as consumers on women, the working classes, and ethnic groups. Their qualified empowerment further undermined older social and cultural hierarchies. The class lines preserved by genteel authorities often blurred in customers' desires and commercial pastimes. In the process, genteel demands for moral and social restraint as the basis of civility were leavened by commercialized encouragements of gratification and self-indulgence. Class lines and social segmentation persisted, to be sure, but they would be redefined (and disguised) as sectors of national markets. The notion of a common public life based on shared civic values, already deeply eroded in the nineteenth century, further crumbled. As private lives were publicized, public life was privatized into market preferences. The "American Way of Life" became defined as one, not of vital political commitments, but of abundant commodity choices. And this proliferation of choices, with its attendant proliferation and fragmentation of needs, further undermined any notion of a stable, cohesive self.

In such a fluid cultural setting, it is hardly surprising that efforts to achieve a common code of public conduct—the dream that nineteenth-century advisers so vainly pursued—encountered even more frustration. From almost the beginning of the new century, social observers complained of a decay of manners and confusedly pointed in all directions in the search for causes (and villains): to the surge of new immigrants; to the vulgarity of the very rich; to the insolence of the working classes; to a decline in deference toward women; to women themselves aggressively entering the work force; to the conditions of urban life in general.[3] In such fashion they began a modern chorus of laments on the state of American manners that has continued to the present day. Successive generations of commentators have been no clearer in explaining the disarray of conventions of conduct, variously assigning blame to myriad factors including the First World War, Prohibition, jazz, the movies, the automobile, radio, the Depression, the Second World War, television, permissive child-rearing techniques, rock music, contraceptive pills, the Vietnam War, student radicalism, the women's movement, psychological therapies, and fast food. Viewing modern consumer culture piecemeal rather than as a whole, they seize upon symptoms and scapegoats.

All the while, new guides to self-improvement and social success (expanding from print to other media, including radio, television, and videotapes) have poured forth in ever-greater numbers. Their growth is yet another sign of the power and fragmentation of the consumer culture and the multiple social and individual divisions it encourages. For all the wailing over the death of manners, the production of etiquette books continued unabated from the extraordinarily popular guides by Lillian Eichler (1921) and Emily Post (1922) up to our own time. Contemporary etiquette writers from Leticia Baldrige and Charlotte Ford to "Miss Manners" (Judith Martin) wear, with varying degrees of earnestness and irony, the mantle of authority donned by their predecessors as they characteristically attempt balancing acts of their own between nods to democratic pieties and the desire for social distinction and protection of class privilege. Admittedly, some matters within the purview of nineteenth-century preceptors have shrunk, such as advice on managing household servants. But the gap has been more than filled by a flood of counsel on personal relationships of all kinds: parental, marital, and sexual, especially. Meanwhile, other strategists, urging the cultivation of manners, deportment, and emotional management as essential to success in social and business dealings alike, have further encouraged readers to regard their very personalities as commodities to be sold. A key book in this development, Dale Carnegie's stupendously popular *How to Win Friends and Influence People* (1936), preached a gospel of positive emotional management to disarm potential enemies. In response to mounting pressures of competition, current guides often coach readers in the development of a devastating emotional backhand as well, in order to "win through intimidation." Concurrently, as individuals have come to view their own bodies as commodities, other "experts" have sprung forward with programs for physical self-improvement through diet, exercise, dress, and grooming techniques—and, for dropouts, self-acceptance. Ironically, from yet another quarter a vast array of guides on psychic self-help and "self-fulfillment" promise aid in recovering the "authentic," "spontaneous" feelings that have been twisted out of shape by the demands of both work and personal life. Some contend that as etiquette has penetrated deeper into emotional life, these are the truest successors in the twentieth cen-

tury to etiquette books in the nineteenth.[4] Finally, advertising itself
has acquired a major role in shaping norms of conduct and feeling
as it has broadened its mission from describing a product's features
to associating it with the potential consumer's "lifestyle," hopes,
fears, desires, and fantasies.

Meanwhile, the larger challenges of civility in American urban
and public life generally persist—and while they are not solvable
simply by the achievement of a full and humane democratic social
order, one wonders how anything less can ever suffice.

Notes

To save space, nineteenth-century and early-twentieth-century etiquette books listed in the Selected Bibliography are cited in shortened form in the Notes.

Introduction

1. Alexis de Tocqueville, *Democracy in America*, ed. J. P. Mayer, trans. George Lawrence (Garden City, N.Y.: Doubleday/Anchor Books, 1969), 605–6.
2. Erving Goffman, "The Nature of Deference and Demeanor," in *Interaction Ritual* (Garden City, N.Y.: Doubleday/Anchor Books, 1967), 91.
3. See, e.g. Judith Martin, *Common Courtesy* (New York: Atheneum, 1985), 9.
4. Among the significant exceptions are two books that appeared after this one was well launched: Karen Halttunen's important and perceptive study *Confidence Men and Painted Women: A Study of Middle-Class Culture in America, 1830–1870* (New Haven: Yale University Press, 1982), and Lawrence W. Levine's brilliant *Highbrow/Lowbrow: The Emergence of Cultural Hierarchy in America* (Cambridge: Harvard University Press, 1988).
5. I take the phrase "anticipatory self" from Philip Fisher, *Hard Facts: Setting and Form in the American Novel* (New York: Oxford University Press, 1985), 157–62.

Chapter One: Manners before the Nineteenth Century

1. Norbert Elias, *The Civilizing Process: The History of Manners*, originally published in German in 1939, trans. Edmund Jephcott (New York: Urizen Books, 1978), 129, 144, 86, 153, 130, 131, 138, 162. The second volume of Elias's *Civilizing Process* appeared in English as *Power and Civility*, trans. Edmund Jephcott (New York: Pantheon Books, 1982).
2. Elias, *Power and Civility*, 232; Elias, *History of Manners*, 164, 189–90.
3. Among the most perceptive (and appreciative) review essays that appeared upon the English translation of *The Civilizing Process* was Keith Thomas, "The Rise of the Fork," *The New York Review of Books* 25 (March 9, 1978): 28–31.
4. Elias, *History of Manners*, 140, 187.
5. R. W. Vail, "Moody's *School of Good Manners*: A Study in American Colonial Etiquette," in *Studies in the History of Culture* (Menasha, Wis.: George Banta, 1942), 261–72; Mary Reed Bobbitt, "A Bibliography of Etiquette Books Published in America Before 1900," *Bulletin of the New York Public Library* 51 (December 1947): 709–10. Vail traces Moody's book to *Civilité Puérile*, specifically the edition of 1564, *L'A, B, C, ou instruction pour les petis enfans*.
6. Eleazar Moody, *The School of Good Manners* (Portland: Thomas B. Wait, 1786), 7, 8, 10.
7. John Allen Murray, ed., *George Washington's Rules of Civility and Decent Behaviour in Company and Conversation* (New York: G. P. Putnam's Sons, 1942), 10, 11, 30, 32. Material enclosed in parentheses is as it appears in this edition; material enclosed in brackets represent my own added punctuation. Moncure Daniel Conway, *George Washington's Rules of Civility Traced to Their Sources and Restored* (London: Chatto and Windus, 1890), 12–23.
8. Jacques Pierre Brissot de Warville, *New Travels in the United States of America, 1788* (first published in 1791), trans. Mara Soceanu Vamos and Durand Echeverria; ed. Durand Echeverria (Cambridge: Harvard University Press, Belknap Press, 1964), 347; Ferdi-

nand-M. Bayard, *Travels of a Frenchman* . . . , trans. and ed. Ben C. McCary (Williams-burg, Va.: Ben C. McCary, 1950), 47n.

9. On this subject see David H. Flaherty, *Privacy in Colonial New England* (Charlottesville: University Press of Virginia, 1972), 76–79; Jack Larkin, *The Reshaping of Everyday Life, 1790–1840* (New York: Harper & Row, 1988), 124–25; William Byrd, as quoted in Edmund S. Morgan, *Virginians at Home: Family Life in the Eighteenth Century* (Williams-burg, Va.: Colonial Williamsburg, 1952), 73; Andrew Burnaby, *Travels through the Middle Settlements in North-America, in the Years 1759 and 1760*, 2d ed. (1775; reprint ed. Ithaca: Cornell University Press, Great Seal Books, 1960), 103n.

10. Melville, chap. 3, "The Spouter-Inn," and chap. 4, "The Counterpane," *Moby-Dick*; Joshua F. Speed, "Incidents in the Early Life of A. Lincoln," quoted in Charles B. Strozier, *Lincoln's Quest for Union* (New York: Basic Books, 1982), 41–42.

11. Elliott J. Gorn, " 'Gouge and Bite, Pull Hair and Scratch': The Social Significance of Fighting in the Southern Backcountry," *American Historical Review* 90 (February 1985): 19; *Journal and Letters of Philip Vickers Fithian, 1773–1774: A Plantation Tutor of the Old Dominion*, ed. Hunter Dickinson Farish (Williamsburg, Va.: Colonial Williamsburg, 1943), 240–41. Most of this passage is cited by Gorn. See also Bertram Wyatt-Brown, *Southern Honor: Ethics and Behavior in the Old South* (New York: Oxford University Press, 1982).

12. Gorn, " 'Gouge and Bite,' " 38.

13. Charles Francis Adams, *Three Episodes of Massachusetts History*, 2 vols., rev. ed. (Boston: Houghton, Mifflin, 1894), 2:802.

14. Of his great-grandfather the President, Adams noted, "To the end of his life a large tankard of hard cider was John Adams' morning draught before breakfast" (ibid., 2:686).

15. Ibid., 2:682, 724–26, 780–82, 785–86, 790–91, 807. For Mather's advice, see *Dr. Cotton Mather's Student and Preacher. Intituled, Manuductio ad Ministerium* (London: Charles Dilly, 1781), 141.

16. Alice Morse Earle, *Customs and Fashions in Old New England* (New York: Charles Scribner's Sons, 1893), 62–63, 73–74, 237–38, 251–53, 369–72; George Francis Dow, *Domestic Life in New England in the Seventeenth Century* (Topsfield, Mass.: Perkins Press, 1925), 22–23; see also 26; *National Cyclopaedia of American Biography* (New York: James T. White, 1937), s.v. "Dow, George Francis."

17. Thomas Nelson Page, "On the Decay of Manners," *Century Magazine* 81 (April 1911): 882.

18. Peter N. Stearns with Carol Z. Stearns, "Emotionology: Clarifying the History of Emotions and Emotional Standards," *American Historical Review* 90 (October 1985): 813–36, esp. 819. For a summary of recent scholarship, see ibid., 817–19; and Carol Zisowitz Stearns and Peter N. Stearns, *Anger: The Struggle for Emotional Control in America's History* (Chicago: University of Chicago Press, 1986), 32–35.

19. Harold Perkin, *The Origins of Modern English Society, 1780–1880* (London: Routledge & Kegan Paul, 1974), 17, 23–25, 38–39, 49, 55, 57; Johnson is quoted in James Boswell, *Boswell's London Journal, 1762–1763*, ed. Frederick A. Pottle (New York: McGraw-Hill, 1950), 320; *Dictionary of National Biography*, s.v. "Holles, John, first Earl of Clare."

20. James Henretta, "Wealth and Social Structure," in Jack P. Greene and J. R. Pole, eds., *Colonial British America: Essays in the New History of the Early Modern Era* (Baltimore: Johns Hopkins University Press, 1984), 278, 281.

21. Richard L. Bushman, "American High-Style and Vernacular Cultures," in Greene and Pole, eds., *Colonial British America*, 349–52; [John Oldmixon], *The British Empire in America*, 2 vols. (1741; reprint ed. New York: Augustus M. Kelley, 1969), 1:197; see also Edgar de N. Mayhew and Minor Myers, Jr., *A Documentary History of American Interiors from the Colonial Era to 1915* (New York: Charles Scribner's Sons, 1980), 17–18.

22. Rhys Isaac, *The Transformation of Virginia, 1740–1790* (Chapel Hill: University of North Carolina Press, 1982), 72–73.

23. Ibid., 73–74.

24. *The Journal of Madam Knight* (Boston: David R. Godine, 1972), 13.

25. Robert Blair St. George, " 'Set Thine House in Order': The Domestication of the Yeomanry in Seventeenth-Century New England," in Jonathan L. Fairbanks and Robert

L. Trent, eds., *New England Begins: The Seventeenth Century*, 3 vols., exhibition catalogue (Boston: Museum of Fine Arts, 1982), 2:159–88.
26. Carl Bridenbaugh, ed., *Gentleman's Progress: The Itinerarium of Dr. Alexander Hamilton, 1744* (Chapel Hill: University of North Carolina Press, 1948), 31.
27. Ibid., 124. Other genteel travelers also complained of the impertinent curiosity of the "lower class." One Philadelphian journeying through New England about this same time grew so exasperated with the barrage of questions he faced at every inn that as soon as he entered he "inquired for the master, the mistress, the sons, the daughters, the men-servants and the maid-servants; and having assembled them all together, he began in this manner. 'Worthy people, I am B. F. of Philadelphia, by trade a ———, and a bachelor; I have some relations at Boston, to whom I am going to make a visit: my stay will be short, and I shall then return and follow my business, as a prudent man ought to do. This is all I know of myself, and all I can possibly inform you of; I beg therefore that you will have pity upon me and my horse, and give us both some refreshment' " (Burnaby, *Travels through the Middle Settlements in North-America*, 101–2).
28. Hamilton, *Itinerarium*, 164.
29. Ibid., 12–13. Other yeomen and artisans beside Morison were offended if served food beneath their station. William Byrd II noted in his diary for March 2, 1711, "The boatwright was affronted that I gave him pone instead of English bread for breakfast and took his horse and rode away without saying . . . a word" (*The Secret Diary of William Byrd of Westover, 1709–1712*, ed. Louis B. Wright and Marion Tinling [Richmond: Dietz Press, 1941], 308).
30. St. George, " 'Set Thine House in Order,' " 2:159–60; for the observation that Morison might have told the story to his own advantage, see Bushman, "American High-Style and Vernacular Cultures," 375; Hamilton, *Itinerarium*, 16.
31. Hamilton, *Itinerarium*, 8, 10.
32. On Jarratt and his memoirs, see Douglass Adair, ed., "The Autobiography of the Reverend Devereux Jarratt, 1732–63," *William and Mary Quarterly*, 3d ser., 9 (July 1952): 346–93; and Rhys Isaac's penetrating discussion, to which I am indebted, in *Transformation of Virginia*, 43–44, 48, 65, 80, 116–17, 124–31, 262, 311.
33. *The Life of the Reverend Devereux Jarratt . . . Written by Himself . . .* (Baltimore: Warner & Hanna, 1806), 13, 14. Barefoot rural boyhood would become by the mid-nineteenth century a nostalgic token of liberty, before the "civilizing process" of growing up was complete. Samuel G. Goodrich, who was born in Ridgefield, Connecticut, in 1793, later wrote of his youth, "I recollect few things in life more delightful than, in the spring, to cast away my shoes and stockings, and have a glorious scamper over the fields. . . . In these exercises I felt as if stepping on air—as if leaping aloft on wings. I was so impressed with the exultant emotion thus experienced, that I repeated them a thousand times in happy dreams, especially in my younger days. Even now, these visions sometimes come to me in sleep, though with a lurking consciousness that they are but a mockery of the past—sad monitors of the change which time has wrought upon me" (*Recollections of a Lifetime* [New York: Miller, Orton, and Mulligan, 1856], 1:28). John Greenleaf Whittier's "The Barefoot Boy" was collected in *The Panorama* the same year Goodrich's *Recollections* appeared. Mark Twain, of course, would make shoes the dreaded mark of civilization that Huckleberry Finn resists.
34. Jarratt, *Life*, 14.
35. Ibid., 25, 26.
36. Ibid., 32.
37. Ibid., 31, 30, 31, 33, 35, 36.
38. Ibid., 40, 15, 81.
39. Both Jarratt's epistolary form and many of the specific details of his narrative, as well as the overarching theme of his rise from humble obscurity to a position of importance, appear modeled on Franklin's *Autobiography*. Jarratt refers explicitly to Franklin's "memoirs" on 141.
40. J. A. Leo Lemay and P. M. Zall, eds., *Benjamin Franklin's Autobiography: An Authoritative Text, Backgrounds, Criticism* (New York: W. W. Norton, 1986), 20; Charles Coleman Sellers, *Benjamin Franklin in Portraiture* (New Haven: Yale University Press, 1962),

96–103; see also Robert Ralph Davis, Jr., "Diplomatic Plumage: American Court Dress in the Early National Period," *American Quarterly* 20 (Summer 1968): 167–68.

41. *Autobiography*, 54.
42. Ibid., 75; Franklin here referred specifically to the virtue of humility.
43. Ibid., 73.
44. Ibid., 13–14.
45. Ibid., 64.
46. Adam Smith, *The Wealth of Nations* (New York: Random House, Modern Library, 1937), 14.
47. Joyce Appleby, *Capitalism and a New Social Order: The Republican Vision of the 1790s* (New York: New York University Press, 1984), 31–32.
48. *Autobiography*, 56.
49. Jeffrey Williamson and Peter H. Lindert, "Long Term Trends in American Wealth Inequality," in *Modeling the Distribution and Intergenerational Transmission of Wealth*, ed. James D. Smith (Chicago: University of Chicago Press, 1980), 9–93, esp. 10, table 1.3, and 12–37.

Chapter Two: Etiquette Books and the Spread of Gentility

1. Margaret Hunter Hall, *The Aristocratic Journey: Being the Outspoken Letters of Mrs. Basil Hall Written during a Fourteen Months' Sojourn in America, 1827–1828*, ed. Una Pope-Hennessy (New York: G. P. Putnam's Sons, 1931), 56; see also 89.
2. Hugh Henry Brackenridge, *Modern Chivalry*, ed. Claude M. Newlin (Part I originally published in 1792; New York: Hafner, 1962), 6, 14, 16.
3. Gordon S. Wood, ed., *The Rising Glory of America, 1760–1820* (New York: Braziller, 1971), 1–22.
4. See esp. Jeffrey Williamson and Peter H. Lindert, "Long Term Trends in American Wealth Inequality," in *Modeling the Distribution and Intergenerational Transmission of Wealth*, ed. James D. Smith (Chicago: University of Chicago Press, 1980), 9–93, esp. 10, table 1.3, and 12–37.
5. The historical and historiographical issues raised here are lucidly explored in Stuart M. Blumin, "The Hypothesis of Middle-Class Formation in Nineteenth-Century America: A Critique and Some Proposals," *American Historical Review* 90 (April 1985): 299–338.
6. Blumin, "Hypothesis of Middle-Class Formation," 313–18.
7. Mary Kelley, *Private Woman, Public Stage: Literary Domesticity in Nineteenth-Century America* (New York: Oxford University Press, 1984), 8.
8. David D. Hall, "Introduction: The Uses of Literacy in New England, 1600–1850," and Robert B. Winans, "Bibliography and the Cultural Historian: Notes on the Eighteenth-Century Novel," both in William L. Joyce et al., eds., *Print and Society in Early America* (Worcester, Mass.: American Antiquarian Society, 1983), 7–9 and 174–85.
9. Stephen Botein, "The Anglo-American Book Trade before 1776: Personnel and Strategies," in Joyce et al., eds., *Print and Society*, 50; the quotation is from the London bookseller William Strahan in 1750.
10. In this and the following discussion of the transformation in the culture of print and styles of reading, I am indebted to Hall's penetrating essay "Uses of Literacy," 1–47.
11. Samuel G. Goodrich, *Recollections of a Lifetime*, 2 vols. (New York: Miller, Orton, and Mulligan, 1856), 2:284.
12. Ibid., 1:60–61.
13. Ibid., 1:165–66.
14. This point is made in Hall, "Uses of Literacy," 21–26; see also David D. Hall, "The World of Print and Collective Mentality in Seventeenth-Century New England," in John Higham and Paul K. Conkin, eds., *New Directions in American Intellectual History* (Baltimore: Johns Hopkins University Press, 1979), 166–80.
15. Botein, "Anglo-American Book Trade," 64.
16. Goodrich, *Recollections*, 1:157.
17. Ibid., 1:86.

18. Hall, "Uses of Literacy," 24, 28–35.
19. Cynthia Z. Stiverson and Gregory A. Stiverson, "The Colonial Retail Book Trade: Availability and Affordability of Reading Material in Mid-Eighteenth-Century Virginia," in Joyce et al., eds., *Print and Society*, 169–70.
20. Goodrich, *Recollections*, 2:533, 333–34.
21. "Try, Try Again," *Merry's Museum* 35 (1858): 172; as quoted in Rex Burns, *Success in America: The Yeoman Dream and the Industrial Revolution* (Amherst: University of Massachusetts Press, 1976), 44.
22. Hall, "Uses of Literacy," 42–48. See Goodrich's list of his publications in Note I of the Appendix, *Recollections*, 2:537–52.
23. See Goodrich's ambiguous assessments of the transformation of Ridgefield, *Recollections*, esp. 1:59–89, 115–32, 300–19.
24. On popular manuals and the hunger for instruction, see Carl Bode, *The Anatomy of American Popular Culture, 1840–1861* (Berkeley: University of California Press, 1959), 119–31.
25. See Sam Bass Warner, Jr., *The Private City: Philadelphia in Three Periods of Its Growth* (Philadelphia: University of Pennsylvania Press, 1968), 66. On this point see Richard D. Brown, *Modernization: The Transformation of American Life, 1600–1865* (New York: Hill and Wang, 1976), and Nathan Rosenberg, *Technology and Economic Growth* (New York: Harper & Row, 1972).
26. See Richard L. Bushman and Claudia L. Bushman, "The Early History of Cleanliness in America," *Journal of American History* 74 (March 1988): 1213–38.
27. Arthur M. Schlesinger, *Learning How to Behave: A Historical Study of American Etiquette Books* (New York: Macmillan, 1946), 18, 34.
28. The most complete (but by no means definitive) bibliography of American etiquette books lists 236 separate titles, a number issued in multiple editions, published in the United States before 1900. Some books, however, were published under more than one title, so that the list contains repetitions. See Mary Reed Bobbitt, "A Bibliography of Etiquette Books Published in America Before 1900," *Bulletin of the New York Public Library* 51 (December 1947): 687–720.
29. This issue of the *Operator* was for July 16, 1883; Edwin Gabler, *The American Telegrapher: A Social History, 1860–1900* (New Brunswick: Rutgers University Press, 1988), 101.
30. On "subscription books," see "The Subscription Book Trade," *Publishers' Weekly* 2 (July 25, 1872): 93–94; Donald Sheehan, *This Was Publishing: A Chronicle of the Book Trade in the Gilded Age* (Bloomington: Indiana University Press, 1952), 190–98; Judy Hilkey, " 'The Way to Win': The Search for Success in the New Industrial Order, 1870–1910," Ph.D. diss., Rutgers University, 1980. For techniques of subscription agents, see O. A. Browning, *O. A. Browning's Confidential Instructions, Rules and Helps for His Agents . . .* (Toledo, Ohio: O. A. Browning, 1881); Ebenezer Hannaford, *Success in Canvassing* (Saint Louis: N. D. Thompson and Co., 1884); and W. Willis Houston, *The General Agent's Guide to Success* (Chicago: International Publishing Co., 1896).
31. *Beadle's Book of Etiquette*; Willis, *Etiquette*.
32. Carroll, *Art Stationery and Usages of Polite Society*.
33. *100 Rules of Etiquette*.
34. *Points on Good Behavior*.
35. Goodrich, *Recollections*, 2:388–89. Goodrich's estimate is accepted in Hellmut Lehmann-Haupt et al., *The Book in America*, 2d ed. (New York: R. R. Bowker, 1951), 124, 195.
36. This estimate is based upon my reading of nineteenth-century etiquette books; see Selected Bibliography.
37. Bayle-Mouillard, *The Gentleman and Lady's Book of Politeness*.
38. Edward T. James, et al., eds., *Notable American Women, 1600–1950* (Cambridge: Harvard University Press, Belknap Press, 1971), s.v. "Leslie, Eliza"; Frank Luther Mott, *A History of American Magazines*, 5 vols. (Cambridge: Harvard University Press, Belknap Press, 1957, 1968), 2:353, 584, 733–34.
39. *Notable American Women*, s.v. "Hale, Sarah Josepha Buell"; Mott, *History of American Magazines*, 2:349–51, 580–94; Mary Alice Wyman, ed., *Selections from the Autobiography of Elizabeth Oakes Smith* (Lewiston, Maine: Lewiston Journal, 1924), 98.

40. *Notable American Women*, s.v. "Sedgwick, Catharine Maria"; Kelley, *Private Woman, Public Stage*, passim.
41. *Notable American Women*, s.v. "Farrar, Eliza Ware Rotch."
42. On Arthur's life, see Donald A. Koch, ed., *Ten Nights in a Bar-Room, and What I Saw There* (Cambridge: Harvard University Press, Belknap Press, 1964), v–xliii.
43. *Dictionary of American Biography*, s.v. "Wells, Samuel Roberts."
44. *Dictionary of American Biography*, s.v. "Leland, Charles Godfrey."
45. *Notable American Women*, s.v. "Moore, Clara Sophia Jessup."
46. Ibid., s.v. "Sherwood, Mary Elizabeth Wilson."
47. Mott, *History of American Magazines*, 3:418–20.
48. David MacKenzie and W. B. Blankenburg, "Preface," Thomas E. Hill, *Never Give a Lady a Restive Horse: A 19th Century Handbook of Etiquette* (Berkeley: Diablo Press, 1967), 5–6.
49. Raymond Williams, *Marxism and Literature* (Oxford: Oxford University Press, 1977), 116.
50. Thomas Lee Bucky, with Joseph P. Blank, "Einstein: An Intimate Memoir," *Harper's* 229 (September 1964): 43–48, esp. 44.
51. Armstrong, *On Habits and Manners*; Woods, *Negro in Etiquette*.
52. For an exception, see Hervey, *Principles of Courtesy*.
53. *Guide to Good Behaviour*, 5–6.
54. *American Code of Manners*, i.
55. Maxwell, *Manners and Customs*, 366–67.
56. William Dean Howells, *The Rise of Silas Lapham* (Boston: Ticknor & Brothers, 1885), 257–61.
57. Maxwell, *Manners and Customs*, 188; see also Smiley, *Modern Manners*, 353–54.
58. *Our Manners at Home and Abroad*, 54–57.
59. See, e.g., *Our Manners at Home and Abroad*, 56; Bunce, *Don't*, 66, 70–71. On the issue of linguistic decorum in this period, see Kenneth J. Cmiel's fine study, "Democratic Eloquence: Language, Education and Authority in Nineteenth-Century America," Ph.D. diss., University of Chicago, 1986.
60. [Longstreet], *Social Etiquette of New York*.
61. Johnson, *New York Fashion Bazar Book*.
62. Learned, *Etiquette of New York To-day*.
63. [Germain?], *Complete Bachelor*, v.
64. *Art of Pleasing*, vii.
65. *Book of Manners*, 9.
66. Smiley, *Modern Manners*, 306.
67. Judith N. Shklar, *Ordinary Vices* (Cambridge: Harvard University Press, Belknap Press, 1984), 101.
68. Quoted in Esther B. Aresty, *The Best Behavior* (New York: Simon and Schuster, 1970), 193.
69. Frances Trollope, *Domestic Manners of the Americans*, ed. Donald Smalley (1832; New York: Knopf, 1949), 186.
70. Margaret Bayard Smith, *The First Forty Years of Washington Society*, ed. Gaillard Hunt (New York: Charles Scribner's Sons, 1906), 295–97.
71. Conkling, *American Gentleman's Guide*, 330.
72. [Tomes], *Bazar Book of Decorum*, 13.
73. Sherwood, *Manners and Social Usages*, 29.
74. L. E. White, *Success in Society*, 8.
75. Stevens, *Usages of the Best Society*, 3. See also [Longstreet], *Social Etiquette of New York*, 8; Bryson, *Every-Day Etiquette*, 130; and Dewey, *Lessons on Manners*, 5.
76. Howard, *Excelsior*, 49.
77. *Our Manners at Home and Abroad*, 23.
78. Bryson, *Every-Day Etiquette*, 22.
79. [Hall], *Social Customs*, 9; Holmes, *The Common Law*, appeared in 1881.
80. Quotation from Burke's *Letters on a Regicide Peace* in Beezley, *Our Manners and Social Customs*, 30. For discussions of the theory of "influence," see Ann Douglas, *The Fem-*

inization of American Culture (New York: Knopf, 1977), and Steven Mintz, *A Prison of Expectations: The Family in Victorian Culture* (New York: New York University Press, 1983), 30–39.

81. Richard L. Bushman, "American High-Style and Vernacular Cultures," in Jack P. Greene and J. R. Pole, eds., *Colonial British America: Essays in the New History of the Early Modern Era* (Baltimore: Johns Hopkins University Press, 1984), 345–83.
82. Review of [Tomes], *Bazar Book of Decorum, Atlantic Monthly* 26 (July 1870): 122.
83. Mark Twain, *Letters from the Earth*, ed. Bernard DeVoto (New York: Harper & Row, 1962), 194, 199–200.
84. Nathaniel Parker Willis, *Hurry-Graphs* (New York: Charles Scribner, 1851), 326.
85. Joan Annett and Randall Collins, "A Short History of Deference and Demeanor," in Randall Collins, *Conflict Sociology: Toward an Explanatory Science* (New York: Academic Press, 1975), 186; Williams, *Marxism and Literature*, 128–35.
86. Dewey, *How to Teach Manners*, 26–27.
87. Wharton, *A Backward Glance* (New York: D. Appleton-Century Co., 1934), 52, 56–57.
88. Ibid., 21–22.
89. Anthony F. C. Wallace, *Rockdale* (New York: Knopf, 1978), 19.
90. Egan, *Gentleman*, 15.
91. Young, *Our Deportment*, 20.
92. William Mathews, *Getting On in the World; or Hints on Success in Life* (Chicago: S. C. Griggs, 1889), 153.
93. Young, *Our Deportment*, 21.
94. T. L. Haines, *Work and Wealth; On the Art of Getting, Saving, and Using Money* (New York: Standard Publishing House, 1884), 127. See also Mathews, *Getting On*, 143; Julia E. Loomis McCanaughy, *Capital for Working Boys* (Boston: James H. Earle, 1883); William Drysdale, *Helps for Ambitious Boys* (New York: Thomas Y. Crowell, 1899), 1–2; Dewey, *How to Teach Manners*, 96; and Allan Horlick, *Country Boys and Merchant Princes: The Social Control of Young Men in New York* (Lewisburg, Pa.: Bucknell University Press, 1975), 153. The social observer quoted is the young F. L. Olmsted in 1845; Charles Cappen McLaughlin, ed., *The Papers of Frederick Law Olmsted*, vol. 1 (Baltimore: Johns Hopkins University Press, 1977), 219. On work and the commercialization of emotions in our own time, see Arlie Russell Hochschild, *The Managed Heart: Commercialization of Human Feeling* (Berkeley: University of California Press, 1983).

Chapter Three: Reading the City: The Semiotics of Everyday Life

1. Henry James, *The American Scene* (1907; reprint ed. Bloomington: Indiana University Press, 1968), 121–22; on Balzac, see Peter Brooks, "The Text of the City," *Oppositions* 8 (1977): 7–11; on Engels, see Steven Marcus, "Reading the Illegible," in H. J. Dyos and Michael Wolff, eds., *The Victorian City: Images and Realities* (London: Routledge & Kegan Paul, 1973), 1:257–76; Steven Marcus, *Engels, Manchester, and the Working Class* (New York: Random House, 1974); on Poe, see the discussion of "The Man of the Crowd" below.
2. Blake McKelvey, *American Urbanization: A Comparative History* (Glencoe, Ill.: Scott, Foresman, 1973), 6–11; Charles N. Glaab and A. Theodore Brown, *A History of Urban America* (New York: Macmillan, 1967), 25–26.
3. McKelvey, *American Urbanization*, 24, 37; Richard E. Fogelsong, *Planning the Capitalist City: The Colonial Era to the 1920s* (Princeton: Princeton University Press, 1986), 60.
4. Glaab and Brown, *History of Urban America*, 107–11; McKelvey, *American Urbanization*, 73.
5. McKelvey, *American Urbanization*, 40–41; Fogelsong, *Planning the Capitalist City*, 61.
6. Fogelsong, *Planning the Capitalist City*, 62; David Harvey, *Consciousness and the Urban Experience* (Baltimore: Johns Hopkins University Press, 1985), 14.
7. Anselm L. Strauss, *Images of the American City* (New York: Free Press, 1961), 6; Roland Barthes, *The Eiffel Tower, and Other Mythologies*, trans. Richard Howard (New York: Hill and Wang, 1980), 8–9; Harriet Martineau, *Retrospect of Western Travel*, 2 vols.

(London: Saunders and Otley, 1838), 1:228. On early photography of the city, see Peter B. Hales, *Silver Cities: The Photography of American Urbanization, 1839–1915* (Philadelphia: Temple University Press, 1984), esp. 27–39, 62–63, 73–91; and Beaumont Newhall, *Airborne Camera: The World from the Air and Outer Space* (New York: Random House, 1969).

8. John W. Reps, *Cities on Stone: Nineteenth Century Lithograph Images of the Urban West* (Fort Worth: Amon Carter Museum, 1976), 2–35; see 14 for quotations from John J. Ingalls, 1858, who was duped by a bird's-eye view of Sumner, Kansas.

9. Joseph Holt Ingraham, *The Miseries of New York* (Boston: "Yankee" Office, 1844); [Edward Z. C. Judson], *The Mysteries and Miseries of New York* (New York: Berford & Co., 1848); [Edward Z. C. Judson], *The Mysteries and Miseries of New Orleans* (New York: Akarman and Ormsly, 1851); George G. Foster, *New York by Gas-Light: With Here and There a Streak of Sunshine* (New York: Dewitt & Davenport, 1850); Matthew Hale Smith, *Sunshine and Shadow in New York* (Hartford: J. B. Burr, 1868); James Dabney McCabe, *New York by Sunlight and Gaslight* (Philadelphia: Douglass Brothers, 1882); James Dabney McCabe, *Lights and Shadows of New York Life* (Philadelphia: National Publishing Co., 1872); Benjamin E. Lloyd, *Lights and Shadows in San Francisco* (San Francisco: A. L. Bancroft, 1876); Samuel Paynter Wilson, *Chicago by Gaslight* (n.p., n.d.); and Henry Morgan, *Boston Inside Out! Sins of a Great City!* (Boston: Shawmut Publishing Co., 1880). The conventions and even the titles of some of these works are part of a tradition extending back in English to at least the turn of the sixteenth century, with such guides to the urban underworld as Thomas Dekker's *English Villainies Discovered by Lantern and Candlelight* (1608)—a point brought to my attention by Jean-Christophe Agnew.

10. [James Dabney McCabe], *The Secrets of the Great City: A Work Descriptive of the Virtues and the Vices, the Mysteries, Miseries and Crimes of New York City* (Philadelphia: Jones, Brothers, 1868), 15–16.

11. Carole Groneman Pernicone, " 'The Bloody Olde Sixth': A Social Analysis of a New York City Working-Class Community in the United States," Ph.D. diss., University of Rochester, 1973, 184. Pernicone argues that contemporary journalists and reformers vastly exaggerated the social disorganization of the Five Points community in New York.

12. Foster, *New York by Gas-Light*, 5.

13. On this point see Christine Stansell, *City of Women: Sex and Class in New York, 1789–1860* (New York: Knopf, 1986), esp. 193–216; and Susan G. Davis, *Parades and Power: Street Theatre in Nineteenth-Century Philadelphia* (Philadelphia: Temple University Press, 1986). For application of the "dark continent" analogy to nineteenth-century English cities, see Deborah Epstein Nord, "The Social Explorer as Anthropologist: Victorian Travellers Among the Urban Poor," in William Sharpe and Leonard Wallock, eds., *Visions of the Modern City* (New York: Heynman Center for the Humanities, Columbia University, 1983), 118–30.

14. Peter Stryker, *The Lower Depths of the Great American Metropolis* (New York: Schermerhorn, Bancroft, 1866), 3, 4.

15. Joseph Alexander, Graf von Hübner, *Promenade autour du monde, 1871*, 2 vols. (Paris: Librairie Hachette, 1874), 1:61–62; my translation.

16. Franklin Walker and G. Ezra Dane, eds., *Mark Twain's Travels with Mr. Brown* (New York: Knopf, 1940), 259.

17. McCabe, *New York by Sunlight and Gaslight*, 57.

18. Champfleury (Jules-François-Félix-Husson) as quoted in Judith Wechsler, *A Human Comedy: Physiognomy and Caricature in 19th Century Paris* (Chicago: University of Chicago Press, 1982), 112. Wechsler's book is a fascinating study on this topic.

19. John Patrick Diggins, "The Three Faces of Authority in American History," in Diggins and Mark E. Kann, eds., *The Problem of Authority in America* (Philadelphia: Temple University Press, 1981), 24.

20. "The Man of the Crowd" in *Collected Works of Edgar Allan Poe*, ed. Thomas Ollive Mabbott, vol. 2, *Tales and Sketches, 1831–1842* (Cambridge: Harvard University Press, Belknap Press, 1978), 506, 507. The illegible early German book to which Poe refers is the *Ortulus anime cum oratiunculis*, printed by Johann Reinhard Gruinger in 1500.

21. Ibid., 508, 509; Brooks, "Text of the City," 8.

22. "Man of the Crowd," 508.
23. Ibid., 511.
24. Ibid., 511, 513, 515.
25. Walter Benjamin, "The Paris of the Second Empire in Baudelaire," in *Charles Baudelaire: A Lyric Poet in the Era of High Capitalism*, trans. Harry Zohn (London: New Left Books, 1973), 37–40, 48; Poe, "Man of the Crowd," 507, 511, 512, 515. On the dialectical relationship between subject and object, see James W. Fernandez, "Reflections on Looking into Mirrors," *Semiotica* 20 (1980): 27–39; and Kevin Dwyer, *Moroccan Dialogues: Anthropology in Question* (Baltimore: Johns Hopkins University Press, 1982), 255–69.
26. Melville's "Bartleby" was originally published in 1853; I follow the text as printed in *The Piazza Tales and Other Prose Pieces, 1839–1860*, ed. Harrison Hayford et al., *The Writings of Herman Melville*, vol. 9 (Evanston and Chicago: Northwestern University Press and Newberry Library, 1987), 13–45.
27. Ibid., 14.
28. Ibid., 13; on the literary fragment and modern life, see Steven Marcus's discussion of Freud's "Fragment of an Analysis of a Case of Hysteria" in *Freud and the Culture of Psychoanalysis* (Boston: George Allen & Unwin, 1984), 54–55.
29. In 1846; it ceased functioning in July 1847. Melville's father, Allan, was an Examiner in Chancery with an office on Wall Street. In addition, the story was no doubt influenced by Dickens's great novel of the abuses of the English Court of Chancery, *Bleak House* (published serially in 1852–53), in which a scrivener also figures.
30. "Bartleby," 14; Alonzo C. Paige, *Reports of Cases Argued and Determined in the Court of Chancery of the State of New York*, 3d ed. (New York: Banks and Brothers, 1883), 385–894; Roscoe Pound, *The Spirit of the Common Law* (Boston: M. Jones Co., 1921), 57.
31. "Bartleby," 15–18.
32. Ibid., 19.
33. Ibid., 20.
34. Elizabeth Hardwick, "Bartleby in Manhattan," *The New York Review of Books* 28 (July 16, 1981): 27.
35. On this point, see William B. Dillingham, *Melville's Short Fiction, 1853–1856* (Athens: University of Georgia Press, 1977), 48–49.
36. "Bartleby," 28, 29.
37. Ibid., 32, 35, 37.
38. Ibid., 38, 40, 41.
39. My interpretation is influenced by Allan Silver's illuminating article "The Lawyer and the Scrivener," *Partisan Review* 48 (1981): 409–24.
40. See the discussion of "minimal altruism" and "the cutoff for heroism" in James S. Fishkin, *The Limits of Obligation* (New Haven: Yale University Press, 1982).
41. Ibid., 20, 49–50.
42. Moore, *Sensible Etiquette*, xv; Edith Wharton, *The Age of Innocence* (1920; New York: Scribner's, 1970), 45.
43. Jonathan Culler, "In Pursuit of Signs," *Daedalus* 106 (Fall 1977): 104.
44. Warren Susman illuminates another aspect of character and its transformation in his stimulating essay " 'Personality' and the Making of Twentieth-Century Culture," in John Higham and Paul K. Conkin, eds., *New Directions in American Intellectual History* (Baltimore: Johns Hopkins University Press, 1979), 212–26. He cites the Emerson quotation and attests to its popularity on 214.
45. In this connection see George Gonos, " 'Situation' versus 'Frame': The 'Interactionist' and the 'Structuralist' Analyses of Everyday Life," *American Sociological Review* 42 (December 1977): 865; and Fredric Jameson, "On Goffman's Frame Analysis," *Theory and Society* 3 (1976): 131–32.
46. Giovanni Morelli, *Italian Painters: Critical Studies of Their Works*, trans. Constance Jocelyn Ffoulkes (London: John Murray, 1892), 47; Arthur Conan Doyle, "The Man with the Twisted Lip," as quoted in Marcello Truzzi, "Sherlock Holmes: Applied Social Psychologist," in Umberto Eco and Thomas A. Sebeok, eds., *The Sign of Three: Dupin, Holmes, Peirce* (Bloomington: Indiana University Press, 1983), 64; Sigmund Freud, "Fragment of an Analysis of a Case of Hysteria" (1905) in *Dora: An Analysis of a Case of Hysteria*

(New York: Crowell-Collier, 1963), 96. For some of the general thrust of this and the following paragraph and especially for the specific linkages connecting Morelli, Freud, and Sherlock Holmes, I am indebted to Carlo Ginzberg's brilliant essay "Morelli, Freud and Sherlock Holmes: Clues and Scientific Method," *History Workshop Journal* 9 (1980): 5–36; also collected in Eco and Sebeok, eds., *Sign of Three*, 81–118.

47. Goodrich, *What to Do and How to Do It*, 28; [De Valcourt], *Illustrated Manners Book*, 57.
48. *Collected Papers of Charles Sanders Peirce* (Cambridge: Harvard University Press, 1931–58), 8 vols., vol. 7, Arthur W. Burks, ed. (1958), 115. This instance is cited in Thomas A. Sebeok and Jean Umiker-Sebeok, " 'You Know My Method': A Juxtaposition of Charles S. Peirce and Sherlock Holmes," in Eco and Sebeok, eds., *Sign of Three*, 38–39.
49. Samuel R. Wells, *New Physiognomy* (New York: American Book Co., 1871), 321.
50. *Our Manners at Home and Abroad*, 87–88; Young, *Our Deportment*, 22. This passage is closely paraphrased in William Mathews, *Getting On in the World; or, Hints on Success in Life* (Chicago: S. C. Griggs, 1889), 143.
51. *Young Man's Own Book*, 139; *Book of Manners*, 67; for examples of urban detection on the street and in omnibuses, see Johnson, *New York Fashion Bazar Book*, 17, and *Art of Conversing*, 49–50.
52. Nicholas B. Wainwright, ed., *A Philadelphia Perspective: The Diary of Sidney George Fisher Covering the Years 1834–1871* (Philadelphia: Historical Society of Pennsylvania, 1967), 530–31.
53. Thomas Knox, Pt. II, in Helen Campbell et al., *Darkness and Daylight; or, Lights and Shadows of New York Life* (Hartford: A. D. Worthington, 1892), 599.
54. William W. Sanger, *The History of Prostitution* (1859; reprint ed. New York: Eugenic Publishing Co., 1939), 29–30; see also 549–59, 566–69; Smith, *Sunshine and Shadow in New York*, 375; William F. Howe, *In Danger; or, Life in New York* (New York: J. S. Ogilvie, 1888), 127; McCabe, *Secrets of the Great City*, 201–2, 215, 208–9.
55. Howe, *In Danger*, 180.
56. *New York Herald*, July 8, 1849, 2, col. 3. For the testimony of Thompson's victims at the trial, see ibid., October 9, 1, col. 6, and October 10, 1849, 4, col. 4. The incident and the discussion it prompted, culminating in Herman Melville's novel *The Confidence-Man: His Masquerade*, are discussed in two articles: Johannes Dietrich Bergmann, "The Original Confidence Man," *American Quarterly* 21 (Fall 1969): 560–677; and Michael S. Reynolds, "The Prototype for Melville's Confidence-Man," *Publications of the Modern Language Association* 6 (October 1971): 1009–13.
57. " 'The Confidence Man' on a Large Scale," *New York Herald*, July 11, 1849, 2, cols. 1–2; reproduced in Bergmann, "Original Confidence Man," 562–65.
58. George W. Matsell, *Vocabulum; or, The Rogue's Lexicon* (New York: George W. Matsell, 1859), 20.
59. On the literature of roguery in late-sixteenth- and early-seventeenth-century England, see Jean-Christophe Agnew, *Worlds Apart: The Market and the Theater in Anglo-American Thought, 1550–1750* (Cambridge: Cambridge University Press, 1986), 63–66. Between 1874 and 1884 a total of sixteen detective books were published under Pinkerton's name, of which *Thirty Years a Detective* (New York: G. W. Carleton, 1884) is the most comprehensive. Pinkerton himself did not write them, but dictated stories and anecdotes that were sent to a ghost writer, then edited the completed manuscript; see Frank Morn, *"The Eye That Never Sleeps": A History of the Pinkerton National Detective Agency* (Bloomington: Indiana University Press, 1982), 80.
60. Thomas Byrnes, *Professional Criminals of America* (New York: Cassell & Cassell, 1886), 270, 274, 40–41. In this last passage, Byrnes very closely paraphrases Philip Farley, *Criminals of America; or, Tales of the Lives of Thieves* (New York: Philip Farley, 1876), 142–45; see also Pinkerton, *Thirty Years*, 190–91.
61. Byrnes, *Professional Criminals*, 98, 112, 170.
62. Ibid., 54–55; see also Pinkerton, *Thirty Years*, 86, 108, 134, 165–66, 264. Allan Pinkerton, *Professional Thieves and the Detective* (New York: G. W. Carleton, 1886), similarly abounds in stories of gentlemanly bearing and demeanor and particularly stresses the

relation between criminals' talents and those of honorable professions; see, e.g., 141, 156, 166.

63. Pinkerton, *Thirty Years*, 193–94; Farley, *Criminals of America*, 206; Byrnes, *Professional Criminals*, 30–32; see also Howe, *In Danger*, 60.

64. Erving Goffman, *The Presentation of Self in Everyday Life* (Garden City, N.Y.: Doubleday/ Anchor Books, 1959), 18n., 59.

65. Byrnes, *Professional Criminals*, 53; Pinkerton, *Thirty Years*, 27. Although the subtitle of Farley's book claimed it would enable "every one to be his own detective," nothing in the book supports this claim.

66. Pinkerton's boast that the detective could teach actors their profession is quoted in Morn, *"Eye That Never Sleeps,"* 84–85. In a similar vein, Jacob A. Riis called Thomas Byrnes "a great actor, and without being that no man can be a great detective" (Riis, *The Making of an American* [New York: Macmillan, 1901], 343). Pinkerton describes the skills of the model detective in *Thirty Years*, 18–19.

Chapter Four: Venturing Forth: Bodily Management in Public

1. Theodore Dreiser, *Sister Carrie*, ed. Neda M. Westlake et al., unexpurgated Pennsylvania Edition (Philadelphia: University of Pennsylvania Press, 1981), 18.

2. William H. Gilman et al., eds., *The Journals and Miscellaneous Notebooks of Ralph Waldo Emerson*, vol. 7 (Cambridge: Harvard University Press, 1969), 158–59. I have omitted Emerson's cancellations from the quotation.

3. Quoted in Howard Gadlin, "Private Lives and Public Order: A Critical View of the History of Intimate Relations in the U.S.," *Massachusetts Review* 17 (Summer 1976): 309–10.

4. Edoardo Weiss, *Agoraphobia in the Light of Ego Psychology* (New York: Grune and Stratton, 1964), esp. 40–41, 64–65; see also Abram de Swaan, "The Politics of Agoraphobia," *Theory and Society* 10 (May 1981): 359–85; on the "built-in identity crisis" of modern society, see Peter L. Berger, Brigitte Berger, and Hansfried Kellner, *The Homeless Mind: Modernization and Consciousness* (New York: Random House, 1973), 92.

5. I here paraphrase Erving Goffman: "One assumes that embarrassment is a normal part of normal social life, the individual becoming uneasy not because he is personally maladjusted but rather because he is not" ("Embarrassment and Social Organization," *Interaction Ritual* [Garden City, N.Y.: Doubleday/Anchor Books, 1967], 109).

6. Ibid., 105–8; Edward Gross and Gregory P. Stone, "Embarrassment and the Analysis of Role Requirements," *American Journal of Sociology* 70 (July 1964): 14; Andre Modigliani, "Embarrassment and Embarrassibility," *Sociometry* 31 (1968): 313; Richard Sennett, *Authority* (New York: Knopf, 1980), 46–47, 94–95.

7. Bertram Wyatt-Brown, *Southern Honor: Ethics and Behavior in the Old South* (New York: Oxford University Press, 1982), 14, 20; Helen Merrell Lynd, *On Shame and the Search for Identity* (New York: Harcourt, Brace, 1958), 22, 26.

8. I here closely follow Harry M. Clor's two related definitions of obscenity in *Obscenity and Public Morality: Censorship in a Liberal Society* (Chicago: University of Chicago Press, 1969), 225. See also Carl D. Schneider's discussion, based on Clor's, in *Shame, Exposure, and Privacy* (Boston: Beacon Press, 1977), 50–51.

9. *Young Lady's Own Book*, 246; see Erving Goffman, "Embarrassment and Social Organization," 109–10; and Goffman, "The Territories of the Self," *Relations in Public* (New York: Basic Books, 1971), 28–61.

10. [Longstreet], *Social Etiquette of New York*, 8–9; see Herbert Morris, *On Guilt and Innocence: Essays in Legal Philosophy and Moral Psychology* (Berkeley: University of California Press, 1976), 60–62.

11. The concern with strategies to avoid embarrassment is a prominent theme in much of Erving Goffman's work. In this connection, see particularly, "On Face-work," *Interaction Ritual*, 15–18; also Lynd, *On Shame*, 184–85; Kurt Riezler, "Comments on the Social Psychology of Shame," *American Journal of Sociology* 48 (January 1943): 459.

12. Issues of sincerity and hypocrisy are sensitively explored in Karen Halttunen, *Confidence Men and Painted Women: A Study of Middle-Class Culture in America, 1830–1870* (New Haven: Yale University Press, 1982).

13. [Longstreet], *Social Etiquette of New York*, 9; [De Valcourt], *Illustrated Manners Book*, 80. On protective and defensive practices, see Erving Goffman, *The Presentation of Self in Everyday Life* (Garden City, N.Y.: Doubleday/Anchor Books, 1959), 13–14.

14. [Anne Royall], *Sketches of History, Life, and Manners in the United States* (1826; reprint ed. New York: Johnson Reprint Corp., 1970), 260–61; Abram C. Dayton, *Last Days of Knickerbocker Life in New York* (New York: George W. Harlan, 1882), 97. See Christine Stansell, *City of Women: Sex and Class in New York, 1789–1860* (New York: Knopf, 1986), 69; John A. Kouwenhoven, *The Columbia Historical Portrait of New York* (New York: Columbia University Press, 1953), 138; May Van Rensselaer, *The Social Ladder* (New York: Henry Holt, 1924), 45; Celia Morris Eckhardt, *Fanny Wright: Rebel in America* (Cambridge: Harvard University Press, 1984), esp. 171–74; Doris G. Yoakam, "Women's Introduction to the American Platform," in William Norwood Brigance, ed., *A History and Criticism of American Public Address*, 2 vols. (1943; reprint ed. New York: Russell & Russell, 1960), 1:153–92.

15. Bugg, *Lady*, 55; Smiley, *Modern Manners*, 153; Thompson Westcott, "The Physiology of Dandyism," *Graham's Magazine* 40 (February and May 1852): 122, 470; Bunce, *Don't*, 27.

16. Contemporary description of John Hancock, quoted in Alice Morse Earle, *Customs and Fashions in Old New England* (New York: Charles Scribner's Sons, 1983), 327.

17. Dayton, *Last Days*, 119–20; [De Valcourt], *Illustrated Manners Book*, 466; John Berger, *About Looking* (New York: Pantheon Books, 1980), 34.

18. Bryson, *Every-Day Etiquette*, 38. On walking stick and umbrella, see *Complete Bachelor*, 6–7, and T. S. Crawford, *A History of the Umbrella* (New York: Taplinger Publishing Co., 1970). On beards and mustaches, see Alison Lurie, *The Language of Clothes* (New York: Random House, 1981), 65–66.

19. [Farrar], *Young Lady's Friend*, 102; Charles Dickens, *American Notes for General Circulation* (1842; New York: Viking Penguin, 1972), 128–29; Maxwell, *Manners and Customs*, 208. On the scrupulous attendance to dress, see F. Hartley, *Ladies' Book of Etiquette*, 109; Cooke, *Social Etiquette*, 409. On jewelry, see, e.g., *Beadle's Book of Etiquette*, 22; [Longstreet], *Good Form*, 57. On heavy perfumes, see, e.g., [Richards], *At Home and Abroad*, 28; [Colesworthy], *Hints on Common Politeness*, 10–11; Smiley, *Modern Manners*, 142.

20. Bunce, *What to Do*, 26; Lyn H. Lofland, *A World of Strangers: Order and Action in Urban Public Space* (New York: Basic Books, 1973), 151–56.

21. A. R. White, *Twentieth Century Etiquette*, 141; Westcott, "Physiology of Dandyism," 470, 123; *Perfect Gentleman*, 215; Howard, *Excelsior*, 80; Osmun, *Mentor*, 58–59.

22. For these and similar phrases, see, e.g., F. Hartley, *Ladies' Book of Etiquette*, 109, 114; *Beadle's Book of Etiquette*, 44; *Etiquette for Ladies: With Hints on . . . Female Beauty*, 44–45; Thornwell, *Lady's Guide to Perfect Gentility*, 78; [Ruth], *Decorum*, 122; *Our Manners at Home and Abroad*, 98; L. E. White, *Success in Society*, 188; R. A. Wells, *Manners*, 132; A. R. White, *Polite Society*, 36; A. R. White, *Twentieth Century Etiquette*, 138.

23. The quotation concerning loud talking appears in F. Hartley, *Ladies' Book of Etiquette*, 113; quotations on how to speak to a gentleman are taken from *Art of Conversing*, 54; F. Hartley, *Ladies' Book of Etiquette*, 112; L. E. White, *Success in Society*, 188.

24. Mary Douglas, *Natural Symbols: Explorations in Cosmology* (New York: Random House, 1973), 12; see idem, *Purity and Danger*; and idem, "Do Dogs Laugh? A Cross-Cultural Approach to Body Symbolism," *Implicit Meanings* (London: Routledge & Kegan Paul, 1975), 87.

25. [Tomes], *Bazar Book of Decorum*, 112–13; virtually the same passage appears in L. E. White, *Success in Society*, 85.

26. [De Valcourt], *Illustrated Manners Book*, 61. On spitting and its abuse, see Dickens, *American Notes*, 144, 160; Margaret Hunter Hall, *The Aristocratic Journey: Being the Outspoken Letters of Mrs. Basil Hall Written during a Fourteen Months' Sojourn in America, 1827–1828*, ed. Una Pope-Hennessy (New York: G. P. Putnam's Sons, 1931), 65, 188, 197,

206; David Macrae, *Americans at Home*, 2 vols. (Edinburgh: Edmonston and Douglas, 1870), 2:148–51; Sedgwick, *Morals of Manners*, 25–26; Howard, *Excelsior*, 61–62; *Complete Bachelor*, 7; Gerald Carson, *The Polite Americans* (New York: William Morrow, 1966), 88.

27. Conkling, *American Gentleman's Guide*, 343; Bunce, *Don't*, 35–36; Osmun, *Mentor*, 76. See Erving Goffman's discussion of social and self-involvement in *Behavior in Public Places* (New York: Free Press, 1963), 33–79.

28. L. E. White, *Success in Society*, 83; Goffman, *Behavior in Public Places*, 83–88; [De Valcourt], *Illustrated Manners Book*, 268, 267.

29. *Independent Mechanic*, May 1811, as quoted in Stansell, *City of Women*, 27; mid-nineteenth-century comic valentine, published in New York City, collection of American Antiquarian Society, Worcester, Massachusetts.

30. Westcott, "Physiology of Dandyism," 470–71. The staring of spectators was an international theme for caricaturists. See, e.g., Grandville's brilliant drawing *Venus at the Opera* (1844), in which he presents the viewers with single eyes for heads; reproduced in Judith Wechsler, *A Human Comedy: Physiognomy and Caricature in 19th Century Paris* (Chicago, University of Chicago Press, 1982), 102.

31. *Bad Breaks in Good Form*, 34, 36; *Ladies and Gentlemen's American Etiquette*, 32; [Leland], *Art of Conversation*, 95; *Beadle's Book of Etiquette*, 18.

32. *Manners That Win*, 288; Smiley, *Modern Manners*, 262; Moore, *Sensible Etiquette*, 508.

33. Young, *Our Deportment*, 145–46. For very similar advice, see, e.g., [Ruth], *Decorum*, 122; *Our Manners at Home and Abroad*, 98; Houghton et al., *Rules of Etiquette*, 103; R. A. Wells, *Manners*, 132.

34. Lofland, *World of Strangers*, 151–56; [Cogswell], *Perfect Etiquette*, 34; *Manners That Win*, 286–87; [Ruth], *Decorum*, 122; R. A. Wells, *Manners*, 132; Beezley, *Our Manners and Social Customs*, 139; A. R. White, *Twentieth Century Etiquette*, 138; Martine, *Hand-Book of Etiquette*, 119; *Points of Etiquette*, 32; Bugg, *Lady*, 222.

35. George G. Foster, *New York by Gas-Light: With Here and There a Streak of Sunshine* (New York: Dewitt & Davenport, 1850), 107–8; Stansell, *City of Women*, esp. 93–100, 171–92.

36. Martine, *Hand-Book of Etiquette*, 119; A. R. White, *Polite Society*, 36.

37. Dreiser, *Sister Carrie*, 323.

38. [Hall], *Social Customs*, 288; Smiley, *Modern Manners*, 262; McCabe, *National Encyclopaedia*, 412; Thornwell, *Lady's Guide to Perfect Gentility*, 78; Beezley, *Our Manners and Social Customs*, 139–40; Cooke, *Social Etiquette*, 336; [Marbury] *Manners*, 45; *Practical Etiquette*, 134.

39. James Thurber, *Alarms and Diversions* (New York: Harper & Brothers, 1957), 99. On chaperons and escorts, see, e.g., Smiley, *Modern Manners*, 318, 363–64; Bugg, *Lady*, 263–64; Sherwood, *Manners and Social Usages*, 222; *Practical Etiquette*, 72.

40. I am indebted to David Scobey for suggesting the importance of such illustrations.

41. "Crossing Broadway," *Harper's Weekly* 14 (March 12, 1870): 171; "Broadway During a Thaw," *Harper's Weekly* 26 (March 9, 1872): 189.

42. "The Recent 'Hot Wave' in the Metropolis," *Frank Leslie's Illustrated Newspaper* 52 (August 27, 1881): 425; my analysis of ritualized subordination in these illustrations draws upon Erving Goffman, *Gender Advertisements* (New York: Harper & Row, 1979), esp. 5.

43. John Allen Murray, ed., *George Washington's Rules of Civility and Decent Behaviour in Company and Conversation* (New York: G. P. Putnam's Sons, 1942), 18; Dixon Wecter, *The Saga of American Society: A Record of Social Aspiration, 1607–1937* (New York: Scribner's, 1937), 161; Orest Ranum, "Courtesy, Absolutism, and the Rise of the French State, 1630–1660," *Journal of Modern History* 52 (September 1980): 431.

44. Frances Trollope, *Domestic Manners of the Americans*, ed. Donald Smalley (1832; New York: Knopf, 1949), 100; Frederick Marryat, *A Diary in America, with Remarks on Its Institutions*, ed. Sydney Jackman (1839; reprint ed. Westport, Conn.: Greenwood Press, 1973), 461; Rudyard Kipling, *American Notes*, ed. Arrell Morgan Gibson (1891; Norman: University of Oklahoma Press, 1981), 17.

45. *Sister Carrie*, 43–44.

46. Ibid., 312, 361, 368, 463, 457.
47. Walter A. Wyckoff, *The Workers: An Experiment in Reality*, 2 vols., *The East* (New York: Charles Scribner's Sons, 1898), 5, 6.
48. Stevens, *Usages of the Best Society*, 4; [Delano and Arnold], *Simplex Munditiis*, 170.
49. *American Chesterfield*, 61; *Laws of Etiquette*, 61. For examples criticizing the snubbing of inferiors, see *Polite Present*, 26–27; Smiley, *Modern Manners*, 263; A. R. White, *Twentieth Century Etiquette*, 69.
50. On the question of whether to bow or simply greet servants, see [Conkling], *American Gentleman's Guide*, 130; Maxwell, *Manners and Customs*, 403; [Hall], *Social Customs*, 291–92; Cleveland, *Social Mirror*, 40–41.
51. Leslie, *Miss Leslie's Behaviour Book*, 66–67.
52. For versions referring to Washington, see [S. R. Wells], *How to Behave*, 69; *Perfect Gentleman*, 212; Martine, *Hand-Book of Etiquette*, 155; Gow, *Good Morals and Gentle Manners*, 208–9; *American Code of Manners*, 102; Smiley, *Modern Manners*, 35; A. R. White, *Twentieth Century Etiquette*, 144. This story of Washington is also alluded to in William Mathews, *Getting On in the World; or Hints on Success in Life* (Chicago: S. C. Griggs, 1889), 157. For versions concerning Clay, see *Beadle's Book of Etiquette*, 20; [Cogswell], *Perfect Etiquette*, 14; Cooke, *Social Etiquette*, 34; *Gentle Manners*, 61. With fine impartiality, Timothy Howard tells the story about both Washington and Clay in *Excelsior*, 72–73. For versions concerning Webster, see Johnson, *New York Fashion Bazar Book*, 15; L. E. White, *Success in Society*, 9. For an English version attributing the show of courtesy to Sir William Johnson, see [Thomas Hughes], *Notes for Boys (and Their Fathers) on Morals, Mind, and Manners* (Chicago: A. C. McClurg, 1888), 54–55.
53. Marryat, *Diary in America*, 75; see also Trollope, *Domestic Manners*, 100; [De Valcourt], *Illustrated Manners Book*, 103; [Tomes], *Bazar Book of Decorum*, 145–47; Edmund Morris, *The Rise of Theodore Roosevelt* (New York: Coward, McCann & Geoghegan, 1979), 27; *The Autobiography of William Allen White* (New York: Macmillan, 1946), 404–5.
54. *Blunders in Behavior Corrected*, 29; *Manners That Win*, 68.
55. For examples of such advice, see *Laws of Good Breeding*, 25; *Good Behavior for Ladies*, 27–28; [De Valcourt], *Illustrated Manners Book*, 103; *Ladies and Gentlemen's American Etiquette*, 28; *Bad Breaks in Good Form*, 39. Other etiquette writers suggested that rather than standing on formalities of precedence, acquaintances should "bow the instant their eyes meet" (Smiley, *Modern Manners*, 258).
56. Smiley, *Modern Manners*, 33.
57. Cooke, *Social Etiquette*, 31.
58. *Bad Breaks in Good Form*, 43.
59. Osmun, *Mentor*, 62.
60. [Lavin], *Good Manners*, 39.
61. See, e.g., [Hall], *Social Customs*, 222; Smiley, *Modern Manners*, 28; Cooke, *Social Etiquette*, 25; A. R. White, *Twentieth Century Etiquette*, 71.
62. See, e.g., Day, *American Ladies' and Gentleman's Manual*, 125–26; [De Valcourt], *Illustrated Manners Book*, 122; Willis, *Etiquette*, 11.
63. *Advice to a Young Gentleman*, 271; see also [Longstreet], *Social Etiquette of New York*, 238. On the bane of familiar address, see J. G. Holland, *Every-Day Topics*, 2d series (New York: Charles Scribner's Sons, 1882), 288–91.
64. The criticism of cutting appears in Rayne, *Gems of Deportment*, 79; defenses in Moore, *Sensible Etiquette*, 281; [Hall], *Social Customs*, 291. For an early-nineteenth-century satire on the art of cutting, see *The Cutter*.
65. *American Code of Manners*, 103; Moore, *Sensible Etiquette*, 282–83; see also Cleveland, *Social Mirror*, 76; [Hall], *Social Customs*, 292; [Delano and Arnold], *Simplex Munditiis*, 113. For the art of dropping an acquaintance, see, e.g., Day, *American Ladies' and Gentleman's Manual*, 19–20; F. Hartley, *Ladies' Book of Etiquette*, 113; Moore, *Sensible Etiquette*, 279, 281; McCabe, *National Encyclopaedia*, 488; A. R. White, *Polite Society*, 37; [Delano and Arnold], *Simplex Munditiis*, 113; *Practical Etiquette*, 136.

Chapter Five: Emotional Control

1. Arlie Russell Hochschild, *The Managed Heart: Commercialization of Human Feeling* (Berkeley: University of California Press, 1983), 57 and note 3, 250–51. On the importance of the distinction between the emotional *experience* of individuals and groups, on the one hand, and the collective emotional *standards* of a society, on the other, see Peter N. Stearns with Carol Z. Stearns, "Emotionology: Clarifying the History of Emotions and Emotional Standards," *American Historical Review* 90 (October 1985): 813–36; and Carol Zisowitz Stearns and Peter N. Stearns, *Anger: The Struggle for Emotional Control in America's History* (Chicago: University of Chicago Press, 1986), esp. 14. Stearns and Stearns advocate using their neologism "emotionology" instead of Hochschild's "feeling rules," but I find the term idiosyncratic and ungainly.

2. Norbert Elias, *The Civilizing Process*, vol. 1: *The History of Manners*, trans. Edmund Jephcott (New York: Urizen Books, 1978). On the expanding shelf of recent studies, see Stearns and Stearns, *Anger*, 24–28.

3. Ward McAllister, *Society as I Have Found It* (New York: Cassell, 1890), 256; Henry Adams, *Democracy: An American Novel* (New York: Farrar, Straus and Young, 1952), 144. On feeling, feigning, and emotional dissonance, see Hochschild, *Managed Heart*, 90.

4. Smiley, *Modern Manners*, 372; *Handbook of the Man of Fashion*, 32–33; [De Valcourt], *Illustrated Manners Book*, 205.

5. Samuel R. Wells, *New Physiognomy, or, Signs of Character* (New York: American Book Co., 1871), iii.

6. *Advice to a Young Gentleman*, 84, 134.

7. Charles Darwin, *The Expression of the Emotions in Man and Animals*, in Westminster ed., *Selected Works of Charles Darwin* (1872; New York: D. Appleton, 1900), 237.

8. Darwin, *Expression of Emotions*, 350, 356.

9. William James, *Psychology: The Briefer Course*, ed. Gordon Allport (1892; New York: Harper & Row, Harper Torchbook, 1961), xv.

10. William James, *The Principles of Psychology*, 2 vols. (New York: Henry Holt, 1890), 2:449–50.

11. James, *Briefer Course*, 249–50.

12. Ralph Barton Perry, *The Thought and Character of William James*, 2 vols. (Boston: Little, Brown, 1935), 2:90; James, *Briefer Course*, 1; James, *Principles of Psychology*, 1:122, 120.

13. James, *Principles of Psychology*, 1:121.

14. Ibid., 1:294.

15. John Henry Newman, *The Idea of a University*, ed. I. T. Ker (Oxford: Oxford University Press, Clarendon Press, 1976), 179. The addition, "unintentionally," often attributed to Oscar Wilde, is credited by various scholars to Oliver Herford. Francis W. Crowninshield plays the witticism as his own in *Manners for the Metropolis: An Entrance Key to the Fantastic Life of the 400* (New York: D. Appleton, 1909), 66.

16. [De Valcourt], *Illustrated Manners Book*, 271; Arthur, *Advice to Young Men*, 128; Hervey, *Principles of Courtesy*, 63.

17. Bryson, *Every-Day Etiquette*, 13; *Manners That Win*, 51; Osmun, *Mentor*, 190–91.

18. McCabe, *National Encyclopaedia*, 419.

19. John E. Mason, *Gentlefolk in the Making: Studies in the History of English Courtesy Literature and Related Topics from 1531 to 1774* (Philadelphia: University of Pennsylvania Press, 1935), 293; see, e.g., *Blunders in Behavior Corrected*, 28; Martine, *Hand-Book of Etiquette*, 159; *Our Manners at Home and Abroad*, 44–45; Smiley, *Modern Manners*, 273.

20. And women were encouraged to stay away from such topics. Advised Eliza Leslie in 1859, "Generally speaking, it is injudicious for ladies to attempt arguing with gentlemen on political or financial topics. All the information that a woman can possibly acquire or remember on these subjects is so small, in comparison with the knowledge of men, that the discussion will not elevate them in the opinion of masculine minds" (*Miss Leslie's Behaviour Book*, 197).

21. Don H. Doyle, "Rules of Order: Henry Martyn Robert and the Popularization of

American Parliamentary Law," *American Quarterly* 32 (Spring 1980): 3–18, esp. 16–17.
22. Frederick Marryat, *A Diary in America, with Remarks on Its Institutions*, ed. Sydney Jackman (1839; reprint ed. Westport, Conn.: Greenwood Press, 1973), 461.
23. Osmun, *Mentor*, 170; [Delano and Arnold], *Simplex Munditiis*, 174–75, 171; *Bad Breaks in Good Form*, 47. For a related discussion of the relationship between status and expressions of feeling, see Hochschild, *Managed Heart*, esp. 172.
24. [Farrar], *Young Lady's Friend*, 324; the same advice is closely paraphrased in Abell, *Woman in Her Various Relations*, 133; Hale, *Manners*, 319; [Ruth], *Decorum*, 204.
25. *Young Lady's Own Book*, 201; Leslie, *Miss Leslie's Behaviour Book*, 209–10. See the discussion of anger as treated in early- and mid-nineteenth-century marriage manuals and popular fiction in Stearns and Stearns, *Anger*, 36–68.
26. Rayne, *Gems of Deportment*, 66.
27. See Erving Goffman, *Behavior in Public Places* (New York: Free Press, 1963), 166–70.
28. Smiley, *Modern Manners*, 37; *Etiquette for Ladies: With Hints on . . . Female Beauty*, 91; [De Valcourt], *Illustrated Manners Book*, 251; A. R. White, *Polite Society*, 55; Cooke, *Social Etiquette*, 36; Griffin, *Young Folks' Book of Etiquette*, 28; [De Valcourt], *Illustrated Manners Book*, 125; *Gentle Manners*, 63; see also *Bad Breaks in Good Form*, 39; *Our Manners at Home and Abroad*, 93; Morton, *Etiquette*, 148; [Richards], *At Home and Abroad*, 63–64.
29. Keith Thomas, "The Place of Laughter in Tudor and Stuart England," *Times Literary Supplement* (January 21, 1977): 90; Mason, *Gentlefolk in the Making*, 297; [Philip Stanhope], *The Letters of the Earl of Chesterfield to His Son*, ed. Charles Strachey, 2d ed., 2 vols. (London: Metheun, 1924), 1:212. Thomas notes that in 1754 William Pitt gave his nephew identical advice.
30. For reiterations of Chesterfield's advice on laughter, see, e.g., *Guide to Good Manners*, 97, and *Polite Present*, 46; the passage appears with attribution in *American Chesterfield*, 136. On laughter's good effects, see Conkling, *American Gentleman's Guide*, 301. For the quotation warning against over much laughing, see Cooke, *Social Etiquette*, 48.
31. [Hall], *Social Customs*; for other examples, see [Farrar], *Young Lady's Friend*, 331–33; Abell, *Woman in Her Various Relations*, 135; F. Hartley, *Ladies' Book of Etiquette*, 113; Rayne, *Gems of Deportment*, 316; [Ruth], *Decorum*, 122; L. E. White, *Success in Society*, 188; Smiley, *Modern Manners*, 277; Beezley, *Our Manners and Social Customs*, 191.
32. Dewey, *How to Teach Manners*, 75; [Delano and Arnold], *Simplex Munditiis*, 135.
33. Bryson, *Every-Day Etiquette*, 24; see also Mackellar, *Treatise on Politeness*, 110.
34. For the text of the speech as well as reactions, see Henry Nash Smith's classic account, " 'That Hideous Mistake of Poor Clemens's,' " *Harvard Library Bulletin* 9 (Spring 1955): 145–80. On jokes and comic recognition, see Mary Douglas, "Jokes," in *Implicit Meanings* (London: Routledge & Kegan Paul, 1975), esp. 98–103.
35. Here I quote from Thomas, "Place of Laughter in Tudor and Stuart England," 77; and Mary Douglas, "Do Dogs Laugh?," in *Implicit Meanings*, 87.
36. Bryson, *Every-Day Etiquette*, 22.
37. Leslie, *Miss Leslie's Behaviour Book*, 31–32; Cooke, *Social Etiquette*, 46–47. On mirrors in the household, see Margaret B. Schiffer, *Chester County, Pennsylvania, Inventories, 1684–1850* (Exton, Pa.: Schiffer Publishing, 1934), 119; Edgar de N. Mayhew and Minor Myers, Jr., *A Documentary History of American Interiors: From the Colonial Era to 1915* (New York: Charles Scribner's Sons, 1980), 133; Kenneth L. Ames, "Meaning in Artifacts: Hall Furnishings in Victorian America," *Journal of Interdisciplinary History* 9 (Summer 1978): 19–46, esp. 34–35. On mirrors and the self, see Benjamin Goldberg, *The Mirror and Man* (Charlottesville: University Press of Virginia, 1985), esp. 247; and Robert Coles, *Privileged Ones: The Well-Off and the Rich in America* (Boston: Little, Brown, 1977), 363, 380–81.
38. See, e.g., Smiley, *Modern Manners*, 295; *Practical Etiquette*, 102.
39. Bryson, *Every-Day Etiquette*, 136; Gow, *Good Morals and Gentle Manners*, 194; L. E. White, *Success in Society*, 184.
40. John Newberry, *A Little Pretty Pocket-Book . . .* (1744; facsimile of 1767 ed., New York: Harcourt, Brace & World, 1967), 10; see the discussion of this passage in Stearns and Stearns, *Anger*, 22–23.
41. *Gentle Manners*, 54, Bennett, *Family Manners*, 5, 9.

42. "Traffic" in "The Crown of Wild Olive," E. T. Cook and Alexander Wedderburn, eds., *The Works of John Ruskin*, vol. 18 (London: George Allen, 1904), 434–35; A. J. Downing, *The Architecture of Country Houses* (New York: D. Appleton, 1850), 25.

43. On goods as ritual adjuncts, see Mary Douglas and Baron Isherwood, *The World of Goods: Toward an Anthropology of Consumption* (New York: Basic Books, 1979), esp. 65.

44. See Peter Gay, *The Bourgeois Experience: Victoria to Freud*, vol. 1: *Education of the Senses* (New York: Oxford University Press, 1984), 198.

45. Martine, *Hand-Book of Etiquette*, 165; Leslie, *Miss Leslie's Behaviour Book*, 47–48; the allusion is to Shakespeare's *Midsummer Night's Dream*.

46. David M. Katzman, *Seven Days a Week: Women and Domestic Service in Industrializing America* (New York: Oxford University Press, 1978), 44–95, 108–10; Daniel E. Sutherland, *Americans and Their Servants: Domestic Service in the United States from 1800 to 1920* (Baton Rouge: Louisiana State University Press, 1981), 114–17; on servants as nonpersons, see Erving Goffman, *The Presentation of Self in Everyday Life* (Garden City, N.Y.: Doubleday/Anchor Books, 1959), 151.

47. *Laws of Etiquette*, 185; Sherwood, *Manners and Social Usages*, 375; see also [Ruth], *Decorum*, 342.

48. [Tomes], *Bazar Book of Decorum*, 233; [Germain?], *Complete Bachelor*, 95.

49. Stevens, *Usages of the Best Society*, 198; see also Bryson, *Every-Day Etiquette*, 143; Learned, *Etiquette of New York To-day*, 283.

50. Helen Campbell, *Prisoners of Poverty: Women Wage-Workers, Their Trades and Their Lives* (Boston: Robert Brothers, 1887), 226, 230; Libbie to Margaret Scott, May 14, 1887, as quoted in Sutherland, *Americans and Their Servants*, 117; see also Lucy Maynard Salmon, *Domestic Service* (New York: Macmillan, 1897), esp. 151–66.

51. See Katherine C. Grier, *Culture and Comfort: People, Parlors, and Upholstery, 1850–1900* (Amherst: University of Massachusetts Press, 1988), 69 and note 31; Ames, "Meaning in Artifacts," 42–45.

52. This discussion draws heavily on Kenneth L. Ames, "Meaning in Artifacts," 19–46; the quotation is from Clarence Cook, *The House Beautiful* (New York: Scribner, Armstrong, 1878), 33.

53. See, for example, *Ladies' Science of Etiquette*, 9; *Good Behavior for Ladies*, 21.

54. Cook, *The House Beautiful*, 48–49; Cook himself preferred the term "living room" to "parlor." In this discussion of parlor furnishings and their "rhetoric" I owe much to Katherine Grier's brilliant study *Culture and Comfort*, esp. 1, 15, 80–82, 88–89, 143, 203–6.

55. *Art of Conversing*, 27. This book uses the word "drawing-room" rather than "parlor."

56. This subject is sensitively explored in Karen Halttunen, *Confidence Men and Painted Women: A Study of Middle-Class Culture in America, 1830–1870* (New Haven: Yale University Press, 1982), esp. 102–7; and Grier, *Culture and Comfort*, esp. 80–102.

57. [Harriet Beecher Stowe], *House and Home Papers* (Boston: Ticknor and Fields, 1865), 1–22, esp. 18, 20, 21. The contents of this volume were first published in *Atlantic Monthly* in 1864.

58. Clifford Edward Clark, Jr., *The American Family Home, 1800–1960* (Chapel Hill: University of North Carolina Press, 1986), 67–70; Joseph S. Van Why, "The Harriet Beecher Stowe House" (Hartford: Stowe-Day Foundation, 1982).

59. This entire paragraph is indebted to Hochschild's *Managed Heart*, esp. 20–21, 35, 119, 139, 156–59, 163–72, 186–87.

Chapter Six: Table Manners and the Control of Appetites

1. Garrick Mallery, "Manners and Meals," *The American Anthropologist* 1 (July 1888): 195. Mallery notes that this article was based upon a more extended paper presented before the Society in April of 1886. The distinction between brutes, barbarians, and cultured men is a variation of a celebrated aphorism of Jean Anthelme Brillat-Savarin. See his *Physiology of Taste; or Meditations on Transcendental Gastronomy*, trans. M. F. K. Fisher (New York: Knopf, 1971), 3.

2. Carl D. Schneider, *Shame, Exposure, and Privacy* (Boston: Beacon Press, 1977), 66–67.
3. See Roland A. Delattre, "The Rituals of Humanity and the Rhythms of Reality," *Prospects* 5 (New York: Burt Franklin, 1980): 35–49.
4. Norbert Elias, *The Civilizing Process*, vol. 1: *The History of Manners*, trans. Edmund Jephcott (New York: Urizen Books, 1978), 67. On medieval European table manners, see also Bridget Ann Henisch, *Fast and Feast: Food in Medieval Society* (University Park: Pennsylvania State University Press, 1976), esp. 147–205.
5. On the etiquette of nose blowing during this time, see Elias, *History of Manners*, 143–45.
6. Bernard Rudofsky, *Now I Lay Me Down to Eat* (Garden City, N.Y.: Doubleday/Anchor Books, 1980), 26–27; Arthur Burkhard, *The Herrenberg Altar of Jörg Ratgeb* (Munich: F. Bruckmann, 1965); Harold Osborne, ed., *The Oxford Companion to Art* (New York: Oxford University Press, 1970), 644–45.
7. Desiderius Erasmus, "On Good Manners for Boys," trans. Brian McGregor, in *Collected Works of Erasmus*, vol. 25, ed. J. K. Sowards (Toronto: University of Toronto Press, 1985), 283; Elias, *History of Manners*, 57.
8. George Francis Dow, *Domestic Life in New England in the Seventeenth Century* (Topsfield, Mass.: Perkins Press, 1925), 11; Edgar de N. Mayhew and Minor Myers, Jr., *A Documentary History of American Interiors: From the Colonial Era to 1915* (New York: Charles Scribner's Sons, 1980), 12–16; Alice Morse Earle, *Customs and Fashions in Old New England* (New York: Charles Scribner's Sons, 1893), 136–38.
9. Daniel Drake, *Pioneer Life in Kentucky, 1785–1800*, ed. Emmet Field Horone (New York: Henry Schuman, 1948), 213.
10. *Autobiography of Peter Cartwright* (1856; Centennial ed., New York: Abingdon Press, 1956), 169–70; Jack Larkin, *The Reshaping of Everyday Life, 1790–1840* (New York: Harper & Row, 1988), 132–33, 180.
11. J. E. Alexander, *Transatlantic Sketches*, 2 vols. (London: Richard Bentley, 1833), 2:102.
12. Charles Dickens, *American Notes for General Circulation* (1842; New York: Viking Penguin, 1972), 203.
13. Margaret Hunter Hall, *The Aristocratic Journey: Being the Outspoken Letters of Mrs. Basil Hall Written during a Fourteen Months' Sojourn in America, 1827–1828*, ed. Una Pope-Hennessy (New York: G. P. Putnam's Sons, 1931), 112–13.
14. Calvert A. Vaux, *Villas and Cottages: A Series of Designs Prepared for Execution in the United States* (1857; reprint ed. New York: Da Capo Press, 1968), 145.
15. *Six Hundred Dollars a Year: A Wife's Effort at Low Living, Under High Prices* (Boston: Ticknor and Fields, 1867), 22, 29, 53; Clifford E. Clark, Jr., "The Vision of the Dining Room: Plan Book Dreams and Middle-Class Realities," in Kathryn Grover, ed., *Dining in America, 1850–1900* (Amherst: University of Massachusetts Press and Margaret Woodbury Strong Museum, 1987), 154–55.
16. Susan Williams, *Savory Suppers and Fashionable Feasts: Dining in Victorian America* (New York: Pantheon Books, 1985), 63–68.
17. On Post, see Joan M. Seidl, "Consumers' Choices: A Study of Household Furnishings, 1880–1920," *Minnesota History* 48 (Spring 1983): 183–97, esp. 188–91; and Clark, "Vision of the Dining Room," 163–66. The quotations are from Post to his father, cited by both Seidl and Clark.
18. Williams, *Savory Suppers and Fashionable Feasts*, 37; Noel D. Turner, *American Silver Flatware, 1837–1910* (South Brunswick, N.J.: A. S. Barnes, 1972), 55–58, 63, 175–206.
19. Writing in *Harper's New Monthly Magazine* 37 (September 1868), James Parton remembered that "in the United States, as recently as 1835, [the use of silver forks] was confined to persons who possessed considerable wealth. They were not common at that time in any but the best hotels, and not one person in ten had ever seen them used" (quoted in Turner, *American Silver Flatware*, 176).
20. Richard J. Hooker, *Food and Drink in America: A History* (Indianapolis: Bobbs-Merrill, 1981), 97–98.
21. However, Esther B. Aresty speculates that Europeans were as right-handed in their use of forks as Americans until around the 1840s, when it began to be fashionable to keep

the fork in the left hand; see *The Best Behavior* (New York, Simon and Schuster, 1970), 175. James Deetz offers still another explanation of the idiosyncratic American use of the fork. He suggests that since forks came into general use much later in colonial New England than in England, even while the colonies imported round-ended knives instead of the pointed blades of old, Americans came to use spoons far more than the English to eat their food. When at last forks were adopted in the eighteenth century, Americans proceeded to employ them, once they cut their food, like spoons (*In Small Things Forgotten: The Archaeology of Early American Life* [Garden City, N.Y.: Anchor Press/Doubleday, 1977], 123).

22. Elizabeth F. Ellet, *Court Circles of the Republic* (Philadelphia: Philadelphia Publishing Co., 1872), 148.

23. Nicholas B. Wainwright, ed., *A Philadelphia Perspective: The Diary of Sidney George Fisher Covering the Years 1834–1871* (Philadelphia: Historical Society of Pennsylvania, 1967), 50.

24. Alexander, *Transatlantic Sketches*, 2:63–64.

25. D. C. Johnston, "The farmers [*sic*] son metamorphosed into a finished exquisite," *Scraps*, No. 6 (Boston: D. C. Johnston, 1835), plate 4, American Antiquarian Society. See also Johnston's caricature of a dandy swooning at the sight of a wooden spoon in "Sensibility," *Scraps*, No. 8 (Boston: D. C. Johnston, 1840), plate 3.

26. Dickens, *American Notes*, 192; see also Hall, *Aristocratic Journey*, 33–37.

27. [Farrar], *Young Lady's Friend*, 346–47.

28. *Art of Good Behavior*, 28.

29. *Art of Pleasing*, 48–49. At roughly the same time, Eliza Leslie observed, "Much of this determined fork-exercise may be considered foolish. But it is fashionable" (*Miss Leslie's Behaviour Book*, 128).

30. *The Family and Householder's Guide; or, How to Keep House . . .* (Auburn, N.Y.: Auburn Publishing Co., 1859), 29, as discussed in Louise Conway Belden, *The Festive Tradition: Table Decorations and Desserts in America* (New York: W. W. Norton, 1983), 27–28.

31. Russell Lynes, *The Domesticated Americans* (New York: Harper & Row, 1963), 182, quoting a source from the 1860s.

32. Sherwood, *Manners and Social Usages*, 361.

33. Arthur M. Schlesinger, *Learning How to Behave: A Historical Study of American Etiquette Books* (New York: Macmillan, 1946), 41.

34. Or as a writer for *Harper's* put it, "Show me the way people dine and I will tell you their rank among civilized beings" ("Silver and Silver Plate," *Harper's New Monthly Magazine* 37 [September 1868]: 434).

35. Smiley, *Modern Manners*, 203–4, 300; Armstrong, *On Habits and Manners*, 8. Nathan D. Urner enjoined men, "Never appear at breakfast, even in sultry weather, without your coat, waistcoat, collar and necktie. Are you a gentleman or a Hottentot?" (*Never*, 23).

36. Armstrong, *On Habits and Manners*, 10.

37. Griffin, *Young Folks' Book of Etiquette*, 53–54.

38. Leslie, *Miss Leslie's Behaviour Book*, 291.

39. Catharine E. Beecher and Harriet Beecher Stowe, *The American Woman's Home* (1869; reprint ed. Watkins Glen, N.Y.: American Life Foundation, 1979), 207.

40. See Mary Douglas, *Purity and Danger: An Analysis of the Concept of Pollution and Taboo* (New York: Praeger, 1966), 120–24; idem, *Natural Symbols: Explorations in Cosmology* (New York: Random House, 1973), esp. 12; and idem, "Do Dogs Laugh? A Cross-Cultural Approach to Body Symbolism," in *Implicit Meanings* (London: Routledge and Kegan Paul, 1975), 87; and also Peter Stallybrass and Allon White, *The Politics and Poetics of Transgression* (London: Methuen, 1986), esp. 7–8, 20–22.

41. Luke 16:19–31.

42. Roger Butterfield, *The American Past* (New York: Simon and Schuster, 1947), 258.

43. See Pierre Bourdieu, *Distinction: A Social Critique of the Judgement of Taste*, trans. Richard Nice (Cambridge: Harvard University Press, 1984), 179–200.

44. [Richards], *At Home and Abroad*, 26.

45. Bryson, *Every-Day Etiquette*, 97.

46. McCabe, *National Encyclopaedia*, 428.
47. Ibid. Cf. *Guide to Good Manners*, 78, where dinner etiquette is called "the *fiery ordeal* by which a person's good breeding is attested."
48. Frederick Townsend Martin, *The Passing of the Idle Rich* (Garden City, N.Y.: Doubleday, Page, 1911), 30–55, quotation on 39; Dixon Wecter, *The Saga of American Society: A Record of Social Aspiration, 1607–1937* (New York: Scribner's, 1937), 180–82.
49. Williams, *Savory Suppers and Fashionable Feasts*, 88.
50. Unidentified author, quoted in A. R. White, *Polite Society*, 183.
51. Sherwood, *Manners and Social Usages*, 314.
52. Ibid., 315. See the similar menu for a "simple dinner" in *American Code of Manners*, 65–66. The author adds: "Such a dinner as this can be given once a week by people of moderate fortune to a party of ten without extravagance."
53. Ward McAllister, *Society as I Have Found It* (New York: Cassell, 1890), 299. McAllister here paraphrased the English wit Sydney Smith.
54. Young, *Our Deportment*, 106. Smiley makes this same point in *Modern Manners*, 162.
55. See [Ruth], *Decorum*, 92.
56. Howard, *Excelsior*, 83.
57. Smiley, *Modern Manners*, 167–68.
58. Howard, *Excelsior*, 84.
59. This remained true even when, by the turn of the century, etiquette advisers were noting that it was no longer as large as previously. E.g.: "Short dinners are the modern fashion. The menu consists, as a general rule, of grapefruit, canapés of caviar, soup, fish, an entrée, a roast with two vegetables, game and salad, dessert and fruit." "Cheese," she added in the next breath, "is sometimes served after the game. If artichokes or asparagus are served they are separate courses" (Learned, *Etiquette of New York To-day*, 85).
60. Smiley, *Modern Manners*, 175.
61. *Journal and Letters of Philip Vickers Fithian, 1773–1774: A Plantation Tutor of the Old Dominion*, ed. Hunter Dickinson Farish (Williamsburg, Va.: Colonial Williamsburg, 1943), entry for July 13, 1774, 185.
62. Belden, *Festive Tradition*, 4–5, 19–21, 33.
63. Henry Bradshaw Fearon, *Sketches of America* (London: Longman, Hurst, Rees, Orme, and Brown, 1818), 112.
64. Belden, *Festive Tradition*, 34.
65. See, e.g., Smiley, *Modern Manners*, 172–73. "Sometimes," Smiley added, "there is one [servant] for each guest, but that is ostentatious."
66. The great French gastronomer Jean Anthelme Brillat-Savarin recommended that "the progress of the . . . [dishes] be from the most substantial to the lightest, and of the . . . [wines] from the simplest . . . to the headiest" (*Physiology of Taste*, 258), and his advice on the conduct of a dinner was often quoted in American etiquette books. However, I am mystified how Noel Turner can attribute the new American fashion of dining in courses solely to the influence of Brillat-Savarin, since it is not a particular concern of his book, and Brillat-Savarin enthusiastically describes meals conducted in the older fashion. See, for example, *Physiology of Taste*, 251–52, and M. F. K. Fisher's note 5 on 258. For Turner's assertion, see *American Silver Flatware*, 176–77.
67. [Catharine Sedgwick], *Letters from Abroad to Kindred at Home*, 2 vols. (New York: Harper & Brothers, 1841), 1:213; see also Sedgwick's experience in Milan, 2:64.
68. Allan Nevins, ed., *The Diary of Philip Hone, 1828–1851*, 2 vols. (New York: Dodd, Mead, 1927), 1:300; see also 1:462. Turner, *American Silver Flatware*, 176–77; Hooker, *Food and Drink in America*, 141–42.
69. Belden, *Festive Tradition*, 33–36. See Mary Douglas, "Deciphering a Meal," in Clifford Geertz, ed., *Myth, Symbol, and Culture* (New York: Norton, 1971), 61–81; Bourdieu, *Distinction*, 196.
70. This is what Mary Douglas has called the "purity rule." See *Natural Symbols*, 12, 16; and idem, *Purity and Danger*.
71. Howard, *Excelsior*, 87.
72. Smiley, *Modern Manners*, 183.

73. Ibid., 174.
74. Ibid., 188–89.
75. "Table Customs," *Scribner's Monthly* 8 (September 1874): 627.
76. Smiley, *Modern Manners*, 186.
77. [Ruth], *Decorum*, 213; see also Smiley, *Modern Manners*, 185; on nose wiping, see Smiley, 184.
78. [Longstreet], *Social Etiquette of New York*, 129.
79. Smiley, *Modern Manners*, 185.
80. Logan et al., *Home Manual*, 47–48.
81. Smiley, *Modern Manners*, 182.
82. Young, *Our Deportment*, 118.
83. "After enjoying the hospitality of another's board, it is not in good taste to depart immediately, as though you were indeed a boarder. . . ." (Howard, *Excelsior*, 89).
84. Smiley, *Modern Manners*, 177.
85. Douglas, *Purity and Danger*, 62–63.
86. Victor Turner, *The Ritual Process: Structure and Anti-Structure* (Ithaca: Cornell University Press, 1969), esp. 131.
87. Victor Turner, *Dramas, Fields, and Metaphors: Symbolic Action in Human Society* (Ithaca: Cornell University Press, 1974), 237.
88. Mark Twain, *The Innocents Abroad*, authorized ed. (New York: Harper & Brothers, 1917), 1:189; Sydney E. Ahlstrom, *A Religious History of the American People* (New Haven: Yale University Press, 1972), 779.
89. The Last Supper, of course, was also horrifying in the context of Jewish dietary laws of its own day; see the illuminating discussion in Gillian Feeley-Harnik, *The Lord's Table: Eucharist and Passover in Early Christianity* (Philadelphia: University of Pennsylvania Press, 1981).
90. Joachim Jeremias, *New Testament Theology*, vol. 1, *The Proclamation of Jesus*, trans. John Bowden (London: SCM Press, 1971), 290. For this reference I am indebted to John Staudenmeier, S.J.
91. See John Murray Cuddihy, *The Ordeal of Civility* (New York: Basic Books, 1974), 158.

Chapter Seven: The Disciplining of Spectatorship

1. This theme is developed with particular richness in Lawrence W. Levine's *Highbrow/Lowbrow: The Emergence of Cultural Hierarchy in America* (Cambridge: Harvard University Press, 1988). Although I prepared a draft of this chapter before reading Levine's study, his work supports and extends much of my discussion.
2. Vera Brodsky Lawrence, *Strong on Music: The New York Music Scene in the Days of George Templeton Strong, 1836–1875*, vol. 1, *Resonances, 1836–1850* (New York: Oxford University Press, 1988), 35–36.
3. See Charles Coleman Sellers, *Mr. Peale's Museum* (New York: W. W. Norton, 1980); and Neil Harris, *Humbug: The Art of P. T. Barnum* (Boston: Little, Brown, 1973).
4. Levine, *Highbrow/Lowbrow*, 21–23.
5. David Grimsted, *Melodrama Unveiled: American Theater and Culture, 1800–1850* (Chicago: University of Chicago Press, 1968), 52–56; Francis Hodge, *Yankee Theatre: The Image of America on the Stage, 1825–1850* (Austin: University of Texas Press, 1964), 38–40. On prostitutes and their importance to the antebellum theater, see Claudia D. Johnson, "That Guilty Third Tier: Prostitution in Nineteenth-Century American Theaters," in Daniel Walker Howe, ed., *Victorian America* (Philadelphia: University of Pennsylvania Press, 1976), 111–20.
6. Washington Irving, *Letters of Jonathan Oldstyle, Gent.*, ed. Bruce I. Granger and Martha Hartzog (Boston: Twayne, 1977), 12–18.
7. Frances Trollope, *Domestic Manners of the Americans*, ed. Donald Smalley (1832; New York: Knopf, 1949), 133–34, 233–34, 271, 339–40.
8. *New-York Mirror* 10 (September 29, 1832): 103; also 13 (December 12, 1835): 191. See Donald Smalley's note to *Domestic Manners*, 134n; also, for another instance, [De Val-

court], *Illustrated Manners Book*, 247. The Irish actor Tyrone Power painted a far milder portrait of American audiences, observing, "I saw no coats off, no heels up, no legs over boxes—these times have passed away" (*Impressions of America: During the Years 1833, 1834, and 1835*, 2 vols. [Philadelphia: Carey, Lea & Blanchard, 1836], 1:47).

9. Robert C. Toll, *On with the Show: The First Century of Show Business in America* (New York: Oxford University Press, 1976), 7.

10. See for example, Fanny Kemble Wister, ed., *Fanny: The American Kemble; Her Journals and Unpublished Letters* (Tallahassee: South Pass Press, 1972), 96–97, 99.

11. *New-York Mirror* 10 (June 8, 1833): 387. See also Trollope, *Domestic Manners*, 134; Irving, *Jonathan Oldstyle*, 14.

12. The outstanding study in this regard is Peter George Buckley, "To the Opera House: Culture and Society in New York City, 1820–1860" (Ph.D. diss., State University of New York at Stony Brook, 1984).

13. Ibid., 164–65.

14. Ibid., 168–80.

15. See ibid., 186–93.

16. On the Astor Place riot, see esp. Buckley, "Opera House"; Richard Moody, *The Astor Place Riot* (Bloomington: Indiana University Press, 1956); Montrose J. Moses, *The Fabulous Forrest: The Record of an American Actor* (Boston: Little, Brown, 1929); and Alan S. Downer, *The Eminent Tragedian: William Charles Macready* (Cambridge: Harvard University Press, 1966).

17. *The Diaries of William Charles Macready, 1833–1851*, ed. William Toynbee, 2 vols. (London: Chapman and Hall, 1912), 2:327.

18. Letter to *The* (London) *Times*, March 22, 1846; reprinted in Moses, *Fabulous Forrest*, 221–22.

19. Macready, *Diaries*, 2:229–30.

20. As Alan Downer notes, Macready had consistently opposed hereditary privilege and monarchical power; *Eminent Tragedian*, 268.

21. The "upper ten" was an abbreviation of the "upper ten thousand," who constituted the New York elite, a phrase coined by Nathaniel Parker Willis in 1844. The "codfish aristocracy" was a disparaging term for the nouveaux riches; it referred specifically to those Massachusetts families who owed their fortunes to the codfish industry. The phrase was popularized in 1849 by James Gordon Bennett of the *New York Herald*. See Lawrence, *Strong on Music*, 1:298; Nancy Laroche, ed., *Picturesque Expressions: A Thematic Dictionary* (Detroit: Gale Research Co., 1980), 325.

22. Macready, *Diaries*, 2:407–8.

23. Ibid., 2:410.

24. Ibid., 2:420.

25. Richard Grant White, "Opera in New York," *Century Illustrated Monthly* 23 (April 1882): 869; for a similar comparison between the Park Theater and its refurbished and reformed successor, see [George William Curtis], "Editor's Easy Chair," *Harper's New Monthly Magazine* 40 (March 1870): 605–7.

26. [Nathaniel Parker Willis], "After-Lesson of the Astor-Place Riot, *Home Journal* 17 (May 26, 1849): 2.

27. White, "Opera in New York," 879–81; Buckley, "Opera House," 263–67; Jay R. S. Teran, "The New York Opera Audience: 1825–1974" (Ph.D. diss., New York University, 1974), 19.

28. Letter from Prescott to John Kenyon, June 8, 1849, New-York Historical Society, quoted in Buckley, "Opera House," 249. This coincidence of a "triple target" of Macready, the "codfish aristocracy," and Opera House is extensively analyzed by Buckley's work.

29. [Willis], "After-Lesson," 2.

30. Macready, *Diaries*, 2:422–24; *New York Herald*, May 8, 1849.

31. In his detailed analysis of the forty-seven signers, Peter Buckley concludes that "all but four had pronounced Whig sympathies and twelve had been party candidates or office holders" ("Opera House," 214).

32. Richard Moody states that thirty-one people died; Peter Buckley argues that this figure

is erroneous and that only twenty-two died altogether; Moody, *The Astor Place Riot*, 216; Buckley, "Opera House," 3, 5–6.

33. Richard Sennett, *The Fall of Public Man* (New York: Knopf, 1977), esp. 75–76; on audiences in eighteenth-century London, see James J. Lynch, *Box, Pit, and Gallery: Stage and Society in Johnson's London* (Berkeley: University of California Press, 1953), esp. 199–207.

34. Peter Anthony Bloom, "The Public for Orchestral Music in the Nineteenth Century," in Joan Peyser, ed., *The Orchestra: Origins and Transformations* (New York: Charles Scribner's Sons, 1986), 279; see also William Weber, *Music and the Middle Class: The Social Structure of Concert Life in London, Paris, and Vienna* (New York: Holmes & Meier, 1975), 3.

35. On this transformation and the professionalization of the theater, see Benjamin McArthur, *Actors and American Culture, 1880–1920* (Philadelphia: Temple University Press, 1984), esp. 3–26; and Bruce McConachie, "Pacifying American Theatrical Audiences, 1820–1900," in Richard Butsch, ed., *For Fun and Profit: The Transformation of Leisure into Consumption* (Philadelphia: Temple University Press, 1990), forthcoming.

36. Charles Edward Russell, *The American Orchestra and Theodore Thomas* (Garden City, N.Y.: Doubleday, Page, 1927), 27–29; Bloom, "The Public for Orchestral Music," 270; Weber, *Music and the Middle Class*, 21, 58–59; Harold C. Schonberg, *The Great Conductors* (New York: Simon and Schuster, 1967), 71–74.

37. Philip Hart, *Orpheus in the New World: The Symphonic Orchestra as an American Cultural Institution* (New York: W. W. Norton, 1973), 3.

38. John H. Mueller, *The American Symphony Orchestra: A Social History of Musical Taste* (Bloomington: Indiana University Press, 1951), 37–51; Howard Shanet, *Philharmonic: A History of New York's Orchestra* (Garden City, N.Y.: Doubleday, 1975), 79–220. Strong's assessment of the 1843 audience appears in Lawrence, *Strong on Music*, 1:194; his 1856 judgment is quoted in Shanet, *Philharmonic*, 123–24.

39. See M. A. De Wolfe Howe, *The Boston Symphony Orchestra, 1881–1931* (Boston: Houghton Mifflin, 1931); quotation from John Sullivan Dwight, "The Orchestra Problem Well-Nigh Settled," *Dwight's Journal of Music* (April 9, 1881), reprinted in Irving Sablosky, ed., *What They Heard: Music in America, 1852–1881, from the Pages of "Dwight's Journal of Music"* (Baton Rouge: Louisiana University Press, 1986), 251.

40. Adam Carse, *The Life of Jullien* (Cambridge, England: W. Heffer & Sons, 1951), 74, 83, 101–2, 113–14, 117; Theodore Thomas, *A Musical Autobiography*, ed. George P. Upton, 2 vols. (Chicago: A. C. McClurg, 1905), 1:26–27.

41. Joseph Horowitz, *Understanding Toscanini* (New York: Knopf, 1987), 22.

42. Thomas, *Musical Autobiography*, 1:58.

43. Ibid., 1:215, 243.

44. On Thomas's physical presence, see Russell, *Theodore Thomas*, 41; on uniform bowing, see the comment by the *Boston Journal* music critic reviewing three concerts by Thomas and the Chicago Orchestra in 1898: "The uniformity in bowing is a delight to the eye" (quoted in Rose Fay Thomas, *Memoirs of Theodore Thomas* [New York: Moffat, Yard, 1911], 478). Lilli Lehmann made a similar comment in *My Pathway through Life*, trans. Alice Benedict Seligman (New York: G. P. Putnam's Sons, 1914), 344.

45. Russell, *Theodore Thomas*, 283–84.

46. Ibid., 287.

47. As the Chicago *Standard* wrote on the occasion of Thomas's death in 1905, "He not only disciplined his musicians but he disciplined the public, educating it sometimes perhaps against its will" (quoted in Rose Thomas, *Memoirs*, 562).

48. "Music and Cigars," *New York Times*, June 2, 1873, 4; Thomas, *Musical Autobiography*, 1:133; I am indebted to Roy Rosenzweig for the first reference.

49. Russell, *Theodore Thomas*, 67–68; Lehmann, *Pathway through Life*, 345.

50. Thomas, *Musical Autobiography*, 2:18–19, 1:133; Rose Thomas, *Memoirs*, 77, 239, 314–15; Russell, *Theodore Thomas*, 82–83.

51. Thomas, *Musical Autobiography*, 2:20–23. Cf. Gustav Mahler's campaign against latecomers in Vienna and Arturo Toscanini's enforcement of audience discipline at La Scala in Milan; Horowitz, *Understanding Toscanini*, 45–48.

52. Thomas, *Musical Autobiography*, 1:152, 2:3; Russell, *Theodore Thomas*, 88–89; Rose Thomas, *Memoirs*, 258; J. Peter Burkholder, "The Twentieth Century and the Orchestra as Museum," in Peyser, ed., *Orchestra*, 410–11.
53. Quoted in Henry Edward Krehbiel, *The Philharmonic Society of New York* (New York: Novello, Ewer, 1892), 64–65.
54. Allan Nevins and Milton Halsey Thomas, eds., *The Diary of George Templeton Strong*, 4 vols. (New York: Macmillan, 1952), 2:389.
55. Ibid., 4:353–54; see also 327, 330, 340.
56. Ibid., 4:353.
57. Program, Theodore Thomas, Summer Nights Concert, Central Park Garden, New York, June 5, 1874, New-York Historical Society, Box—Large Programs, 1870s, N–Z.
58. Program, Mendelssohn Glee Club, Chickering Hall, New York, April 17, 1877, New-York Historical Society, Box—Large Programs, 1870s, N–Z.
59. Howe, *Boston Symphony Orchestra*, 96.
60. Playbill, Booth's Theatre, New York, January 29, 1876, New-York Historical Society, Box—Large Programs, 1870s, N–Z.
61. Playbill, Carter Zouave Troupe, Charlestown City Hall, July 1864, Harvard Theatre Collection, Minstrels, Box Ca–Ce.
62. Playbill, Carncross & Dixey's Minstrels, New Eleventh Street Opera House, Philadelphia, 1876–77 season, Harvard Theatre Collection, Minstrels, Box Ca–Ce. The same rule of the hall appears on playbills in the Harvard Theatre Collection as early as May 1868.
63. E.g., Playbill, Campbell's Minstrelsy, St. Nicholas Exhibition Room, New York, March 16, 1853, Harvard Theatre Collection, Minstrels, Box Ca–Ce.
64. On boxing in the nineteenth century, see Elliott J. Gorn, *The Manly Art: Bare-Knuckle Prize Fighting in America* (Ithaca: Cornell University Press, 1987).
65. Smiley, *Modern Manners*, 283.
66. See Dewey, *Lessons on Manners*, 91; Cleveland, *Social Mirror*, 36; Frederic Dan Huntington, *Good Manners a Fine Art* (Syracuse: Wolcott & West, 1892), 35; and L. E. White, *Success in Society*, 54.
67. Dewey, *Lessons on Manners*, 87.
68. Cleveland, *Social Mirror*, 35–36.
69. Helen L. Roberts, *Putnam's Handbook of Etiquette* (New York: G. P. Putnam's Sons, 1913), 289–90.
70. Edward Baxter Perry, "Mutual Courtesy Between Artist and Audience," *Music* 2 (July 1892): 246–55.
71. Bruce A. McConachie, "New York Operagoing, 1825–1850: Creating an Elite Social Ritual," *American Music* 6 (Summer 1988): 181–92; Levine, *Highbrow/Lowbrow*, 85–104; Michael Hays, "Theater History and Practice: An Alternative View of Drama," *New German Critique* 12 (Fall 1977): 85–97, esp. 93; Teran, "New York Opera Audience," 47, 55–64; William Weber, "Wagner, Wagnerism, and Musical Idealism," in David C. Large and William Weber, eds., *Wagnerism in European Culture and Politics* (Ithaca: Cornell University Press, 1984), 28–71, esp. 35; Charles Dana Gibson, *The Social Ladder* (New York: R. H. Russell, 1902); [George William Curtis], "Editor's Easy Chair," *Harper's New Monthly Magazine* 69 (July 1884): 802–3; also ibid. 60 (February 1880): 463–64; 66 (April 1883): 793–94; for a defense of noisy boxholders, see "About the World," *Scribner's Magazine* 19 (April 1896): 525–26; a palliative view is in Katherine Metcalf Root, "The Opera Singer and the American Audience," *Craftsman* 9 (March 1906): 802–10, esp. 806.
72. [George William Curtis], "Editor's Easy Chair," *Harper's New Monthly Magazine* 72 (April 1886): 803; Perry, "Mutual Courtesy," 246–55; on the sacralization of art and its implications for audiences, see Levine's fine discussion in *Highbrow/Lowbrow*, esp. 186–95.
73. Philip G. Hubert, Jr., "The Abuse of Applause," *Century Illustrated Monthly* 38 (May 1889): 158–59; on Wagner's role in this sacralization, see Large and Weber, eds., *Wagnerism*.

74. George Gladden, "Is Applause Necessary?," *Music* 8 (September 1895): 431–36; Wagner's distinction between looking and listening is quoted in Weber, "Wagner, Wagnerism, and Musical Idealism," 42; see also Anne Dzamba Sessa, "At Wagner's Shrine: British and American Wagnerians," in Large and Weber, eds., *Wagnerism*, 246–77.

75. Mark Twain, "At the Shrine of St. Wagner" (1891), in *What Is Man?*, authorized ed. (New York: Harper & Brothers, 1917), 224–25; Gladden, "Is Applause Necessary?," 436.

76. Irving Kolodin, *The Metropolitan Opera, 1883–1966* (New York: Knopf, 1966), 3–6, 49–55; Mary Ellis Peltz, *Behind the Gold Curtain; The Story of the Metropolitan Opera: 1883–1950* (New York: Farrar, Straus, 1950), 7–11; Mary C. Henderson, *The City and the Theatre: New York Playhouses from Bowling Green to Times Square* (Clifton, N.J.: James T. White, 1973); New York *Evening Post*, October 23, 1883; Robert A. M. Stern, Gregory Gilmartin, and John Montague Massengale, *New York 1900: Metropolitan Architecture and Urbanism, 1890–1915* (New York: Rizzoli, 1983), 203.

77. Charles C. Baldwin, *Stanford White* (New York: Dodd, Mead, 1931), 199–207; Stern et al., *New York 1900*, 203.

78. Harris, *Humbug*, 244–45.

79. Robert C. Toll, *Blacking Up: The Minstrel Show in Nineteenth-Century America* (New York: Oxford University Press, 1974), 145–52; idem, *On with the Show*, 106–8.

80. B. F. Keith, "The Vogue of the Vaudeville," *National Magazine* 9 (November 1898): 146–53, reprinted in Charles W. Stein, ed., *American Vaudeville as Seen by Its Contemporaries* (New York: Knopf, 1984), 17. On the origins of vaudeville, see Stein, x–5; Robert William Snyder, "The Voices of the City: Vaudeville and the Formation of Mass Culture in New York Neighborhoods, 1880–1930" (Ph.D. diss., New York University, 1986), 27–59; Robert C. Allen, "B. F. Keith and the Origins of American Vaudeville," *Theatre Survey* 21 (November 1980): 105–15; Elizabeth Kendall, *Where She Danced* (New York: Knopf, 1979), 37–38; Toll, *On with the Show*, 271–72.

81. Edwin Milton Royle, "The Vaudeville Theatre," *Scribner's Magazine* 26 (October 1899): 487.

82. Douglas Gilbert, *American Vaudeville* (New York: Whittlesey House, 1940), 204–5. See also B. F. Keith's account of his lecture to a demonstrative gallery in Providence in Albert F. McLean, Jr., "Genesis of Vaudeville: Two Letters from B. F. Keith," *Theatre Survey* 1 (1960): 82–95, esp. 93–94.

83. Royle, "Vaudeville Theatre," 488; Gilbert, *American Vaudeville*, 244.

84. Levine recounts the Forrest incident in *Highbrow/Lowbrow*, 30; the anecdote concerning Adler is in Irving Howe, *World of Our Fathers* (New York: Simon and Schuster, 1976), 484.

85. Hutchins Hapgood, "The Foreign Stage in New York: The Yiddish Theatre," *Bookman* 11 (June 1900): 348–58, esp. 349.

86. John Corbin, "How the Other Half Laughs," *Harper's New Monthly Magazine* 98 (December 1898): 30–48.

87. See John F. Kasson, *Amusing the Million: Coney Island at the Turn of the Century* (New York: Hill and Wang, 1978).

88. Russell Merritt, "Nickelodeon Theaters 1905–1914: Building an Audience for the Movies," in Tino Balio, ed., *The American Film Industry* (Madison: University of Wisconsin Press, 1976), 62–63; Charles Stelzle, "How One Thousand Workingmen Spend Their Spare Time," *Outlook* 106 (April 4, 1914): 762.

89. Roy Rosenzweig, *Eight Hours for What We Will: Workers and Leisure in an Industrial City, 1870–1920* (Cambridge: Cambridge University Press, 1983), 201–3; Jane Addams, *The Spirit of Youth and the City Streets* (New York: Macmillan, 1910), 86.

90. John Collier, "Leisure Time, the Last Problem of Conservation," *Playground* 6 (June 1912): 94.

91. Merritt, "Nickelodeon Theaters," 73–79; Lary May, *Screening Out the Past: The Birth of Mass Culture and the Motion Picture Industry* (New York: Oxford University Press, 1980), 147–52.

92. Rosenzweig, *Eight Hours*, 212, 217.

93. See Robert B. Westbrook, "Politics as Consumption: Managing the Modern American

Election," in Richard Wightman Fox and T. J. Jackson Lears, eds., *The Culture of Consumption: Critical Essays in American History, 1880–1980* (New York: Pantheon Books, 1983), 143–73.

Epilogue

1. Arlie Russell Hochschild, *The Managed Heart: Commercialization of Human Feeling* (Berkeley: University of California Press, 1983), 22.
2. For the key shift in emphasis between "character" and "personality" after the turn of the century, see Warren I. Susman, " 'Personality' and the Making of Twentieth-Century Culture," in John Higham and Paul K. Conkin, eds., *New Directions in American Intellectual History* (Baltimore: Johns Hopkins University Press, 1979), 212–26.
3. See, e.g., Thomas Nelson Page, "On the Decay of Manners," *Century Illustrated Monthly* 81 (April 1911): 881–87.
4. Hochschild, *Managed Heart*, 192.

Selected Bibliography of Etiquette Books, 1800–1910

I list here books on etiquette published in the United States in the nineteenth century and the first decade of the twentieth century that I have found useful. I have avoided listing more than one edition of each work and identical works by an author under different titles, as well as more general essays and stories on manners, books on housekeeping, success, health, and other related works of advice.

Abell, Mrs. L. G. *Woman in Her Various Relations: Containing Practical Rules for American Females.* . . . 1851; New York: R. T. Young, 1853.

Advice to a Young Gentleman, on Entering Society. Philadelphia: Lea & Blanchard, 1839.

The American Chesterfield, or Way to Wealth, Honour and Distinction. . . . 1827; Philadelphia: Lippincott, Grambo, 1852.

The American Code of Manners. . . . New York: W. R. Andrews, 1880.

Antrim, Minna Thomas. *Don'ts for Girls: A Manual of Mistakes.* Philadelphia: Henry Altemus, 1902.

Armstrong, Mary Frances. *On Habits and Manners.* Rev. ed. Hampton, Va.: Normal School Press, 1888.

The Art of Conversing. . . . Boston: James French, 1846.

The Art of Good Behavior, and Letter Writer on Love, Courtship and Marriage. . . . New York: C. P. Huestis, 1845.

The Art of Pleasing; or, The American Lady and Gentleman's Book of Etiquette. 1852; Cincinnati: H. M. Rulison, 1855.

Arthur, Timothy S. *Advice to Young Men on Their Duties and Conduct in Life.* 1847; Boston: Phillips, Sampson, 1853.

Bad Breaks in Good Form. . . . New York: Brentano's, 1897.

Baker, George Augustus, Jr. *The Bad Habits of Good Society.* 1876; New York: White, Stokes, & Allen, 1886.

Bayle-Mouillard, Elisabeth Felicie [Mme. Celnart, pseud.]. *The Gentleman and Lady's Book of Politeness and Propriety of Deportment, Dedicated to the Youth of Both Sexes.* 1833; 5th American ed., Philadelphia: Grigg, Elliot, 1849.

Beadle's Dime Book of Practical Etiquette for Ladies and Gentlemen. . . . New York: Irwin P. Beadle, 1859.

Beezley, Charles F. [Daphne Dale, pseud.]. *Our Manners and Social Customs.* . . . Chicago: Elliott & Beezley, 1891.

Bennett, Mary E. [Elizabeth Glover, pseud.]. *Family Manners.* New York: Thomas Y. Crowell, 1890.

———. [Elizabeth Glover, pseud.]. *The Gentle Art of Pleasing.* New York: Baker and Taylor, 1898.

Blunders in Behavior Corrected. . . . New York: Garrett, Dick & Fitzgerald, [n.d.].

The Book of Manners: A Guide to Social Intercourse. New York: Carlton & Phillips, 1854.

Book of Politeness. Philadelphia: Fisher & Brother, [1850?].

Brown, James Baldwin. *Our Morals and Manners.* New York: Thomas Nelson, 1871.

Bryson, Louise Fiske. *Every-Day Etiquette: A Manual of Good Manners.* New York: W. D. Kerr, 1890.

Buel, James William. *Buel's Manual of Self Help.* . . . Chicago: National Publishing Co., 1894.

Bugg, Lelia Hardin. *A Lady. Manners and Social Usages.* New York: Benziger Brothers, 1893.

Bunce, Oliver Bell [Censor, pseud.]. *Don't: A Manual of Mistakes and Improprieties More or Less Prevalent in Conduct and Speech.* New York: D. Appleton, 1883.

Bunce, Mrs. Oliver Bell. *What to Do: A Companion to "Don't."* New York: D. Appleton, 1892.

Butler, Charles. *The American Gentleman.* Philadelphia: Hogan & Thompson, 1836.

———. *The American Lady.* 1836; Philadelphia: Hogan & Thompson, 1841.

Carroll, George D. *The Art of Correspondence, and Usages of Polite Society.* New York: Dempsey & Carroll, 1880. 2 vols. bound together.

———. *Art Stationery and Usages of Polite Society.* New York: Dempsey & Carroll, 1879.

Clapp, Eleanor Bassett. *Social Usage and Etiquette.* . . . New York: Home Circle Library, 1904.

Cleveland, Rose E. *The Social Mirror: A Complete Treatise on the Laws, Rules and Usages that Govern our Most Refined Homes and Social Circles.* Detroit: F. B. Dickerson, 1886.

[Cogswell, Albert.] *Perfect Etiquette; or How to Behave in Society. A Complete Manual for Ladies and Gentlemen.* . . . New York: A. Cogswell, 1877.

[Colesworthy, Daniel Clement.] *Hints on Common Politeness.* Boston: D. C. Colesworthy, 1867.

The Complete Bachelor: Manners for Men. New York: D. Appleton, 1896.

Conkling, Margaret Cockburn [Henry Lunettes, pseud.]. *The American Gentleman's Guide to Politeness and Fashion; or, Familiar Letters to His Nephews.* . . . New York: Derby & Jackson, 1857.

Cooke, Maud C. *Social Etiquette or Manners and Customs of Polite Society Containing Rules of Etiquette for All Occasions.* . . . Philadelphia: J. H. Moore 1896.

Correct Social Usages: A Course of Instruction in Good Form, Style & Deportment, by Eighteen Distinguished Authors. . . . 8th rev. ed., New York: The New York Society of Self-Culture, 1907. 2 vols. bound in one.

Cunliffe-Owen, Marguerite [The Marquise de Fontenoy, pseud.]. *Eve's Glossary: The Guide-book of a "Mondaine."* Chicago: Herbert S. Stone, 1897.

The Cutter, in Five Lectures Upon the Art and Practice of Cutting Friends, Acquaintances, and Relations. New York: Longworth, 1808.

The Daughter's Own Book; or Practical Hints from a Father to his Daughter. Boston: Lilly, Wait, Colman, and Holden, 1833.

Day, Charles William. *The American Ladies' and Gentleman's Manual of Elegance, Fashion, and True Politeness.* Auburn, N.Y.: James M. Alden, 1850.

[Delano, Mortimer, and Reginald Harvey Arnold.] *Simplex Munditiis. Gentlemen.* New York: De Vinne Press, 1891.

[De Valcourt, Robert.] *The Illustrated Manners Book: A Manual of Good Behavior and Polite Accomplishments.* New York: Leland, Clay, 1855.

Dewey, Julia M. *How to Teach Manners in the School-Room*. New York: E.L. Kellogg, 1888.

———. *Lessons on Manners; Arranged for Grammar Schools, High Schools, and Academies*. New York: Hinds & Noble, 1899.

Duffey, Elizabeth Bisbee. *The Ladies' and Gentlemen's Etiquette: A Complete Manual of the Manners and Dress of American Society*. . . . Philadelphia: Potter & Coates, 1877.

Dunbar, M. C. *Dunbar's Complete Handbook of Etiquette*. . . . New York: Excelsior, 1884.

Egan, Maurice Francis. *A Gentleman*. 2d ed., New York: Benziger Brothers, 1893.

Etiquette for Americans, by a Woman of Fashion. Chicago: Herbert S. Stone, 1898.

Etiquette for Ladies: A Manual of the Most Approved Rules of Conduct in Polished Society. . . . Philadelphia: J. & J. L. Gihon, 1843.

Etiquette for Ladies: With Hints on the Preservation, Improvement, and Display of Female Beauty. Philadelphia: Lea & Blanchard, 1838.

Everett, Marshall. *The Etiquette of Today: A Complete Guide to Correct Manners and Social Customs in Use Among Educated and Refined People of America*. N.p: Henry Well, 1902.

[Farrar, Eliza Ware.] *The Young Lady's Friend*. Boston: American Stationers' Co., 1837.

Ferrero, Edward. *The Art of Dancing, Historically Illustrated. To Which Is Added a Few Hints on Etiquette*. . . . New York: Dick & Fitzgerald, 1859.

Forbes-Lindsay, Margaret Osborne [Mrs. Charles Harcourt, pseud.]. *The Blue Book of Etiquette for Women*. Philadelphia: John C. Winston, 1907.

Gentle Manners: A Guide to Good Morals. 3d ed. East Canterbury, N.H.: n.p., 1899.

[Germain, Walter?] *The Complete Bachelor: Manners for Men*. . . . New York: D. Appleton, 1896.

The Girls' Manual: Comprising a Summary View of Female Studies, Accomplishments, and Principles of Conduct. New York: D. Appleton, 1850.

Good Behavior for Ladies. The Laws of Etiquette. . . . Rochester, N.Y.: D. M. Dewey, 1850.

Good Manners; A Manual of Etiquette in Good Society. [Plagiarism from English work *Good Society*, 1869.] Philadelphia: Porter & Coates, 1870.

Goodrich, Samuel G. [Peter Parley, pseud.]. *What to Do and How to Do It; or Morals and Manners Taught by Examples*. 1843; New York: Sheldon, 1865.

Good Society. A Complete Manual of Manners by the Right Hon. the Countess of . . . New York: George Routledge & Sons, 1869.

Gow, Alexander Murdoch. *Good Morals and Gentle Manners. For Schools and Families*. New York: American Book Co., 1873.

Green, Walter C. *A Dictionary of Etiquette: A Guide to Polite Usage for All Social Functions*. 1904. New York: Brentano's, 1912.

Griffin, Caroline S. *The Young Folks' Book of Etiquette*. Chicago: A. Flanagan, 1905.

Guide to Good Behaviour. Being a Complete Book of Instructions on the Subjects of Dress, Conversation, Balls, Parties, Dinners, Dancing, etc. . . . Philadelphia: John B. Perry, 1856.

A Guide to Good Manners: Containing Hints on Etiquette, Business, Morals, Dress, Friendship, Weddings, Balls, Dinners, Parties, Compliments, and Letter Writing. 1847; Fitchburg, Mass.: Shepley, 1848.

A Guide to Men and Manners. Consisting of Lord Chesterfield's Advice to his Son. To Which Is Added a Supplement. . . . 1818; Philadelphia: B. Warner, 1821.

The Habits of Good Society: A Handbook for Ladies and Gentlemen. . . . 1860; New York: Carleton, 1864.

Hale, Sarah Josepha. *Manners; or, Happy Homes and Good Society All the Year Round.* Boston: J. E. Tilton, 1868; reprint ed. New York: Arno Press, 1972.

[Hall, Florence Marion Howe.] *The Correct Thing in Good Society.* Boston: Estes & Lauriat, 1888.

————. *Social Customs.* 1881; Boston: Estes & Lauriat, 1887.

Hand-book of Good Manners and Guide to Politeness. . . . New York: Hurst, n.d.

The Handbook of the Man of Fashion. 1839; Philadelphia: Lindsay and Blakiston, 1847.

[Hardy, Edward John.] *Manners Makyth Man.* New York, Charles Scribner's Sons, 1887.

Harrison, Constance. *The Well-bred Girl in Society.* 1898; Garden City, N.Y.: Doubleday, Page, 1905.

Hartley, Cecil B. *The Gentlemen's Book of Etiquette, and Manual of Politeness. . . .* 1860; Boston: J. S. Locke, 1873.

Hartley, Florence. *The Ladies' Book of Etiquette, and Manual of Politeness. . . .* 1860; Boston: J. S. Locke, 1876.

Hervey, George Winfred. *The Principles of Courtesy: With Hints and Observations on Manners and Habits.* New York: Harper & Brothers, 1852.

Hill, Thomas Edie. *Hill's Manual of Social and Business Forms: A Guide to Correct Writing. . . .* 1873; 33d ed. Chicago: Hill Standard Book Co., 1882.

Holt, Emily. *Encyclopaedia of Etiquette. . . . A Book of Manners for Everyday Use.* Garden City, N.Y.: Doubleday, Page, 1902.

Houghton, Walter, R., et al. *Rules of Etiquette and Home Culture; or, What to Do and How to Do It.* 1882; 28th ed., rev. and extended, Chicago: Rand, McNally, 1889.

Howard, Timothy Edward. *Excelsior; or, Essays on Politeness, Education, and the Means of Attaining Success in Life. Part I.—For Young Gentlemen, by T. E. Howard. . . . Part II.—For Young Ladies, by a Lady (R.V.R.).* Baltimore: Kelly and Piet, 1868.

How to Behave; or, The Spirit of Etiquette. . . . 5th ed. New York: Dick & Fitzgerald [18—].

How to Do It; or Book of Etiquette by a Member of Society. New York: Frank Tousey, 1902.

Johnson, Sophie Orne [Daisy Eyebright, pseud.]. *A Manual of Etiquette with Hints on Politeness and Good Breeding.* 1873; New York: G. P. Putnam's Sons, 1874.

————. *The New York Fashion Bazar Book of Etiquette. A Compendium of Social Knowledge.* New York: George Monro, 1887.

Kingsland, Florence. *The Book of Good Manners. "Etiquette for All Occasions." . . .* 1901; Garden City, N.Y.: Doubleday, Page, 1910.

Ladies and Gentlemen's American Etiquette. With the Rules of Polite Society. . . . Boston: J. Buffum [187?].

The Ladies' Science of Etiquette. By an English Lady of Rank [Countess de Calabrella?]. New York: Wilson, 1844.

The Lady's Companion; or, Sketches of Life, Manners, and Morals, at the Present Day. Philadelphia: H. C. Peck & Theo. Bliss, 1852.

[Lavin, Eliza M.] *Good Manners.* 1888; 3d ed., New York: Butterick Publishing Co., 1889.

The Laws of Etiquette; or, Short Rules and Reflections for Conduct in Society. New ed., Philadelphia: Carey, Lea & Blanchard, 1836.

The Laws of Good Breeding; or, The Science of Etiquette, for Ladies and Gentlemen. . . . Cincinnati: Hayward, James, 1848.

Learned, Ellin Craven. *The Etiquette of New York To-Day.* . . . New York: F. A. Stokes, 1906.

[Leland, Charles Godfrey.] *The Art of Conversation, with Directions for Self Education.* 1864; New York: Carleton, 1865.

Leslie, Eliza. *Miss Leslie's Behaviour Book.* . . . 1853; Philadelphia: T. B. Peterson and Brothers, 1859; reprint ed. New York: Arno Press, 1972.

Logan, Mary Simmerson Cunningham, et al. *The Home Manual. Everybody's Guide in Social, Domestic, and Business Life.* Chicago: H. J. Smith, 1889.

Longstreet, Abby Buchanan. *Cards, Their Significance and Proper Uses, as Governed by the Usages of New York Society.* New York: Frederick A. Stokes & Brother, 1889.

[————.] *Good Form: Manners Good and Bad, at Home and in Society.* New York: Frederick A. Stokes, 1890.

[————.] *Social Etiquette of New York.* . . . 1879; New York: D. Appleton, 1887.

[————.] *Social Life.* New York: Butterick, 1889.

McCabe, James Dabney. *The National Encyclopaedia of Business and Social Forms, Embracing the Laws of Etiquette and Good Society.* . . . 1883; Philadelphia: National Publishing Co., 1884.

Mackellar, D. *A Treatise on the Art of Politeness, Good Breeding, and Manners, with Maxims and Moral Reflections.* Detroit: George E. Pomeroy, 1855.

The Manners That Win: Compiled from the Latest Authorities. Minneapolis: Buckeye, 1880.

A Manual of Politeness, Comprising the Principles of Etiquette, and Rules of Behaviour in Genteel Society, for Persons of Both Sexes. Philadelphia: W. Marshall, 1837.

[Marbury, Elisabeth.] *Manners: A Handbook of Social Customs.* . . . New York: Cassell, 1888.

Martine, Arthur. *Martine's Hand-Book of Etiquette, and Guide to True Politeness.* . . . New York: Dick & Fitzgerald, 1866.

Maxwell, Sara B. *Manners and Customs of To-Day.* . . . Des Moines: Cline, 1890.

Mixing in Society. A Complete Manual of Manners. By Right Hon. The Countess of *****. 1870; New York: George Routledge & Sons, 1872.

[Moody, Eleazar.] *The School of Good Manners. Composed for the Help of Parents in Teaching Their Children How to Behave in Their Youth.* Ca. 1715; revised ed. Boston: Sabbath School Society, 1837.

Moore, Clara Sophia Jessup [Mrs. H. O. Ward, pseud.]. *Sensible Etiquette of the Best Society, Customs, Manners, Morals and Home Culture.* 10th ed., Philadelphia, Porter & Coates, 1878.

———— [Mrs. H. O. Ward, pseud.]. *Social Ethics and Social Duties. Thorough Education of Girls for Wives and Mothers and for Professions.* Boston: Estes & Lauriat, 1892.

Morton, Agnes H. *Etiquette: Good Manners for All People, Especially for Those "Who Dwell Within the Broad Zone of the Average."* 1892; rev. ed. Philadelphia: Penn Publishing Co., 1908.

Newcomb, Harvey. *How to Be a Lady: A Book for Girls, Containing Useful Hints on the Formation of Character.* 14th ed. Boston: Gould and Lincoln, 1860.

100 Rules of Etiquette. Baltimore: Kohler Manufacturing Co., n.d.

Osmun, Thomas Embley [Alfred Ayres, pseud.]. *The Mentor: A Little Book for the Guidance of Such Men and Boys as Would Appear to Advantage in the Society of Persons of the Better Sort.* 1884; New York: Funk & Wagnalls, 1885.

Our Manners at Home and Abroad: A Complete Manual on the Manners, Customs, and Social Forms of the Best American Society. . . . Harrisburg: Pennsylvania Publishing Co., 1883.

The Perfect Gentleman; or Etiquette and Eloquence. . . . New York: Dick & Fitzgerald, 1860.

Points of Etiquette. Designed as a Text Book for the Young. New York, W. H. Sadlier, 1889.

Points on Good Behavior. Rochester, N.Y.: Published for Dr. Walker, n.d.

The Polite Present; or Manual of Good Manners. 1831; Boston: William H. Hill, Jr., [1865?].

[Pollard, Josephine?] *Good Manners: A Few Hints About Behavior. By J—— P——.* Chautauqua Text-books, no. Forty-Three. New York: Phillips & Hunt, 1883.

Power, Susan C. *Art of Good Manners; or Children's Etiquette.* 1893; New York: Werner, 1899.

[———.] *Behaving; or Papers on Children's Etiquette.* Boston: D. Lothrop, 1877.

Practical Etiquette. By N.C. Revised ed. Chicago: A. Flanagan, 1899.

Rayne, Martha Louise. *Gems of Deportment and Hints of Etiquette.* . . . Detroit: Tyler, 1881.

Richards, Cornelia Holroyd [Mrs. Manners, pseud.]. *At Home and Abroad; or, How to Behave.* New York: Evans and Brittan, 1853.

Roy, George. *The Art of Pleasing.* Cincinnati: Robert Clarke, 1875.

[Ruth, John A.] *Decorum: A Practical Treatise on Etiquette and Dress of the Best American Society.* Rev. by S. L. Louis. 1877; New York: Union Publishing House, 1882.

Sedgwick, Catharine Maria. *Morals of Manners; or, Hints for Our Young People.* New York: G. P. Putnam, 1846.

Shearer, William John. *Morals and Manners; or, Elements of Character and Conduct.* New York: Richardson, Smith, 1904.

Sherwood, Mary Elizabeth Wilson. *Manners and Social Usages.* 1884; rev. ed. New York: Harper & Brothers, 1897; reprint ed. New York: Arno Press, 1975.

[Shields, Sarah Annie Frost.] *Frost's Laws and By-laws of American Society. A Condensed but Thorough Treatise on Etiquette and Its Usages in America.* . . . New York: Dick & Fitzgrald, 1869.

Smiley, James B. [Mrs. Julia M. Bradley, pseud.]. *Modern Manners and Social Forms: A Manual of the Manners and Customs of the Best Modern Society.* . . . Chicago: James B. Smiley, 1889.

Social Etiquette and Home Culture. The Glass of Fashion: A Universal Hand-book of Social Etiquette and Home Culture for Ladies and Gentlemen. . . . 1878; New York: Harper & Brothers, 1881.

Stevens, Frances. *The Usages of the Best Society. A Complete Manual of the Social Etiquette.* New York: A. L. Burt, 1884.

Thornwell, Emily. *The Lady's Guide to Perfect Gentility.* . . . New York: Derby & Jackson, 1856. xvii + 234 p.

[Tomes, Robert.] *The Bazar Book of Decorum.* New York: Harper & Brothers, 1870.

True Politeness: A Hand-book of Etiquette for Ladies. New York: Leavitt and Allen, 1847.

True Politeness, or Etiquette for Ladies and Gentlemen. Boston: n.p., 1846.

Urner, Nathan D. [Mentor, pseud.]. *Always: A Manual of Etiquette of Either Sex into the Empurpled Penetralia of Fashionable Life.* . . . New York: G. W. Carleton, 1884.

——— [Mentor, pseud.]. *Never: A Handbook for the Uninitiated and Inexperienced Aspirants to Refined Society's Giddy Heights and Glittering Attainments.* New York: G. W. Carleton, 1883.

Wells, Richard A. *Manners, Culture and Dress of the Best American Society.* . . . 1890; Springfield, Mass.: King Richardson, 1894.

[Wells, Samuel Roberts.] *How to Behave: A Pocket Manual of Republican Etiquette, and Guide to Correct Personal Habits.* . . . New York: Fowler & Wells, 1856.

White, Annie Randall. *Polite Society at Home and Abroad.* . . . Chicago: Monarch Book Co., 1891.

———. *Twentieth Century Etiquette.* Chicago: Wabash, 1900.

White, Lydia E. *Success in Society. A Manual of Good Manners, Social Etiquette, Rules of Behavior at Home and Abroad, on the Street, at Public Gatherings, Calls, Conversations, etc.* Boston: James H. Earle, 1889.

Willis, Henry P. *Etiquette, and the Usages of Society.* . . . New York: Dick & Fitzgerald, 1860.

Woods, Elias McSails. *The Negro in Etiquette: A Novelty.* Saint Louis: Buxton & Skinner, 1899.

Young, John H. *Our Deportment, or the Manners, Conduct and Dress of the Most Refined Society.* . . . 1879; rev. ed. Detroit: F. B. Dickerson, 1884.

The Young Lady's Own Book: A Manual of Intellectual Improvement and Moral Deportment. Philadelphia: Key & Biddle, 1833.

The Young Man's Own Book: A Manual of Politeness, Intellectual Improvement, and Moral Deportment. . . . Philadelphia: Key & Biddle, 1833.

Sources of Illustrations

1. *Gleason's Pictorial Drawing-Room Companion* 2 (May 8, 1852): 297. Courtesy Library of Congress.
2. James Dabney McCabe, *The National Encyclopaedia of Business and Social Forms* (Philadelphia: National Publishing Co., 1884), title page. Courtesy University of North Carolina, Chapel Hill.
3. Thomas E. Hill, *Hill's Manual of Social and Business Forms* (1885; reprint Chicago: Quadrangle Books, 1971), 139. Courtesy of the Margaret Woodbury Strong Museum, Rochester, New York.
4. Lithograph by J. Bachmann, Boston, 1877. Courtesy Library of Congress.
5. James Dabney McCabe, *The Secrets of the Great City* (Philadelphia: Jones, Brothers, 1868), frontispiece. Courtesy Duke University.
6. Matthew Hale Smith, *Sunshine and Shadow in New York* (Hartford: J. B. Burr, 1868), frontispiece. Courtesy University of North Carolina, Chapel Hill.
7. Giovanni Morelli, *Italian Painters: Critical Studies of Their Works*, trans. Constance Jocelyn Ffoulkes (London: John Murray, 1892), 78. Courtesy University of North Carolina, Chapel Hill.
8. Helen Campbell et al., *Darkness and Daylight; or, Lights and Shadows of New York Life* (Hartford: A. D. Worthington, 1892), 599. Courtesy University of North Carolina, Chapel Hill.
9. "New-York by Gas-light. Hooking a Victim." Lithographed and published by Serrell & Perkins about 1850. Courtesy Museum of the City of New York.
10. Reprinted from Edward Van Every, *Sins of New York as "Exposed" by the Police Gazette* (New York: Frederick A. Stokes, 1930), 56. Courtesy University of North Carolina, Chapel Hill.
11. Thomas Byrnes, *Professional Criminals of America* (New York: Cassell, 1886), facing 58 and 170. Courtesy University of North Carolina, Chapel Hill.
12. Allan Pinkerton, *Thirty Years a Detective* (New York: G. W. Carleton, 1884), facing 40. Courtesy Duke University.
13. McCabe, *The Secrets of the Great City*, facing 82. Courtesy Duke University.
14. Thompson Westcott, "The Physiology of Dandyism," *Graham's Magazine* 40 (February and May 1852): 120. Courtesy University of North Carolina, Chapel Hill.
15. Advertisement, New York, 1872. Courtesy Library of Congress.
16. Advertisement, B. Altman & Co., New York, spring and summer 1885. Courtesy Archives Center, National Museum of American History, Smithsonian Institution.
17. *Ballou's Pictorial Drawing-Room Companion* 11 (December 27, 1856): 400. Courtesy University of North Carolina, Chapel Hill.
18. Woodcut by N. Orr in [Robert De Valcourt], *The Illustrated Manners Book* (New York: Leland, Clay, 1855). Courtesy Library of Congress.
19. Mid-nineteenth-century comic valentine, published in New York City. Courtesy American Antiquarian Society.
20. Westcott, "Physiology of Dandyism," 471. Courtesy University of North Carolina, Chapel Hill.

21. Drawing by T. de Thulstrup in *Harper's Weekly* 31 (November 5, 1887): 804–5. Courtesy University of North Carolina, Chapel Hill.
22. Drawing by Sol Eytinge, Jr., in *Harper's Weekly* 14 (March 12, 1870): 168. Courtesy University of North Carolina, Chapel Hill.
23. Drawing by W. J. Hennessy in *Harper's Weekly* 16 (March 9, 1872): 189. Courtesy University of North Carolina, Chapel Hill.
24. Drawing by A. B. Shults in *Frank Leslie's Illustrated Newspaper* 52 (August 27, 1881): 421. Courtesy University of Illinois at Urbana-Champaign.
25. "The Age of Brass. or The Triumphs of Womans Rights," lithograph by Currier & Ives, 1869. Courtesy Library of Congress.
26. Rose E. Cleveland, *The Social Mirror* (Detroit: F. B. Dickerson, 1886), 71. Courtesy University of North Carolina, Chapel Hill.
27–28. Charles Darwin, *The Expression of the Emotions in Man and Animals*, in Westminster ed., *Selected Works of Charles Darwin* (New York: D. Appleton, 1900), 52–53, 289. Courtesy University of North Carolina, Chapel Hill.
29. Drawing by A. Kimbel in *Gleason's Pictorial Drawing-Room Companion* 7 (November 11, 1854): 300. Courtesy Library of Congress.
30–31. *Hill's Manual of Social and Business Forms*. Courtesy of the Margaret Woodbury Strong Museum, Rochester, New York.
32. Courtesy Stowe-Day Foundation, Hartford, Connecticut.
33. Courtesy Museum Boymans–van Beuningen, Rotterdam.
34. Reproduced, by permission of copyright holder, from Noel D. Turner, *American Silver Flatware, 1837–1910* (South Brunswick, N.J.: A. S. Barnes, 1972), 190. Courtesy University of North Carolina, Chapel Hill.
35. *Scraps*, No. 6 (Boston: D. C. Johnston, 1835). Courtesy American Antiquarian Society.
36. *Godey's Lady's Book* 58 (March 1859): 267. Courtesy University of North Carolina, Chapel Hill.
37. Drawing by C. Jay Taylor. Reprinted from Roger Butterfield, *The American Past* (New York: Simon and Schuster, 1947), 258. Courtesy University of North Carolina, Chapel Hill.
38. Lithograph by J. Ottmann, after drawing by Joseph Keppler in *Puck* 24 (January 23, 1889): 362–63. Courtesy Library of Congress.
39. Drawing by Thomas Nast, *Harper's Weekly* 16 (August 3, 1872): 608. Courtesy Library of Congress.
40. Lithograph published by White and Bauer, ca. 1870s. Courtesy Library of Congress.
41–42. *Hill's Manual of Social and Business Forms*. Courtesy of the Margaret Woodbury Strong Museum, Rochester, New York.
43. Colored lithograph published by Nathaniel Currier, New York, 1845. Courtesy of the Margaret Woodbury Strong Museum, Rochester, New York.
44. Frances Trollope, *Domestic Manners of the Americans* (London: Whittaker, Treacher, 1832), facing 116. Courtesy University of North Carolina, Chapel Hill.
45. Lithograph by Nagel and Weingaertner, published by Elton, 1849. Courtesy of The New-York Historical Society, New York City.
46. Watercolor by John Searle. Courtesy of The New-York Historical Society, New York City.
47. *The Illustrated London News* 14 (June 2, 1849): 369. Courtesy Library of Congress.
48. Photograph by Max Platz in Rose Fay Thomas, *Memoirs of Theodore Thomas*

(New York: Moffat, Yard, 1911), facing 272. Courtesy University of North Carolina, Chapel Hill.

49. *Harper's Weekly* 10 (February 10, 1866): 89. Courtesy University of North Carolina, Chapel Hill.

50. Lithograph, 1898. Courtesy Library of Congress.

Index

Women's walking costumes (ill.), 122
Woods, Elias M., 54
Working class, 36, 140: and decay of
  manners, 258; and etiquette manuals,
  57; and middle class, 43, 58–60, 78,
  121, 138, 181, 197; and performing
  arts, 218, 222, 227–28, 238, 249, 252–
  55
Working-class women and prostitution,
  130

Wright, Frances, 117
Wyatt-Brown, Bertram, 114
Wyckoff, Walter, 139–40

Yiddish theater (New York), 251–52
Young Folks' Book of Etiquette, The (Grif-
  fin), 194
Young Lady's Friend, The (Farrar), 50, 160
Young Lady's Own Book, The, 161